A PEPYS OF MOGUL INDIA

1653-1708

A Pepys of Mogul India
1653-1708

BEING AN ABRIDGED EDITION
OF THE "STORIA DO MOGOR"
OF NICCOLAO MANUCCI

TRANSLATED BY
WILLIAM IRVINE

ABRIGED EDITION PREPARED BY
MARGARET L. IRVINE

MANOHAR
2026

Due to the academic and scholarly importance of this volume, we are reprinting/republishing it from the original source without any modifications or changes. Therefore, some misprints and errors may occur.

First published 1913
Reprinted 2025, 2026
First eBook edition 2025

ISBN 978-93-6080-882-2 (Hb)
ISBN 978-93-6080-030-7 (ebook)

Published by
Ajay Kumar Jain *for*
Manohar Publishers & Distributors
4753/23 Ansari Road, Daryaganj
New Delhi 110 002

Printed and bound in India

A PEPYS OF MOGUL INDIA

1653—1708

BEING AN ABRIDGED EDITION
OF THE "STORIA DO MOGOR"
OF NICCOLAO MANUCCI

TRANSLATED BY WILLIAM IRVINE

(ABRIDGED EDITION PREPARED BY
MARGARET L. IRVINE)

WITH A FRONTISPIECE

LONDON
JOHN MURRAY, ALBEMARLE STREET, W.
1913

INTRODUCTION

NICCOLAO MANUCCI—THE MAN

Niccolao Manucci, the hero of our narrative, ran away from Venice in 1653, being then fourteen. He hid on board a vessel bound for Smyrna, and was fortunate enough to find a protector in a certain Viscount Bellomont, an English nobleman, then on his way to Persia and India. He followed Bellomont through Asia Minor to Persia, and from Persia to India, meeting with many adventures by sea and land. The sudden death of his master near Hodal, in 1656, left Manucci friendless in a strange land.

He seems to have been a youth of considerable resource, however, and fortune favoured him, for he soon found employment as an artilleryman in the service of Prince Dārā Shukoh, eldest son of the Emperor Shāhjahān. Till Dārā's death, in 1659, Manucci followed his varying fortunes in peace and war, and, refusing to transfer his services to Aurangzeb, he gradually adopted the profession of medicine.

Being offered the post of a captain of artillery by Rajah Jai Singh, he returned to soldiering for some years, till apparently he grew tired of it, and resigned his post. He made his way to Bassain, where he narrowly escaped the Inquisition, and thence to Goa, ultimately returning to Agrah and Dihlī. Here he took service with Kīrat Singh, son of Jai Singh; but when Kīrat Singh was ordered to Kābul, Manucci resolved to move to Lāhor (end of 1670 or early in 1671) and start in practice as a physician. At the end of six or seven years, having made a little money, Manucci decided to remove into European territory, and he made his home at Bandora, on Salsette Island. Before long, however, he lost his money in an unlucky venture, and was obliged to return to the Mogul Court. He obtained an appointment as one of the physicians attached to Shāh 'Ālam, and followed him to the Dakhin when he went there as Governor in 1678. Shāh 'Ālam was recalled in 1680 to take part in a campaign, and from that time they were on the move till early in 1681. Manucci seems to have found his position somewhat irksome, and determined to make his escape to Goa on the pretext of taking leave of absence.

He reached Goa, and was employed by the Portuguese in negotiations with the Mahrattah chief, Sambhā Jī, and also with Shāh 'Ālam, for which services the Governor conferred on him a patent of knighthood in the Portuguese Order of Sant' Iago, 1684. On a second embassy to Shāh 'Alam, Manucci was detained as a deserter from his service. He attempted flight, but was brought back, and had to accompany Shāh 'Ālam through the Ghāts to Aḥmadnagar, and thence on a campaign against the King of Gulkhandah. When at Mālkher, Manucci managed to make his escape into Gulkhandah, and when Shāh 'Ālam occupied Gulkhandah he fled to the European settlements at Narsāpur and Masulipatam. He was brought back to Gulkhandah, but evaded being given up to the agents of Shāh 'Ālam, and, with the help of an

Augustinian friar, he managed to escape once more and took refuge at the English settlement of Fort St. George. He had thought at this time of returning to Europe, but was dissuaded from doing so, and was advised to marry. He acted on this advice, and married in 1686 a Catholic widow named Clarke, daughter of Christopher Hartley and Aguida Pereyra. They had one child, a son, who died in infancy.

During his residence in Madras Manucci was employed by Governors Gyfford and Pitt; by Gyfford in the matter of transmitting letters to the "Great Mogull," and by Thomas Pitt in actual negotiations with Dā,ūd Khān, who invested Madras in 1702. From 1703 onwards for several years Manucci seems to have been quite absorbed in matters ecclesiastical, and he devoted many pages of his memoirs to the discussion of the disputes between the Capuchins and Jesuits, which reached an active stage about that time. In 1706 his wife died, and between 1706 and 1712 Manucci moved his home to Pondicherry.

In that year he was about to make a special journey to Shāh 'Ālam's court at Lāhor as an intermediary on behalf of the Madras Council, who wished to settle various long-standing difficulties, and also to secure fresh privileges. The death of Shāh 'Ālam put an end to these plans, but as a reward for his previous services the Governor and Council on January 14, 1712, conceded to him in perpetuity his leasehold house and garden at Madras, which he had acquired as being heir of Thomas Clarke, having married his widow.

There is no further trace of Manucci at Madras or Pondicherry, and the only date for his death is a reference in the work, "Della Litteratura Veneziano"

(4to, Venice, 1854), by the Doge Marco Nicolò Foscarini, where on p. 441 of the 4th edition, 1854, it is said that Manucci died in India in 1717 as an octogenarian, as he (Foscarini) had heard.

NICCOLAO MANUCCI—THE AUTHOR

Manucci's own life is brimful of adventure, and not less interesting is the story of the vicissitudes through which his manuscript memoirs passed before they were finally presented to the public in 1907 in the masterly edition prepared by my father, the late William Irvine, entitled "Storia do Mogor." The strange story is given by him in the minutest detail in his Introduction to the "Storia," and I must content myself by giving a mere outline of the most essential facts.

Manucci sent home two copies of his manuscript; the first by the hands of a certain Mons. Boureau Deslandes in 1701. This manuscript was lent by Deslandes to a certain Père Catrou, a Jesuit priest, who published in 1705 a book founded upon it, and entitled "Histoire Générale de l'Empire du Mogol depuis sa fondation, sur les Mémoires de M. Manouchi Vénitien."

In 1705 this particular manuscript passed with others into the possession of Baron Gérard Meerman, of the Hague, was bought from his heirs in 1824 by Sir Thomas Philipps, of Middle Hill, Worcester, and was finally acquired by the Königliche Bibliothek at Berlin in 1887.

Some time in 1704, or 1705, Manucci received from Catrou an advance copy of his "Histoire," or of the preface to it. He was intensely indignant at what he considered to be an attempt on the part of the Jesuit Fathers 'to transfer to themselves the glory won by another's labour," and he determined to send to Europe the original draft of his Parts I., II., and III., together with Part IV., on which he had been engaged since 1701. He sent them to the Venetian Senate by the hand of Father Eusebius, of Bourges, a Capuchin, in 1705. We learn that the manuscript was made over to the then Ambassador of the Venetian Senate at Paris, Lorenzo Tiepolo. Tiepolo became librarian of the San Marco Library in 1736, and Manucci's manuscript is entered in the catalogue made during his tenure of office, although we have no record of its transmission to Venice.

With the first manuscript sent to Europe, in 1701, Manucci also sent a volume of portraits. This seems to have passed out of the Jesuits' possession, for Zanetti catalogues it as being in the San Marco Library at Venice in 1741. Since then it has become the property of the French nation, being made over to them in 1797, and is now to be found in the Cabinet des Estampes at the Bibliothèque Nationale in Paris, classed as O.D. No. 45 (réserve).

This brief sketch of the man and his work will serve, I hope, to awaken interest in his story, and perhaps it will not be out of place to state here the reasons which suggested that a volume of selections from the "Storia" might meet with success.

The "Storia do Mogor," as a whole, is very lengthy, and somewhat diffuse; and a great deal of it is interesting only to the student and the scholar. Some passages, such as those dealing with the disputes between the Capuchins and Jesuits, might even be called wearisome, whilst to many people the mere appearance of the four weighty volumes is quite alarming. We hoped, therefore, by making a selection of passages, dealing chiefly with Manucci's own life-story, that we might thus give a sufficiently faithful picture of the man and his career, and introduce him in this way to many readers, who otherwise would never have made his acquaintance.

In conclusion, I wish to express my most cordial thanks to Mr. L. Cranmer-Byng for his kind and able assistance and advice.

M. L. IRVINE.

GRINDELWALD,
January 11, 1913.

CONTENTS

INTRODUCTION . . . . pp. v–x

Departure from Venice—Service with Lord Bellomont—Travel in Turkey—Arrival in Persia—The Shah's banquet—Interview with 'Aẓamat-ud-daulah, his reply on behalf of the King—Negotiations fail—Of the city of Isfahān, Shīrāz, Lār, and Bandar 'Abbāsi, Hormuz Island—The Port of Sūrat, Burhānpur, Sironj—Of Sarāes, Narwar, Gwāliyar, Dholpur, Āgrah—Lord Bellomont dies at Hodal—His property seized—Manucci at Dihlī, Shāhjahān and his audience-hall—Ambassador's property released—Manucci enters Prince Dārā's service . . . . pp. 1–50

Warlike preparations—Dārā and his army set forth—Traitorous advice to Dārā—Dawn of battle day—Course of events—Dārā's defeat and flight—Dārā at Āgrah, Dihlī, and Lāhor—Manucci starts for Dihlī—Adventures on the way—He rejoins Dārā—Dārā leaves for Multan—M. follows—Departure for Bhakkar—Siege of Bhakkar—Evacuation of Bhakkar—At Lāhor, Primavera killed—M. escapes naked, goes to Dihlī, refuses to serve Aurangzeb . . pp. 51–98

Manucci as Médecin Malgré Lui—Aurangzeb's march to Kashmir—Details of march—Plan of encampment—M. at Dihlī, Āgrah, and Allahābād—Bathing in the Ganges—Benares and Patnah—A journey by river—Arrival at Huglī—A marriage proposal—Interference of two friars—M. leaves Huglī—A rescue from Satī; M. enters service of Jai Singh—European modes of fighting on sea and land—M. negotiates with petty rajahs—Spells and sorcery—M. and Shivā Jī; At Bassain and Goa—M. leaves Goa—Attacked by thieves—At Aurangābād, Āgrah, and Dihlī—M. sets up as a physician—His first patient—M. and Muhammad Amīn Khān—A false accusation of theft—He is protected by Fidā,e Khān—M. and Mahābat Khān . . . . pp. 99–150

A royal patient, successful treatment—Use of human fat and flesh—Europeans persecute Manucci—Attempted murder—M. and the Pathan widow—M. as an exorcist—M. leaves Lāhor—An unlucky venture—M. enters service of Shāh 'Ālam—Sambhā Jī plans to seize Goa—M. and the Portuguese—Events at Goa—M's embassy to Sambhā Jī—Sambhā Jī's envoy—M's embassy to the Mogul fleet—Second embassy to Sambhā Jī—Arrival of Shāh 'Ālam—M. and Shāh 'Ālam—M. made a Knight of Sant Iago—M. attempts to leave Shāh 'Ālam—He is recaptured, granted leave, and returns to the royal camp—M. again takes flight, reaches Gulkhandah, is brought back again—A fresh escape—M. reaches Madras—his marriage pp. 151-197

Why Manucci left the Mogul country—His service with Shāh 'Ālam, 1680-85—Royal blood-letting—A merry jest—jealousy of native physicians—Successful cases—Poor rewards—Encounter with an angry slave . . . . pp. 198-213

Manucci in Madras—Employed by Governor Gyfford—Life in San Thome—Jealousy of the Goa doctors—M. as envoy to Shāh 'Ālam—M. tricked by a Portuguese—Dalpat Rao—Life in Goa—M. and the Inquisitor—Life in S. Thome—Bishop Gaspar Alfonço—M. and the Jesuits—M's letter to Dā,ūd Khān—M. and Dā,ūd Khān—Dā,ūd Khan visits Governor Pitt—Dā,ūd Khān departs . . pp. 215-250

Dā,ūd Khan's hostile return—Manucci acts as envoy once more—He assists the French—The French envoy successful—M. visits Dā,ūd Khān—The French and the Moguls—Fortresses and artillery—Vellore fortress—Crocodiles—Dā,ūd Khan visits San Thome—An English deputation—Marriage of François Martin's granddaughter—Illness of François Martin—French pirates—M. and the French doctor's son—Fate of the French doctor—M. as swashbuckler—He recalls his youthful escapades—M's house at Big Mount attacked—M. and Shāh 'Ālam—M. and Muhammad Muqīm—M. hides himself—Friends at Court—A good appointment—Royal blood-letting—M's offended dignity—Accident attributed to skill—A. Legrenzi, physician—Death of M's wife . . . . pp. 251-289

INDEX . . . . pp. 291-310

NOTE

Passages placed in square brackets have been supplied by the Editor to connect the narrative.

A PEPYS OF MOGUL INDIA

PART I

MY JOURNEY TO INDIA

Of My Departure from Venice

When I was still quite young, I had a passionate desire to see the world, but as my father would not allow me to leave Venice, my native place, I resolved to quit it in some way or another, no matter how. Finding that there was a *tartane* just about to leave, although I did not know its destination, I went on board in 1653, at the age of fourteen. The officers of the vessel, thinking that I was the son of one of the merchants who were going on board, did not ask me who I was, but let me pass without question. We had scarcely left Venice before we ran into the teeth of a gale which lasted twenty-four hours—hours of the greatest misery to me, as I was sea-sick, being unaccustomed to the sea. When twenty-four hours had passed, I was forced by hunger to present myself before the captain, who asked under whose protection I was there. I begged for pardon, saying that, having come on board a short time before he put out to sea, I had fallen asleep, and that, finding myself utterly unprovided for, I had come to him. At this he gave orders for me to be looked after; but fortunately for me I found on board an English gentleman in disguise called Lord Bellomont. He had left England to escape death at the hands of

Cromwell, protector of that kingdom, who had condemned him because he belonged to the party of King Charles II., then in France. This person showed me much affection, and when he asked me if I would like to go with him, I inquired of him his destination. He then told me he was going to Turkey, Persia, and India.

I was much rejoiced thereat, and answered that I would gladly go with him, when he at once gave me the keys of his wardrobe, and I served him with great affection, seeing he loved me as if I had been his son. We arrived at Raguza, where we stayed several days on account of a contrary wind. Having at last set sail, we coasted along Dalmatia and past several islands, and finally leaving the Archipelago behind, at the end of four months we arrived in the port of Smyrna.

Smyrna is a Turkish port, and there is a mingling of many nations there—namely, Italians, French, English, Dutch, and many Armenian merchants, who all live by the borders of the sea. At the time when we were at this port it happened that a Turk gave several blows with a stick to the captain of an English vessel. The Englishman swallowed the affront while he remained in the town waiting to embark, and after he had got a little way out to sea he bombarded the town and fled.

We remained seven days at Smyrna; after that we started with a caravan for the town of Burca (Brūsa). On the road we suffered much from cold, owing to the large amount of snow, and we arrived in eight days in good health.

On our arrival at Burca, an ancient town of the Greeks, we were received by an Armenian called Anthoine Cheleby, who acted as governor of the town; and further seeing that we should have to wait a long time before we could meet with a caravan leaving for Persia, we quitted the town and went to live in the country house of the said Anthoine Cheleby.

While our clothes were being carried out, under charge of one of our men called Charles, a Frenchman and a great musician, a couly (*qulī*) carrying one tin case disappeared. In this box was our money, also the best and most valuable of what my master possessed. Great efforts were made to recover the things, but all we could find was the empty box, lying outside the town in the middle of some gardens. In this difficulty Anthoine Cheleby gave us whatever we had need of for the expenses of our journey.

[After fifty days in Burca, Lord Bellomont and his retainers left for Persia.]

We pursued our route along with the caravan, which was a very large one. In it were several Armenian merchants, who looked after our food, also our horses, mules, and camels. We put up in their tents, where we were very well treated; but this was not done without an object, for the Armenians are very fond of their own interest. After some days we arrived at Tocat (Tokat). In this town, which lies among mountains, we remained eight days, after which we started again with the whole caravan, keeping our eyes ever open as we advanced by reason of the robbers who often on these routes attack caravans. This is the reason why men travel armed, and at night sentinels are set on watch on every side, so that no one can come near the encampment. One day it happened that there was a great alarm, some horsemen having appeared who wanted to rob us. Twenty-two of our mounted men went out against them, and prepared to attack them; but the robbers took to flight. Still, one of them was caught; his horse being much out of condition, could not gallop like the others. He was made prisoner.

The next day the robbers sent a message praying that their comrade might be released, and 10,000 *pataques* must be sent. If not, they would attack the caravan, and give quarter to no one. This news caused some apprehension in the caravan; but the leader of it, who was a brave man and experienced in these journeys, showed no fear, but, on the contrary, he sent word to them in a rage that he would come out in pursuit and leave not one alive. Thus the negotiations on both sides were confined to threats and defiance; and this went on for three days, during which the robber horseman was always guarded by two of our mounted men. After three days, one night, while the caravan was asleep, the thief escaped, and the quarrel came to an end.

In these journeys one has to be extremely vigilant, taking care never to go any distance from the caravan, for those who do so run a very great risk of falling into the hands of clever thieves, and of losing both goods and life, as has happened to many. If any traveller intends to make this journey, he will do well to arm himself with a great deal of patience, and take good thought of the hardships and disagreeables which he will have to encounter on these roads. For it is not as in Europe, where there are inns in which all the necessities and comforts requisite for life are to be found. When travelling in Turkey you must sleep on the ground on a piece of carpet, or on the top of some bale of goods, where you suffer from the cold. Then, in the middle of your sleep, you are roused hurriedly to get ready and load up the camels and horses, and start on your way. During the day you are much troubled with the heat of the sun. Often it happens that the Turks seek you out and assail you with much abuse, and subject you to much indignity and shame. In these encounters it is wise to hang your head down like a Capuchin, and not open your mouth. At times it is necessary to bear slaps on the face with humility and even endure beating with a stick, for fear of worse happening. For if a hand is raised by chance against a Turk, such person is forthwith either forced to become a Mahomedan, or he is decapitated. The greatest favour accorded to him would be to let him go free after cutting off his hand. It is requisite to inform all who mean to travel in these regions that they must not wear anything of a green colour. Turks only may wear clothes of that colour. This remark applies to Turkey, for in Persia and in the Mogul Empire Christians can wear any colour they like. But the Turks are very particular about green, it having been liked and approved by the false prophet Mahomed.

No traveller need to expect to find wine on the journey, for only water is drunk. In order never to be without water, it is necessary to have a bottle hanging from, or attached to, the beast on which one rides, and thus be able to have recourse to it in case of need. The bottles so used are easily procurable, and are sold ready for use. The merchants who go on these journeys also carry with them nets, with which they can catch fish. Many buy a kind of boiled sour milk called *jugurd* in the language of the country. It is put in a say (? sieve), so that the water in it may drain away; and in that way it can be kept several days. We ate it several times mixed with water, putting in it biscuits or dry bread, or it was mixed with *pelos* (? pilão). It is very palatable. When any dwellings are met with you can get eggs, butter, fowls, goats, and a few kinds of ripe fruit. But it is advisable to carry with you some dried fruit, meat fried in butter and packed in leather vessels; also sausages and puddings of salted beef, for it is at times impossible to obtain any food. And the best advice that I can give is, not to allow your curiosity to carry you so far as to look into the earthen houses of the country, or to examine the peasants who dwell in them, for thereby one runs the risk of a thousand mishaps and evil fortune.

After having passed over this wearisome road in the midst of dangers and across swamps, we arrived at Erzerūm, where are to be found many Armenians, for it is a town with a great trade, lying upon the Turkish frontier. There we remained six days.

Good bread and plentiful supplies are found in the town, but the Turks there are dishonest boors; they examined our baggage with great severity (a common occurrence in this town, one of which all travellers complain). We were able, however, to conceal several presents that we were carrying for the King of Persia. At the end of the six days we left the town and continued our journey. After marching for two days, we came to a fortress built in the rock on the top of high ground; at its foot was a small town called Hassamcala (Ḥasanqala'h). When we had passed that place, and on the same day, the men of Erzerūm examined our baggage a second time, to see if there were no merchandise hidden by us; and although we had very few things, they insisted on our paying customs dues a second time, finishing up by cursing us as they bade us farewell. However, we had made over to an Armenian the swords that we were taking as a present for the King of Persia; we had also confided to him a box in which were the letters of the embassy. This man had taken another route, and overtook us during the night at a place where we were free from the attempts of such-like people.

Next day we continued our march, and after going on for eight days we reached a stream called the Aras, over which one has to cross several times. In the end, by slow degrees, we arrived on Persian territory, where we had the consolation of being both freer and more honoured than in the country we had just left. In due time we came to Erivan, a region which once on a time belonged to the Armenians, and thus there are still a great many of them living there. Erivan is situated just in front of a great mountain called Ararat. They say that it was on this mountain that the Ark of Noah rested. At a distance of some ten leagues from the town the mountain looked as if entirely covered with ice on its summit, and when the sun shone on it, its appearance was splendid. There are many brooks at the foot of this mountain, and the ground is covered throughout the year with sweet-smelling flowers. The town is enclosed by very thick and strong walls of earth, so that cannon would not be able to do as much damage as they would on a wall of stone, the reason being that the stones fracture while the earth does not. The country round is fresh, fertile, delicious, abounding in oil and fruit. We halted for ten days.

We drew up at a spot near Erivan, whence the Armenians who were with us went to inform the *Cam* (*Khān*), or governor of the place, that an ambassador had come from the King of England, Charles II., son of King Charles I., and was on his way to the King of Persia. On receiving this information the *Khān* sent at once to compliment him on his arrival, and invited him to enter the town. On the following day, according to the usage in regard to all ambassadors who come to the King of Persia, we were well received in the greatest pomp by the governor, who gave a banquet, and presented to the ambassador four horses and several pieces of silk. Then he issued orders that every day our wants were to be carefully attended to; we and our animals were to be fed plentifully. We remained in this place ten days, receiving numerous visits and passing our time agreeably, the pleasure being enhanced by seeing ourselves in a land of plenty, and in the midst of a people more polite than those we had just left behind. When we were ready to make a start, the governor sent a horseman and several armed men on foot to accompany us, as it is the habit to do for all ambassadors. These men go on ahead and get ready whatever is required for food and repose in the villages. Thus we were relieved of all trouble and exertion.

At the end of five days we arrived with our followers at the town of Tauris (Tabrīz). This town is the same as the ancient Ecbatana, built by Arfaxad, King of the Medes, as may be read in the Book of Judith chapter i. At present it is inhabited by people of various nationalities: there are many Armenian merchants; many carpets are manufactured, and also pieces of silk, velvet, and brocade. Although the governor was not actually present in the town, having gone to one of the provinces, my lord was acknowledged as an ambassador, and treated as is the custom for such. We dwelt for some thirty days in this place, where we equipped ourselves and got ready new clothes to be worn on our arrival at the court of the King of Persia. He was then at Casbin (Qazwīn). We were forced to have new clothes, those we had being of Turkish pattern.

Before entering the town I noticed an open place where stood two pillars which marked the distance that a stick had been thrown by Sultan Morad (Murād) the Grand Signor, when he came to take Tabrīz. But it seems almost impossible that a man should be able to throw a stick so far. I noticed also that the town is fairly large, surrounded by gardens which contain fine trees yielding good fruit. There are many mulberry trees, so that they have much silk, of which they make various kinds of stuff.

At the end of thirty days we started again, accompanied as before, and with the same retinue. As we went along, I saw that the land did not produce so many trees, nor was water so plentiful as in Turkey; for in Persia they are forced in many places to bring water from a great distance through underground channels. They make big holes to see if there is running water underneath, and whether it is sufficient. In the open country there are certain dry plants on which the sheep subsist and grow fat. They have very long and broad tails from which much fat is obtained, and their wool is excellent. The skins of these sheep are very soft, and the wool curly; it is usual to make fur coats from them, and also hats. I have also noticed in Persia that there is no firewood, and in place of it they burn cow-dung, also the droppings of camels, horses, asses, and sheep.

How we were sent for Twice to the Royal Palace at Qazwīn

At the end of thirteen days we arrived at the city of Qazwīn, where the king, Xaabas (Shāh 'Abbās), was. We were conducted to a house made ready for the purpose; and after three days a captain came, accompanied by several cavalry soldiers, to visit the ambassador on behalf of the chief ministers of the king. He presented congratulations on our arrival, with many compliments and offers of service. Subsequently the ambassador paid a visit to the chief minister, called Etmadolat ('Aẕamat-ud-daulah), which means "Modesty of Wealth," by whom he was well received with many polite speeches and compliments, in which the Persians are never wanting. Between them there was much conversation in the Turkish language, the chief object of which was directed to finding out what presents we had brought for the King of Persia; secondly, to know the ambassador's rank, so that the proper honours might be paid to his person. Hearing from the Armenians that he (Bellomont) was of a great family, 'Aẕamat-ud-daulah sent to Smyrna to obtain information whether or not he were of the great family that he claimed to be. Meanwhile, after eight days from our arrival, we were sent for to the royal palace, into which we went through numerous gates, ending in a large court-yard, in the midst of which stood two beautiful trees full of shade. Beneath them were two lions fastened with heavy golden chains; before each lion was a large golden basin full of water. Also below each tree stood a well-dressed man with long moustachios reaching to his shoulders, in his hand a short spear all of gold, with his face turned towards the royal seat. We went on our way, and next came to an open hall, which had twenty beautiful gilt pillars, ornamented with many kinds of floral designs and many coloured enamels. Here we seated ourselves in the expectation that the king would come out.

An hour afterwards the king arrived in great state, whereupon all rose to their feet, and crossed their hands on their breasts, and made a bow with lowered heads. This, too, was done by the ambassador, seeing that this was the custom of that court. Then, approaching the king, he delivered to him the letter, which the king took with his own hand, and placed in that of the chief minister, who stood at his side.

The king seated himself in his place, and the master of ceremonies, who was close to the ambassador, pointed out to him his place, which was the fifth on the right hand. He was to sit there. On taking his seat he presented a breastplate, a headpiece (*morion*), and sword-mountings, all of fine work made at Paris. All these were accepted by the king, who looked at the ambassador with a pleased face, saying to him that he was delighted at his coming. All this was spoken through an interpreter, an Armenian, who was in our employ. Then he asked after the health of the King of England, inquiring if he had any brothers, if he were married, how old he was, and whether he was loved by his people. To all these questions the ambassador replied; and after the lapse of one hour the king rose, saying to the ambassador that he should take rest and recover from his fatigues. Meanwhile he forwarded to Espahaõ (Iṣfahān) the letter brought by the ambassador in order to have it translated by a Capuchin friar named Frey Raphael Dumans, well acquainted with the Turkish and Persian languages, a priest of great virtues, loved by the king and all the court.

The letter having been translated, the king sent to the ambassador an invitation to come to court, where he gave him a banquet at his own table. It was given in the hall already described, which was decorated with rich brocade and handsome cushions. In the assembly was the king seated in the midst of ten persons. That is to say, on his right hand 'Aẓamat-ud-daulah, then three of the great officials, and in the fifth place the ambassador, and on his left hand other five men, who were the chief generals then actually present at court.

Below the royal seat, which was raised the height of a foot, there were on each side thirty persons, all men of rank and position.

They placed in front of the king twelve large basins of gold filled with polas (*pulāo*) of various kinds, and four dishes of different roast meats, six porcelain vessels holding various other meats, and several boxes having their covers ornamented with all sorts of precious stones. Each of those who were on the two sides of the king had the half of what the king himself had placed before him, and the sixty who were farther down, away from the king's side, had each of them four basins of *pulao*. At this banquet wine was absent; and although the king knew how to drink a drop or two, on this occasion he refrained as a matter of dignity. When the first course was finished, the second was brought, consisting of much fruit and numerous sweet dishes.

The reader will be pleased to learn what *pulāo* means. *Pulāo* is rice cooked with many spices: cloves, cinnamon, mace, pimento, cardamoms, ginger, saffron, raisins, and almonds, to which is added the flesh of sheep, or fowls, or goats, and the whole dressed with plenty of butter. They make these *pulāos* of many sorts and of different flavours.

When the feast had ended, the king rose and said to the ambassador that he might start for the city of Iṣfahan, for which he himself would set out in a few days. This sending off of milord was because they were waiting for the answer from Smyrna, whether it was true that he had been sent as an ambassador by the King of England, Charles II., and whether he was of the rank that he claimed. At the end of six months the answer came, as I shall mention presently. Meanwhile we had spent fifty days in this city of Qazwīn, and every day there came to us food in abundance for every one of our people, with sufficient wine, and whatever was necessary for our animals.

The city of Qazwīn stands in the midst of several mountains; it has sufficient water, many gardens, and much fruit, a fitting place for the holiday resort of a king, however great he may be, where he can go out after game, with which the country is well supplied.

We came out of Qazwīn to start for Iṣfahān, and neither at the time of leaving nor during the journey were the accustomed supplies delivered to us. None the less, we managed to make our journey in sufficient comfort, and in twelve days we reached Iṣfahān, where there was made over to us as a dwelling a large house with a lovely garden. It was the property of the general of the king's artillery, who was then in Qazwīn. There we fed ourselves at our own expense.

Finally, at the end of three months, when winter had passed, the king arrived at Iṣfahān, and we were obliged to leave that house where the general lived, and they made over to us another. After a few days the ambassador sent a message to 'Aẓamat-ud-daulah that he desired to pay him a visit, but the answer returned was that in these days, the king being newly-arrived, he was very much occupied, and he (the ambassador) must have a little patience, and that notice would be given of the time when they could meet.

Thus matters were kept in suspense till the answer from Smyrna should arrive. Finally, they learnt that without any doubt the Belmont (Lord Bellomont) had been sent as ambassador, and that he was of the rank that he asserted. Three months after the king's arrival at Iṣfahān, 'Aẓamat-ud-daulah sent for the ambassador, and held with him a long conversation. I was present the whole time, quite close to the ambassador, who put me forward as his son.

In the speech he made, he (the ambassador) told how the king, Charles I., was unjustly beheaded by his subjects, who into his place had raised a man of low origin, banishing King Charles II. and his brother James from the kingdom, and persecuting them. He had, therefore, come to His Majesty of Persia to ask for help, in accordance with the friendship which had always existed between the crowns of England and of Persia.

'Aẓamat-ud-daulah asked in what way could his king give aid such as he required. Then the ambassador replied that he should call to mind the word given long ago by the King of Persia to afford help to the King of Great Britain, should occasion arise. That also he still owed for the expenses incurred by the King of England when he sent a fleet to take the fortress of Orumus (Ormuz) from the hands of the Portuguese, and made it over to Persia. It was also most desirable that he should assist King Charles II. at this conjuncture, by expelling from his dominions all the English who were partisans of the rebellion, and compel them to abandon their trade. By thus doing the praise of the generous acts of the famous Persian king would go through all the world. 'Aẓamat-ud-daulah, having listened to this reasoning with a solemn countenance, replied with a smile that he would report to the king all that had been said, and would give an answer afterwards. With this ended the interview.

When eight days had elapsed from the visit to the *wazīr* the ambassador was invited to a grand banquet in a beautiful palace that the king had recently completed. At its gateway stood the large and handsome cannon which were captured at Ormuz. They were near a large reservoir of nice appearance and very pleasant. At this second feast which the king gave him, the ambassador was treated with great honours in deference to his embassy, 'Aẓamat-ud-daulah and a number of officers proceeding to the gates of the palace to meet him, and continuing in his suite until he arrived before the king. The latter caused his guest to be seated in the second place—that is to say, 'Aẓamat-ud-daulah came first, then the ambassador, then three of the king's officers; there being on the left hand five other persons, the greatest of the generals. The seat was larger than in Qazwīn, with greater richness, and the room more beautiful. In it were sundry officials and captains, who stood.

There was not much conversation. The king only asked the ambassador whether the climate of Persia suited him; to which the ambassador replied that, after all, the climate of Persia had much resemblance to that of England, by reason of the frosts and snows that it had. I was standing behind the ambassador, and the king asked who I was. The ambassador answered that he looked upon me as his son. The king said to him that if he chose to make me over to him he would treat me very well, and thus there would be a memorial of him left at the court. The ambassador said that if I were in reality his son he would make me over to His Majesty, but as my parents had placed me in his care, he could not part with me.

This was the conversation that we had until, after one hour had passed, the table was laid; it was much more imposing and more highly adorned than the one at Qazwīn. The place where the king was seated was larger, and the carpets of greater value and more beautiful. The king's whole table vessels were of gold, with covers having handles ornamented with precious stones. In the lower seats were on each side fifty men, all nobles, including a few men of learning. Among these the king ordered me to take my seat. Each person had four plates full of *pulão*, also various dishes of roast and fried meat, and some of pickles. I noticed that all these men were of large frame, tall, and well made, with huge moustachios which some of them had twisted round their ears, so that they might not fall on their shoulders. All were well clad in rich stuffs, and wore enormous turbans. Many of them ate voraciously.

The first course being finished, they set before us the second, consisting of a great quantity of fruit, which in Isfahān is very plentiful. This course lasted two hours, and at the end of it the king rose and entered the female apartments. 'Azamat-ud-daulah conducted the ambassador to the end of the room, holding him by the hand, saying that nothing should be wanting on his part to do him service, with many amicable speeches, in which this kind of people are never deficient.

Some days elapsed after the above invitation, when 'Azamat-ud-daulah sent to the ambassador from the king fifty pieces of gold and silver brocade, velvet, and various-coloured silk, four pairs of handsome carpets, and 2,000 *patacas*, which arrived just at the right time; for the ambassador had run into debt with certain Armenian merchants, and with this money he paid his debt. After a very few days the ambassador went to the house of 'Aẓamat-ud-daulah, where he remained a long time in consultation, the subject being the following:

The ambassador demanded a favourable reply, saying that it was necessary for him to leave. 'Azamat-ud-daulah made use of many friendly expressions, but was not desirous of answering the proposition laid before him. By putting questions he feigned an eagerness to know whether England was a large kingdom, how many men it could place in the field, if there were a route to it by land. He appeared to be much amazed that all the kings of Europe, being themselves Christian, did not afford succour to the King of England.

The ambassador replied to all this, but chiefly to this last question. He said if the King of Persia would pay the money that he owed, the King of England could then, without other assistance, obtain possession of his kingdom, and seize his enemies. Seeing the stiff answer of the ambassador, 'Aẓamat-ud-daulah succeeded in sending him away with pleasant words.

During the time the ambassador was in Isfahān, the king decided to have a parade of his armed force, and make a display of his power. For this affair he sent an invitation to the ambassador. We repaired to the very large royal hall, containing forty pillars, which has an outlook on the great square. In this hall the king takes his seat but rarely, and only when he has a review of his cavalry. These reviews are held twice a year; each time they last three days.

We went one day only. We saw the cavalry enter at one side of the plain and march out at the other. The soldiers, forty thousand in number, were mostly clad in mail, and bore maces; some squadrons had lances, others bows and arrows, others matchlocks. All were mounted on good and swift horses, and they carried standards bearing devices. At the end of the review we saw two Persians bound each on a camel, with their bowels protruding. Their offence was causing a disturbance, after they had drunk too much wine. These men were conducted thus through the city until they died.

The ambassador, although somewhat doubtful of obtaining an answer such as he desired, never desisted from importuning 'Aẓamat-ud-daulah, reminding him that it was close upon a year that he had been in Isfahan without making the smallest advances in the negotiations for which he had come so far. 'Aẓamat-ud-daulah put him off from day to day. At length, tired out by so many remonstrances, he made up his mind to give an answer. With this view he sent a message to the ambassador, requesting him to be good enough to come to his house, as he wanted to speak to him.

We repaired to the house of 'Aẓamat-ud-daulah, who received the ambassador with many gracious words and much politeness. Seating themselves they began a long conversation to the following effect: 'Azamat-ud-daulah began a very long way off by remarking that the King of Persia was a great friend of the King of England, and cherished for him the same amity that he had felt towards the former kings, his ancestors; he greatly desired to assist that king, chiefly owing to the great necessity of the case. This was the reason that he had postponed his reply, while he searched for and considered ways in which he could give assistance. But he could find no manner of so doing. The Persian cavalry and the rest of their troops could not be sent, by reason of the great distance by the land route. On the road were many kingdoms through which they must pass. Thus it was impossible to be of any use by sending an armed force. Then he had sought for some means of helping him by way of the sea; but to send a great fleet he saw was extremely difficult. In Persia they had no ships, and, should they attempt to construct them, they had not sufficient materials for the purpose.

Another reason for the long delay in giving an answer was this: they had used the interval to find out from the nations of Europe—the Portuguese, the Dutch, and even the English themselves—whether they could purchase any ships in which to send reinforcements to the king. But in spite of all the offers they had made, they could not obtain what they wanted. The ambassador knew well that this was all a pretence, but he kept his temper, although showing signs of impatience at all this long-winded and superfluous talk.

When 'Aẓamat-ud-daulah had finished this long speech, the ambassador began as follows: First of all, he expressed his thanks for the great efforts that the King of Persia and 'Aẓamat-ud-daulah had taken to assist the King of England. Then, half making fun of 'Aẓamat-ud-daulah's many words, he said to him that he himself had a much easier method of remedying all this, without giving trouble to the Persian monarch, and without fatiguing the Persian soldiers, so famous throughout Europe. This plan was that the King of Persia should pay, cash down, the money due on the bill owing to the King of England. He had not come all that long journey in search of cavalry, nor a fleet, nor ships, but of a debt in arrears. If he would excuse him, he would say a word or two frankly. To this 'Aẓamat-ud-daulah replied that he might speak as freely as he liked. Upon this the ambassador continued that all that had been said by him showed that his king had no intention of paying the debt. 'Aẓamat-ud-daulah, in a deceptive manner and smiling, said that his king wished to pay, but, seeing that the amount demanded was very large, it would require a great number of beasts of burden, that it would be necessary to pass through other kingdoms, that possibly he might be robbed on his way. Nor was the difficulty met by saying that he could carry the amount by sea, for all the world knew what risks were run at sea, both of being attacked and of being wrecked, whereby the whole amount would be lost.

The ambassador's answer was that, if they gave him the money, he knew quite well how to take care of it and remove it in safety. If they paid over to him a sufficient sum, the King of England, his master, would have no other demand to make. He would hold himself satisfied, according to the orders he had received, as set forth in the letters he had presented. This he said with a certain show of emotion, for by this time he saw that their object was to pay him in words.

'Aẓamat-ud-daulah hung his head down and affected a mild expression of countenance, then said in a low voice: "Necessity is not the most perfect of judges." He added that, as to banishing from the Persian realm the English traders, that could not be; for the king had allowed them willingly to enter his territory —the land of Persia was free to all—and the king declined to turn out any one unless he had been guilty of an offence. All the same, they would grant him (Bellomont) leave to eject them from the kingdom himself by his own forces. The king would back up neither one side nor the other.

Finally, being wearied out, the ambassador said, with a certain amount of passion, that he had not looked for such an answer from a king of such fame in the world, especially after the Persian kingdom had received aid from the King of England, at great cost to the latter. 'Aẓamat-ud-daulah did not change countenance, but endeavoured to pacify the ambassador, saying that such events were sent from above, that never was all that we asked of God granted us, that in due time God would bring to mind his king. Encouraging him and consoling him with kind and soft words, he added that, if he were in any difficulty for expenses, he could send to his interpreter, who would help him. Hearing this, the ambassador said not a single word, but rose hastily, came forth, and returned home. When he had arrived there, he by-and-by gave an order for the sale of some pieces of cloth and some carpets which still remained, to provide for our road expenses.

The above conversation was in Turkish, which I could already speak and understand sufficiently. Listening to everything with the greatest attention, I admired the way in which 'Aẓamat-ud-daulah was able to evade the aggressive answers of the ambassador without betraying any sign of ill-humour.

The firm words of the ambassador were the cause of their giving him his leave to depart after a brief delay. With this intent, eight days after the above-mentioned conversation, he was sent for to court on behalf of the king, when we were given another feast like the one which I have described, and in the same place. At the end of the banquet 'Aẕamat-ud-daulah took the ambassador by the hand and led him in front of the royal seat at a distance of two or three paces, and with his face towards the king. The ambassador was on the left side of 'Aẕamat-ud-daulah. The latter put his hand into his pocket and drew forth a bag of gold brocade, in which was a letter. Lifting this bag with both hands, he placed it on his head, making a profound reverence to the king, bowing his head most deeply. Then he handed the said bag to the ambassador, saying that his king sent that letter to the King of England. He was directed to make obeisance as he had seen the others do. During this short speech 'Aẕamat-ud-daulah held half the bag in his hand, while the other half was in that of the ambassador. As soon as the brief speech was ended the ambassador drew the bag from the hands of 'Azamat-ud-daulah, and quickly turned his back, and without any sort of bow held it out contemptuously to the interpreter. This man at once hastened up to receive the letter with both hands, for the motion made by the ambassador showed that, if he did not hurry near, the ambassador would throw the bag at him.

Then, without any civility, or any sort of bow, he left 'Aẕamat-ud-daulah standing where he was and went out, his head high, while the king sat with cast-down eyes as if he saw nothing of what was passing. All those present remained in silent wonder at such boldness. I was quite close to the ambassador, and came out, notwithstanding with some amount of dread, anticipating that the king would send out some order to have us killed. But we were not interfered with.

On arriving home we took measures to prepare ourselves without delay for continuing our journey—in fact, we did so at the end of nine days; and the ambassador, not being provided with sufficient funds for our expenses, applied to the head of the English factory at Isfahān, who was called Mestre Jhon (Mr. Young), a very short man, but most generous and liberal, as I made note of from the feasts and offerings which several times he had given to the said ambassador.

The city of Isfahān is very large, situated in a great plain at the foot of some low hills. It has four canals of water, which flow through the midst of it, and these serve for irrigating the gardens. These canals issue from a river which flows between Julpha (Zulfah) and Iṣfahān; its name is Senderuth (Zindah-rūd); over it are four bridges somewhat distant from each other. Of the four, two are especially handsome—namely, the one on the road from Iṣfahān to Julpha (Zulfah). You approach it by a long and wide raised way, adorned on both sides with the great and beautiful walled gardens of the king, and with high trees, called in Persian "chenar" (*chanār*), and in European languages "planes." In the midst thereof flows one of the aforesaid canals of water, which fills various reservoirs for the use of the said gardens, and goes on its course until it reaches again the river from which it was taken. Horses are ridden on the raised way.

There are many seats where the Persians imbibe tobacco from crystal "guriguris," called by them "caliaõ" (*qaliyān*), which are long and narrow-necked circular flasks filled with water, having a vessel of tinned copper or of silver in the shape of an open flower of the water-lily stuck into its (the flask's) mouth, and filled with tobacco. With this they sit, telling stories until late, sometimes, without exaggeration, as many as five or six thousand of them.

The second bridge, which is the finest of them all, is called the bridge of Xiras (Shīrāz), thus named because when going from Iṣfahān to Shīrāz you cross over it. The bridge consists of three stories besides the chief one, which is in the middle. The king goes there sometimes with his harem, and he can descend to the water without being seen. By all these stories you can cross from one side of the river to the other. The water runs over dressed stones, made artificially high or low, so as to produce waves pleasing to behold.

I noticed that the houses of Iṣfahān, and those throughout Persia, seen from the front, are not pleasing, being all made of clay; but they are lovely inside, and highly decorated. They have both large and small gardens, with good fruit trees—that is to say, pears, apples, peaches, apricots, mulberries, sweet and sour quinces, like the apples of Europe, vines of Boas Vuas, and vineyards of Vuas, grapes without stones, which are called "quiximis" (*kishmish*), many kinds of plums—and all the varieties of flowers that grow in Europe, for the Armenians are very fond of growing European flowers, and present them to the Persian nobles. The Persians, as also the Moguls, are fond of flowers and perfumes.

In front of the royal palace is a large plain, where throughout the year stand fruit-sellers' booths, and a large quantity of exquisite melons. Here they drink coffee and smoke tobacco; the place is always full of people going and coming. Here are to be seen dancers, wrestlers, and other performers. In one corner of this open square is a palace where musical instruments are played; and there stands the clock found by them in the fortress of Ormuz, which they preserve as a memorial of their victory over the Portuguese. The city is always clean, due to the energy of the gardeners, because with what is removed from the streets they manure their gardens. They collect most industriously the sewage from the houses for the same purpose. This is a great help to keeping the air pure by not allowing dirt to accumulate in the city. There are also many baths, where the body may be washed. The soul also profits (as they believe), for when they wash themselves they imagine themselves to be absolved from their sins. Ablution serves among the Mahomedans—and speaking always with due reverence—like confession and absolution among us Catholics. In the city are two factories—one of the English, the other of the Dutch. There are also four churches—one of the Portuguese Augustinians, which the present king caused to be entirely gilded at his own expense, and he went there several times to see our ceremonial. Another church belongs to the bare-footed Carmelites, another to the Jesuits, another to the Capuchins.

There are also in the city many mosques, among them a dome with two tombs, which are much venerated. The door of this dome is only opened once a year, on the occasion of a great festival, to which flock people from different provinces on the appointed day. One tomb they assert to be that of 'Alī, the other they state to be that of his sons Assen (Ḥasan) and Ossen (Ḥusain), who are revered as martyrs. Others declare they are tombs of the companions of Muḥammad, although he had no court or courtiers.

We were now to continue our journey, wherefore we begged the help of Mestre Jonh (Henry Young), who gave to the ambassador the assistance he required. We wished to leave Iṣfahān in company with the said Mestre Jonh (Henry Young), but we could not conclude our business in time. He left several days before we did, and we left at the end of September, of one thousand six hundred and fifty-two (1652).

During our journey to the town of Xiras (Shīrāz)

we obtained good supplies of food, but the road is somewhat difficult, owing to the mountain ranges which must be crossed, where horses are fatigued not a little in trying to keep their feet. But I must allow there is also some fine open country, notwithstanding there are some very difficult swamps. The mountains are like all those in Persia—that is to say, generally bare of trees, though not wanting in fodder for sheep and goats, which in some places produce the stone called *b'azar* (bezoar). Of these stones I will speak when I come to write of the kingdom of Gulkhandah, where there is an abundance of them.

The sheep of Persia are very prolific; they bring forth young twice a year, by the help of a grain called *chicharos*, on which they are fed at a certain time of the year; and their wool is of the sort already described (p. 8).

Finally, at the end of fifteen days' travel, we arrived at the town of Xiras (Shīrāz), where we stayed for thirty days, the ambassador having fallen ill. He received many visits from a barefooted Carmelite friar, a missionary to the Armenians who dwell here. The air of this town is very fresh; there are many gardens with good fruit, and the country round produces a quantity of grapes; consequently they make a great deal of wine, which is exported to all parts of India. Although the law of the Mahomedans forbids the drinking of wine, still the King of Persia permits the English to make it; but they only produce enough for the company and not to sell to others. In this region there is no deficiency of food produced, of oranges, of lemons, nor, above all, of roses, which they distil, and the rose-water is forwarded in boxes to all parts.

One of the wonderful things round Shīrāz is a famous building standing at a distance approximately of two leagues, where dwelt, as they declare, the great Darius, King of Persia, who was defeated in battle by

Alexander the Great. There is also a mountain in which is a cave where drips a liquid called by the Persians *mumihay* (*mūmiyāī*). This liquid belongs to the king exclusively, and thus the cave is closed by doors and guarded by vigilant sentinels. It is the business of these men to collect the liquid (which drips in minute quantities) and then forward it to the king. When he wishes to make a gift to anyone, he gives them a little of this liquid. This is on account of the admirable results it produces—that is, for all bruises, fractures of bones, and sores.

If what they say is true, though I have not made the experiment, should the leg of a cock or other animal be broken and you take of the above liquid ten to fifteen drops and give it to the animal to drink, at the same time anointing the wounded place with it, then, if it is a true story, in twenty-four hours the bones will unite. I possessed a little, given me by one of the king's eunuchs. He had effected wonderful cures with it. The principal case was the recovery of a stonemason who fell from a great height, and lay with his bones broken, blood pouring from his mouth, nostrils, and ears, the man having entirely lost his senses and being without hope of life. In two days he was perfectly well. There is also a pond (*pauso*) where on the top of the water floats a ready-made gum which is sold by the natives as the royal liquid, thus cheating a few simpletons. It is not devoid of virtues, but they are nothing like so great as those of the royal liquid.

When the ambassador began to recover his health, we quitted Shīrāz, and in nine days we were at the fort of Lār, which they say was formerly much larger, with a great enclosed space. But in the Middle Ages it was quite small, inhabited by many Hindūs, who bought there the goods brought by traders from Iṣfahān and other places, and then exported them to many countries, principally from the ports of Congo and Bandar 'Abbās.

During our journey from Shīrāz as far as Lār we were in excellent health, but were in some concern lest we should not find water for drinking; for on the roads the water which is used is that collected during the rainy season in great cisterns. The earth being salt, the water which flows over it acquires the same property, and therefore is not potable. For this reason they preserve water in cisterns, in which there are all kinds of filth, and it is only out of absolute necessity that one feels inclined to drink.

In spite of this defect of water the country was sufficiently humid, and many places had their gardens of oranges, of palm trees and date trees bearing dates. In Lār we obtained sufficient food supplies, but water only of the quality described. There was water below ground in channels, as is the custom over almost the whole of Persia. The fort of Lār is placed upon a small hill standing in the midst of four other hills of the same size. Thus the fort in time of war is in want of protection from good walls and dependent edifices, for an enemy who occupied the aforesaid hills could easily attack the fort.

After a day's rest we left Lār and journeyed through open and agreeable country, coming to different "sarays" (*sarāes*), where we obtained grapes and melons for our consumption. We moved between hills of salt, we crossed several streams, whose crystal clearness invited us to drink, but their waters were so salt that no one could even pass them over his tongue. Among the rest is a stream called Ryo Salgado (Salt River), over which was a great bridge of more than thirty arches. In nine days, after sufferings enough, we arrived at Gomoram (Gombroon), of which the other name is Bandarabassi (Bandar 'Abbāsi), meaning "Harbour of Shāh 'Abbās"; for, being a port on the sea, it is called "Bander" (*bandar*), and having been established by the Great Shāh 'Abbās, they have added "abassi" and have come to call it Bandarabassi. This harbour was made by Shāh

'Abbās, after having recovered from the hands of the Portuguese, with the aid of the English, the famous island and fort of Orumus (Hormuz).

This island was formerly the greatest and most frequented port on the ocean, where dwelt traders to every region in India—men of great wealth—so that a merchant possessing more than a million of *patacas* (about £100,000) was not a man of very great account. Shāh 'Abbās considered that by making himself master of Hormuz, and transferring the port to the mainland, lying not over a league from the island, he would be able to draw all this wealth into Persia. But he was frustrated in his object because the traders were afraid of his interference. The island has many hills of salt, and the climate is therefore prejudicial to life. Notwithstanding this, the Persians are so jealous about the island that they do not wish a single European to set foot in it.

After we had been at Bandar 'Abbās three days, the ambassador ordered me to go to the English factory to speak to the chief, requesting him to send a trustworthy person to discuss certain negotiations of great importance. The chief sent to him Mestre Pit (Mr. Pitt), who had acted as page to the English gentleman desirous of speaking to Shāh 'Abbās. With him there was a full hour's discussion. Next day the chief himself came with the officials of the factory to visit the ambassador. Offers were made to him to serve him in every way they could. At the time there was an English vessel, belonging to a private owner, about to sail for the port of Surrati (Sūrat). They asked the ambassador to embark in her, as she would be the last vessel to leave Bandar 'Abbās in that monsoon. Then we ate mutton which came from Hormuz, also good and cheap fish caught in the harbour.

The water at Bandar 'Abbās is either rain-water or brackish, and of such bad quality that it disorders the bodily humours, and generates worms as long as your arm, which appear on the hands, jaws, and legs. When they begin to show themselves you must lay hold of them by the head, and pull at them daily, winding them round a *hide* (? twig) or cloth very slowly. For if they break they turn inwards, causing great pain and becoming very difficult to cure. For this reason, everybody who can do it sends to fetch water by camels from inland, three leagues off, at a place called Hixin. The climate of this port is most noxious by reason of the salt ridges, and of certain hot winds, and the noise of the sea. I noted that many of the inhabitants had defective sight and teeth, and I was informed that on this coast, as far as Arabia and Mecca, they suffered from these ailments by reason of the many dates they eat; for the larger number of the inhabitants live upon that fruit in addition to fish.

Two days after the visit that the Englishmen had paid to the ambassador—that is to say, on the fifteenth of December of one thousand six hundred and fifty-two (1652; should be 1655)—we went on board the said vessel. During the whole of our voyage the captain treated us with great politeness and civility. Setting sail, we arrived in twelve days, having favourable winds, at a port in the Great Mogul's territory called Sindī. There the vessel anchored, and we travelled up-stream by the river for a whole night to an inhabited place, which stood twelve hours' journey from the sea. This river is a very large one, it being formed of seven rivers which flow down from the interior of the country, as I will relate hereafter. Here we saw many Arabian and Persian vessels which import great quantities of dates, horses, seed-pearls, incense, gum-mastic, senna-leaves, and Jew's-stones, which come from Mecca. In return they load up with white and black sugar, butter, olive oil, and *cocos*, which medical men call *nos Indica* (Indian Nut). Of this product and its virtues I will make mention farther on. They also export many kinds of white linen (? cotton cloth) and printed goods which are manufactured in the same region. When the business was finished that our captain had to do at this place, we left it, and returned to the vessel. Setting sail, we arrived in a few days at the port of Sūrat on the twelfth of January of one thousand six hundred and fifty-three (1653; correctly 1655–6).

As soon as we anchored milord went ashore secretly, following the advice given to him by our captain and by a private trader to seek a refuge in the town. For the English were going to seize him and put him by force on board one or other of the English vessels, then in harbour and about to sail for England. It produced great astonishment in me to see how milord landed without breathing a word to me. But I heard the reason afterwards when I reached Sūrat, bringing all the baggage which was in my charge. There we found Mestre Jonh (Henry Young), who had left Persia a short time before; and my master announced that he had come as an ambassador from the King to the Great Mogul.

When the Governor of Sūrat heard of the ambassador's arrival, he ordered his secretary to pay him a visit. The message thus brought was that rumour said he had come as ambassador, therefore he was requested to state whether this was true or not. It was necessary for him (the governor) to send a report to the Emperor Xaaiahan (Shāhjahān), then ruling over the Empire of the Great Mogul. The ambassador replied that it was correct, that he could write in all confidence, and announce his arrival. Before I say anything of our stay, I will state something about this port.

I was much amused when I landed to see the greater number of the inhabitants dressed in white clothes, also the many different kinds of people, as well men as women. The latter, mostly Hindūs, do not conceal the face as in Persia and Turkey, where women go about with their faces hidden. It is true that the Mahomedan women do not allow their faces to be seen by anyone, it being contrary to their law to allow themselves to be seen with an uncovered face. But among other things I was much surprised to see that almost everybody was spitting something as red as blood. I imagined it must be due to some complaint of the country, or that their teeth had become broken. I asked an English lady what was the matter, and whether it was the practice in this country for the inhabitants to have their teeth extracted. When she understood my question, she answered that it was not any disease, but (due to) a certain aromatic leaf, called in the language of the country, *pān*, or in Portuguese, *betele.* She ordered some leaves to be brought, ate some herself, and gave me some to eat. Having taken them, my head swam to such an extent that I feared I was dying. It caused me to fall down, I lost my colour, and endured agonies, but she poured into my mouth a little salt, and brought me to my senses. The lady assured me that every one who ate it for the first time felt the same effects.

Betel, or *pān*, is a leaf similar to the ivy leaf, but the betel leaf is longer; it is very medicinal, and eaten by everybody in India. They chew it along with "arrecas" (*areca*), which physicians call *Avelans Indicas* (Indian filberts) and a little *catto* (*kath* or *katthā*), which is the dried juice of a certain plant that grows in India. Smearing the betel leaf with a little of the *kath*, they chew them together, which makes the lips scarlet, and gives a pleasant scent. It happens with the eaters of betel, as to those accustomed to take tobacco, that they are unable to refrain from taking it many times a day. Thus the women of India, whose principal business it is to tell stories and eat betel, are unable to remain many minutes without having it in their mouths.

It is an exceedingly common practice in India to offer betel leaf by way of politeness, chiefly among the great men, who, when anyone pays them a visit, offer betel at the time of leaving as a mark of goodwill, and of the estimation in which they hold the person who is visiting them. It would be a great piece of rudeness to refuse it.

We remained for seventy-five days in that port—*i.e.* Sūrat—the revenues of which had been given by Shāh Jahān to his daughter, Begom Saeb (Begam Saḥib) to meet her expenditure on betel. During this time we were making our preparations for going on to the court of the Great Mogul. I was much gratified at seeing such plenty in this place, for I had never had such a satisfaction since (I left) my Venice, and felt proud at staying some days in this port, especially after the arrival of the French. During the time we stayed the English never ceased to offer a thousand civilities to milord, the ambassador. But his true friends told him not to trust them, for all they did was in order to get hold of him and carry him off to England. They did their very best once to persuade the ambassador to go on board of an English vessel, then about to depart for England, under the pretext of offering him a banquet with all the state befitting his dignity. But the truth was that they wanted to confine him in the ship, and he most politely made excuses. Then we began to get together our baggage, for which purpose the ambassador was in want of funds. Mestre Jonh (Henry Young) secretly offered to supply all that was required, whether in money or in different sorts of goods, among the latter some fine broadcloth, a handsome clock, an Arab horse for a present to the king, with swords, pistols, matchlocks, and numerous playthings. We started from Sūrat bearing a passport given us by the governor, and in fifteen days we reached the town of Brampur (Burhānpur), where was the court of the Prince Aurangzeb, with whom we had much to discuss. We did not meet with him, by reason of his being at that time in Orangabad (Aurangābād).

We found Brampur (Burhānpur) a town of medium size, and without a wall. Aurangzeb, in the year one thousand six hundred and seventy-six, being then absolute king, caused it to be enclosed by a bulwark and wall along the bank of the river which flows beneath it. This river is not very large, but its waters are clear and good. The town is much frequented by Persian and Armenian traders, on account of the many excellent kinds of cloth manufactured there, chiefly various sorts of women's head-dresses (*touca*) and cloth for veils (*beatilha*), scarlet and white, of exceeding fineness; also for the quantity of iron procured there.

In this town there is plenty of fruit, such as *ambah*, or *mangas* (mango)—the best fruit to be found in India—oranges, limes, citrons, and grapes in abundance. There is also in this town, as throughout the kingdom of the Mogul, a large supply of vegetables of various sorts. On the road to this town we found every day different streams and brooks with good water; also villages, shady and pleasant woods, peopled with many varieties of animals of the chase, such as harts, stags, gazelles, wild oxen (*ores*), peacocks, cooing doves, partridges, quail (*cordernizes*), blackbirds (*tordo*), geese (*patto*), ducks (*ades*), widgeon (*marecas*), and many sorts of birds.

I would warn the reader never to stray far from his companions, because he might come across robbers in these woods. When they find any person apart from his company they rob him. I was very near falling into their hands, for, having gone some distance from the rest of the caravan, I had got off my horse. I was about to shoot at a peacock with my matchlock, when all of a sudden there came out towards me two men with bows and arrows, who with signs and calls invited me to approach them. But I, apprehending what they wanted, went on my way in the direction the rest of the company had gone, never ceasing to have an eye upon those men. These, seeing me choose a different direction, placed arrows in their bows and, hastening their pace, came after me, trying to overtake me. Seeing that otherwise I could never escape them, I stopped and put my matchlock to my cheek as if I meant to fire. Frightened at my firmness, they placed their hands on their heads as a sign of politeness, and, turning their backs, fled with even more agility than when they had followed me. I continued on my way in dread of a similar encounter, and thus I learnt nevermore to leave the rest of the travellers, and I put off my longing to go out shooting until we should reach some place or village. Then I went out to shoot, and without hindrance killed whatever I wished, there being no scarcity of things to kill.

We delayed eight days in Burhānpur, then, resuming our journey, we came in six days to a river called the Narbadā, where there was a town called Andia (Hāndiyah); there was also on the bank of the above-named river a little fort, situated at the crossing-place. This river is a great breadth, and full of large stones. Its waters divide the lands of the Dacan (Dakhin) from those of Industan (Hindūstān), which word means "Hindūdom" (*gentilidade*, place of the heathen).

We crossed the river, and after going eight days through jungle, we arrived at a large town called Seronge (Sironj), which in old days was founded by a Hindū prince, but at present the overlord thereof is the Grand Mogul. This town lies in the midst of the territories of several Hindū princes of the Rājput tribe. Of these the nearest and most powerful is the Rajah Champet Bondela (Champat Rāe, Bundelah), whose country extends to twenty leagues from Agra

(Āgrah), and he has command over fifteen thousand horsemen, and three hundred thousand infantry.

For the use of wayfarers there are throughout the realms of the Mogul on every route many "sarais" (*sarāes*). They are like fortified places with their bastions and strong gates; most of them are built of stone or of brick. In every one is an official whose duty it is to close the gates at the going down of the sun. After he has shut the gates he calls out that everyone must look after his belongings, picket his horses by their fore and hind legs, above all that he must look out for dogs, for the dogs of Hindūstān are very cunning, and great thieves. I may find a good opportunity to speak of the cunning of these dogs.

At six o'clock in the morning, before opening the gates, the watchman gives three warnings to the travellers, crying in a loud voice that everyone must look after his own things. After these warnings, if anyone suspects that any of his property is missing, the doors are not opened until the lost thing is found. By this means they make sure of having the thief, and he is strung up opposite the *sarāe.* Thus the thieves when they hear a complaint made, drop the goods somewhere, so as not to be discovered.

These *sarāes* are only intended for travellers (soldiers do not go into them). Each one of them might hold, more or less, from 800 to 1,000 persons, with their horses, camels, carriages, and some of them are even larger. They contain different rooms, halls, verandahs, with trees inside the courtyard, and many provision-shops, also separate abodes for the women and men who arrange the rooms and the beds for the travellers. I will speak hereafter of the deceits of all these, when I come to talk of the Sultan Amayum (Humāyūn).

We halted four days in Sironj, and then went on our way across inaccessible mountains, with numerous beautiful trees, and traversed by crystal streams, whose waters are most wholesome, doing no harm to those who drink them fasting, rather they are beneficial, and most palatable. In six days we reached the town of Narvar (Narwar), which lies at the foot of a great range of hills six leagues in circumference. On the very highest point of these hills is a fortress, which occupies all the level ground on the summit, with a circumference of two miles—a little more or less—with many houses and rooms; a work made long ago by the Hindūs. But in the course of years, and by the inclemency of the weather, the walls are crumbling away through the negligence of the Mogul king. His object is to destroy all the strong places of the Hindūs of which he can get possession, so that their conquered princes may not rebel against him. His only anxiety is to fortify and supply the forts that are on the frontiers of his kingdom.

We did not halt at this place, but pressed onwards. In five days we arrived at the well-known fortress of Gualior (Gwāliyār), where it is usual for the Mogul to keep as prisoners princes and men of rank. This fortress is on the top of a great mountain having a circuit of three leagues. It is in the middle of a fertile plain, and thus there is no other high ground from which it could be attacked.

There is only a single road to ascend it, walled in on both sides, and having many gates to bar the way, each having its guard and sentinels. The rest of the hill is of rock, perpendicular as a wall, though made by Nature. All around this mountain are to be seen many balconies, lanterns (? kiosks), rooms and verandahs in different styles of architecture, with Hindū sculptures—all of this making the view most agreeable and pleasant to the visitor.

On the crest of the mountain is a great plain, on which are sumptuous palaces with many balconies and windows of various kinds of stone, and delightful gardens irrigated from many crystal springs, where cypress and other lovely trees raise their heads aloft, so as to be visible from a distance. Within this fortress is manufactured much oil of jasmine, the best to be found in the kingdom, the whole of the level ground on the summit being covered with that shrub. There are also in this district many iron-mines, of which numerous articles are made and sent to the principal cities in the Mogul country.

In the town, which lies at the foot of the hill, there dwell many musicians, who gain a livelihood with their instruments, and many persons maintain that it was on this mountain that the god Apollo first started Hindū music.

Continuing our route, we came in three days to the river called the Chambal, at which is the town named Dolpur (Dholpur), where Arangzeb gave battle against his brother Darâ (Dārā Shukoh), in the year one thousand six hundred and fifty-six (correctly 1658), at which I was present, and to which, farther on, I shall refer. Thence in four days we arrived at the city of Āgrah, having ended by doing four hundred and sixty leagues, for such is the number reckoned from Sūrat as far as Āgrah. At this place the governor assigned to us a handsome house to stay in.

We remained in this city, of which I will speak on a future occasion, and, a few days after our arrival, the Englishmen who at that time were present at their factory came to visit the ambassador, showing themselves desirous of being useful to him, making him frequent and handsome offers. But these the ambassador would in no way accept. After several visits they invited him to their house, where they gave him a splendid feast, with dressed meats and beverages after their style. The ambassador complained very much of the great heat that has to be endured in that country, and the English offered him a powder, declaring that if he mixed it and drank it he would experience great relief and coolness.

When a few days had passed we resumed our route for Dely (Dihlī), where at that moment the king, Shāhjahān, was living. Then, after three days from our leaving Āgrah, towards the evening, when in sight of the place where we meant to halt for that night, the ambassador called out to me in great pain, asking me for water. Then he expired without allowing me time to give it to him, those being the last words that he uttered. He died on the twentieth of June of one thousand six hundred and fifty-three (correctly 1656), at five o'clock in the evening. We carried the body at once to a *sarāe* called Orel (Hodal), between Āgrah and Dihlī, and, it being already late, we did not bury him that night. The official at the *sarāe* sent notice to the local judicial officer, who hastened to the spot, and, putting his seal on all the baggage, laid an embargo upon it. I asked him why he seized and sealed up those goods. He answered me that it was the custom of that realm, and that he could not release the things until an order came from court, they being the property of an ambassador.

After seven hours of the night had passed we removed the body of the defunct from the palanquin in order to enshroud it, and, as day began to dawn, we proceeded to lay him in the grave. Taking him by the arms I tried to lift him, but, while in my hands, a blister burst, from which exhaled such a fetid odour that all those standing by nearly fainted and fell down. We were forced to cease to lift him, and await the day. When day arose we somehow or other put him into a coffin, with all the haste that the odour compelled, and interred him on the bank of a reservoir which adjoined the town, marking the spot so that his bones might be transported elsewhere, as accorded with the rank of such a person. And as a fact they removed the remains after fifteen months to the city of Agra (Agrah).

Having interred the ambassador, the servants all disappeared, and I was left alone, sad and anxious, having nothing to console me, nor anywhere to turn in order to recover my things, which had been sealed up by the official along with the ambassador's, although all the keys were in my possession.

After we had buried the ambassador I wrote to the English factory at Āgrah, informing them of his death, and of the embargo imposed by the local officials on his property as well as mine, wherefore I prayed them to send me the necessary recommendatory letters. I received no answer; but eight days afterwards two Englishmen appeared, one called Thomas Roch (? T. Roach), and the other Raben Simitt (? Reuben Smith), dressed after the fashion and costume of the country, men in the service of the King Shāhjahān, and captains of the bombardiers in the royal artillery.

They came to visit me, and when I saw them I asked what they had come about. They informed me that they had come under the king's orders to carry away the property of the ambassador, which lapsed to the crown. To that I retorted by asking if they bore any order, whereupon they laughed, and asked who I might be. I told them I was the servant of the ambassador, that the property in question had been made over to me, that I did not mean to let it go without their delivering to me my belongings—that is, two muskets, four pistols, clothes, and other trinkets, which had been set apart. Their answer was that the whole belonged to the king, and without another word they went to find those who had put on the seals, and obtaining their consent made themselves masters of everything, arranging to remove the whole to the city of Dihlī.

I did not mean to abandon the property, and resolved to set out in their company. On the road they showed me not the least little sign of civility, such as Europeans, even of different nations, are accustomed to display in all parts of Asia when they come across each other. Many a time did I entreat them for God's sake to make over to me what was mine; but as they saw I was only a youth they scoffed at me, and said: "Shut your mouth; if you say a word we will take your horse and your arms away." Seeing there was no other way out of it, I dissembled for the time being, but never despaired of getting back what belonged to me.

After three days' journey we arrived at Dihlī, where the Englishmen deposited the property in a *sarāe*, put seals on the room doors, and told me to go about my business. Then I began to make request that they would be so good as to separate my property from that of the ambassador, and make it over to me, for it did not belong to the king. They burst out laughing and mocked me, giving me the customary answer. As I took my leave I prayed them to do me the favour of telling me their names, so that if anyone called me to account about that property I should be able to defend myself by pointing out the persons who had taken possession of it. I expressed my astonishment that they should lock up in a *sarāe* room property that they said belonged to the king. I asked them angrily whether the king had no other place in which to store the goods he owned; but they knew quite well that the property did not belong to them, and that they were taking the king's name in vain, solely in order that they might get hold of other people's goods. They replied that there was no need to know their names. As for my second remark they only set to laughing, and thus went away in apparent triumph, not foreseeing what was to happen to them.

I retired to a room in the same *sarāe*, not far from the one where the property was. Then I found out the names of those two Englishmen, so as to be able to take my own measures. Being anxious to know what was going on, there turned up on a visit to me a Frenchman, called Clodio Malier, a founder employed in the artillery of Dārā, first-born son of Shāhjahān. With him I talked over what had happened to me with those two Englishmen, and said again that it did not seem to me possible that so great a monarch as the Mogul king should possess no other place to store the goods that belonged to him than a mere *sarāe*, where travellers took up their quarters. The Frenchman assured me that the Englishmen had not seized the goods by order of the king, but that Thomas Roach, learning of the ambassador's death, had sent in a petition to the prince Dārā, by whom he was favoured, in the following terms: "A man of my country, a relation of mine, came from Europe, his purpose being to obtain the honour of serving under your highness, but his good fortune was of such little duration and so scanty that he was unable to obtain his desire, being overtaken by death on reaching the *sarāe* of Hodal, whereupon those who govern in that place laid an embargo upon his goods. Therefore I pray as a favour that your highness be pleased to issue orders for their delivery to me."

The prince dealt with this petition as Thomas Roach hoped, but Raben Semitt (Reuben Smith), getting word of what Thomas Roach was about, held it not to be right that he should acquire the whole of the ambassador's property, that it must be divided between the two of them. Thus he (R. Smith) accompanied him (T. Roach) as far as Hoḍal. Should he not consent to a division, he (R. Smith) threatened to tell the whole story to the king. Thomas Roach accepted the situation, so as not to lose the whole. This was the story told me by Clodio Malier, who bade me adieu with much civility and many offers of service. Being thus informed of what was going on, and confiding in my knowledge of the Turkish, but more especially of the Persian language, which is that chiefly used and most current at the court of the Mogul, I resolved to go to the secretary of the king, whose name was Vizircan (Wazīr K͟hān) to lodge a complaint. For this purpose I went to his house, and, obtaining permission to enter, I reported to him what was going on. He directed me to sit down opposite to him, alongside one of his sons, who was of my age.

The secretary asked me if I knew the accustomed mode of making obeisance before the king by those who enter his presence. I answered that I did. As he displayed a desire to see me do this, I arose, stood quite erect, and, bending my body very low until my head was quite close to the ground, I placed my right hand with its back to the ground, then raising it, put it on my head, and stood up straight. This ceremonial I repeated three times, and this is done to the king only. The secretary was delighted to see a foreigner, young in years and newly arrived in the city, make his obeisances so confidently. I was dressed like a Turk, with a turban of red velvet bound with a blue ribbon, and dressed in satin of the same colour; also a waist-cloth of gold-flowered pattern with a red ground. He was amused to see me got up like this, and asked the reason for adopting such a costume, and why I did not adopt the Mogul fashions, whereupon I acquainted him of the journey that I had made and the countries through which I had passed.

During this time a notice reached him that the king had decided to hold an audience that morning. Then, rising at once, he took me with him to the palace, telling me that it was requisite for me to go with him before the king.

He warned me that, when I came into the king's presence, I must perform the same obeisances that I had practised before him. When we got to the palace the king had already taken his seat on the throne. The secretary directed two men to present me to the king, while he (the secretary) should be talking to him. Accordingly they did present me, ordering me to appear in front of the king at a distance of fifty paces, waiting until he should take notice of me before I made my obeisance.

I had noticed that, when the secretary reached the

place where is the railing, he made one bow, such as I had done at his house; then, when close to the throne, he made three bows; and, approaching still nearer, he began to speak to the king. After a few words he raised his hand towards where I was, as if pointing me out. The king raised his eyes towards me, then the courtiers with me told me to make my obeisances, which I did. The secretary went on with his conversation, which I could not overhear by reason of the distance at which I was. All those who were present before the king were standing; only one man was seated at the side of the throne, but his seat was lower, and this was the Prince Dārā, the king's son.

I noted that the throne on which the king, Shāhjahān, was seated stood in front of, and near to, the palace of the women, so that as soon as he came out of its door he reached the throne. It is like a table, adorned with all sorts of precious stones and flowers, in enamel and gold. There are three cushions—a large one, five spans in diameter, and circular, which serves as a support to the back, and two other square ones, one on each side; also a most lovely mattress: for in Turkey, and throughout the whole of Hindūstān, they do not sit upon chairs, but upon carpets or mattresses, with their legs crossed. Around the throne, at the distance of one pace, are railings of gold, of the height of one cubit, within which no one enters except the king's sons. Before they enter they come and, facing the king, go through their obeisance, then enter the palace and come out by the same door from which the king issued. Arriving there, they again make obeisance, and upon a sign from the king they take their seat in the same enclosure, but at the foot of, and on one side of, the throne. Thereupon the pages appear with the umbrella, parasol, betel, spittoon, sword, and fly-brusher.

Below the throne, several feet lower than it, a space is left, sufficient for the secretary (? *wazīr*) and the greatest officials of the court. This space is surrounded by a silver railing. Near it stand "grusberdares" (*gurz-bardārs*)—that is to say, the bearers of golden maces, whose duty it is to carry orders from the court to princes of the blood royal. After a descent of a few more steps there is another space of greater size, where are the captains and other officials, also the "grusberdares" (*gurz-bardārs*) with silver maces, who convey the orders of the court to the governors, generals, and other princes. These are placed with their backs to a railing of wood painted vermilion, which surrounds the space.

The hall in which stood the royal seat is adorned with twenty highly decorated pillars, which support the roof. This roof stretches far enough to cover the spaces enclosed within the silver railing, and is hidden half-way by an awning of brocade. Further, a canopy over the king's throne is upheld by four golden pillars.

Outside the wooden railing is a great square, where, close to the railing, stand nine horses on one side and nine on the other, all saddled and equipped. Near to the pillars are brought certain elephants on every day that the king gives audience, and there they make their obeisance, as I shall describe when I speak of the elephants. Behind the horses already spoken of were four handsomely adorned elephants, and in the square a considerable number of soldiers stand on guard. At the end was a great hall, where were stationed the players on instruments, and these, upon the king's appearing to give audience, played very loudly, to give notice that the king was already in the audience hall.

The silence preserved was astonishing, and the order devoid of confusion. For this purpose there are officials, whose business it is to see that the people are placed in proper order. Some of these officials held gold sticks in their hands, and these came within the silver railing. The others carried silver sticks, and they took great heed that throughout the court nothing was done which could displease the king.

After I had received my permission to go I left in the company of the two courtiers, and returned to the *sarāe.* There I showed them where I had put up, and the room in which was the property. Thereupon they broke the seals, and brought out all the things, and carried them away.

The next day, about nine o'clock in the morning, there came two servants of the secretary (*wazīr*) to fetch me. They took me to his palace, where I found him seated in the same hall where I had spoken to him the day before. As I came in I observed that the ambassador's property was lying there. I made the usual obeisance to the secretary (*wazīr*). Then with a pleasant look on his face he asked me if I identified the two thieves, pointing with his hand to one corner of the hall. Noticing this, I turned my face that way, and saw the two English impostors, loaded with iron, fetters on their feet and shackles on their necks, and very much ashamed, being afraid that they would be decapitated.

Turning again to the secretary, I craved leave to speak to them, and going near to them I said: "It would have been more honest to let me have the little that was mine, but then you wanted to acquire more than was yours; you suffer through your excess of greed, and in your desire to embrace all you are left with nothing. You laughed, you scoffed, and had no tenderness for me, and now I sorrow for love of you, and feel compassion for the miserable condition in which I see you. You may make certain that I shall not fail to deal towards you with more charity and consideration than you showed me on the road from Hoḍal."

Returning to the secretary (*wazīr*), he told me to look at the things, and inform him whether any article was missing, for the prisoners would have to pay for anything deficient. I examined the property in his presence, and ascertained that it was complete. Since my things had been separated and were kept apart I prayed him as a favour to issue orders that they should be returned to me. In addition, most of the ambassador's goods belonged to an English trader, named Mestre Jonh (Mr. Young), dwelling in Sūrat, from whom the ambassador had obtained them, promising to repay him afterwards.

The secretary (*wazīr*) told me to sit down beside his son, who was in front of him; he said he would give me many things, and making me great promises said to me that if I consented to remain in his house he would treat me like a son. In case I did not agree he did not mean to give me anything. My answer was that I could not live in his house, that I cared very little about the loss of my own things, but should grieve a very great deal if he did not give to Mestre Jonh (Mr. Young) those that were his.

Upon this the secretary (*wazīr*) asked me minutely which were the ambassador's and which Mestre Jonh's (Mr. Young's) things. I pointed them all out in detail, one of the secretary's clerks taking the whole down in writing. I told him that besides these goods Mestre Jonh (Mr. Young) had lent the ambassador the sum of four thousand *patacas* (about £800), and an Arab horse, already in the secretary's (*wazīr's*) possession. Finally I begged leave to return to my abode, and he, in sending me off, directed me to return in two days to speak to him in the same place.

Accordingly this I did, and he said to me that he had spoken to the king, who ordered that the property should be sent to the Governor of Sūrat for the purpose of being made over to Mestre Jonh (Mr. Young), with the exception of the Arab horse, which the king kept for himself, giving an order to pay to the said Jonh (Young) one thousand *patacas*, the price at which it had been valued. He took nothing else but the letter which was destined for him.

After this I made a fresh application to the secretary (*wazîr*) that he would order my property to be given to me; but his answer was that the whole must go to Sūrat, and be made over to Mestre Jonh (Mr. Young), who, if he liked, might give them to me. Thus he was unable to dispose in any way of this property. But if I consented to live with him he would give me a great deal more, and repeated that he would cherish me as his son, and many other promises. For all these words and the kindness he had displayed I gave him thanks over and over again; but as for living with him that could never be. It was not right for me to do so, being a Christian. The secretary (*wazîr*) cut short my speech, and, losing his temper, said angrily: "You do not know that you are the king's slave."

Hearing these words I rose to my feet, and answered that Europeans were not and never would be slaves of anyone, and in great haste I left the hall, resolved to give my life rather than live in his house. Coming out at the door, I vaulted lightly on to my horse, and took my way somewhat hurriedly, dreading lest the secretary (*wazîr*) might send someone after me to attack me. Then my groom warned me that two foot soldiers were hurrying after us, trying to overtake us. Then I turned my horse round, and, putting my hand on my cutlass, set off to face them. I asked what they wanted. They made me a bow, and answered that the secretary (*wazîr*) sent me ten gold rupees for the purchase of betel. I took them, and went on my way. I was determined to return to Sūrat that I might find myself among Europeans.

At this time I met Clodio Malier, who carried me off to his house, and there I told him of my resolve. He did not approve. Then by his arguments he succeeded in persuading me. Having got as far as the court, what was the good of leaving it again without first seeing what there was there, so that I might report on the riches and greatness of the kings of the Mogul, exceeding the riches of other kings (as may be seen in the course of this my book)?

As I was a youth carried away by curiosity, but still more by the friendship shown to me by Clodio, and reflecting that I had already in him one friend who could do me some good in this kingdom, and be of help to me in some affair, I determined to remain where I was.

After three days had elapsed, Clodio Malier was sent for to the palace of Prince Dārā, who inquired if he knew of the arrival of a European youth, who had come with the ambassador of England, and a few days before had appeared in the king's presence to make a complaint of injuries done by a captain of artillery and other Englishmen. Clodio answered that he knew me well, that, seeing me unprotected, he had taken me into his house, adding that I was a youth of quality. He wished that, before allowing me to leave the Mogul kingdom, I should see something of the king's and princes' riches, so that on my return to Europe I might declare the wealth and grandeur of the Moguls.

Thereupon the prince said to him that he wanted to speak to me, and thus he must not fail to find a way to bring me to his presence. When Clodio Malier came home, he said to me at once, with a joyous countenance, that I had already captured good fortune, for the eldest prince, a generous man and friendly to Europeans, had shown himself interested about me and wanted to speak to me.

I rejoiced at this good news, knowing that the Europeans who served this prince had a good life of it, and received adequate pay. Thus I, too, was desirous of obtaining some employment at his court. I made up my mind for that reason not to put off my visit, and I asked Clodio if we should have to wait long before complying with the prince's desire. My friendly shelterer replied to me that it was not wise to delay, otherwise we might lose the favourable opportunity. For the resolves of the great were like birds: if the bird-lime stuck to them they were easily caught, but if once they flew away it was very hard to lay hold of them a second time.

For these reasons we started the very same day, and repaired to the court of the above-named prince. As soon as he was informed of our arrival, he gave the order to allow us to enter. When I reached his presence, and had made the usual obeisances, he asked me if I could speak Persian, and put some other questions with a pleased and friendly expression on his face. He was delighted at seeing a youth of not more than eighteen years, and a foreigner, with such quick-wittedness that he had learned to make the proper obeisance without any shyness. Then I answered the questions, showing myself acquainted with Turkey and Persia and other important matters. The whole of my replies were in Persian, by which I proved to the prince that I could speak sufficiently well the language about which he had asked me.

At the conclusion of the above talk he directed that the ambassador's letter be given to me. It had already been opened; and I was directed to translate it into Persian. The letter was in Latin, written in letters of gold, and it differed but little from the letter presented to the King of Persia. Being thus already acquainted with the business, I had little difficulty in translating it. Next the prince asked what the letter was written on, for it seemed to him like a skin and not paper. I answered that it was of vellum skin, and it was the usage of European kings, when forwarding letters to far-off kingdoms, to have the more important matters written on vellum skin, in order that they might be better protected against the inclemencies of the weather and of the journey than they would be if they were on paper.

At the end of this conversation Dārā asked me if I wished to remain for a time in the Mogul country, to which I replied affirmatively. He said to me with a smile on his face: "Would you like to enter my service?" As this was the very question and none other that I was hoping for, I replied that I should have put to very good use the weariness and fatigues of my journey if I had the good fortune to serve under so famous a prince.

He then directed that every month they should give me eighty rupees of pay, a sum equal to forty *patacas.* He ordered them to deliver to me at once, in his presence, a serpao (*sarāpā*), and thirty rupees and a good horse. He put me in charge of one of his trusted eunuchs, called Coja Mosquis (K͟hwājah Miskīn), with instructions to look after the little European and see that he was well trained and educated. I returned thanks to the prince, and seeing how well Dārā was inclined towards me, I prayed leave to entreat another favour—that is to say, the liberty of the two English prisoners; and through the mediation of the prince, they were released in a few days by order of the king.

I came out from the prince's presence. Although Dārā desired that K͟hwājah Miskīn should teach me the court ceremonial in order to turn me into a courtier, I took means to prevent my being made into a Mahomedan. So I did not go to seek out the said K͟hwājah Miskīn, but kept in the company of the Europeans. Some of these were surgeons, but the greater number artillerymen in the Mogul service, an honourable employment. For European artillerymen who took service in that branch had only to take aim; as for the rest—the fatigue of raising, lowering, loading, and firing—this was the business of artificers or labourers kept for the purpose. However, when Aurangzeb came to the throne, he, seeing the insolent behaviour and the drunkenness of such-like men, deprived them of all their privileges, except that of distilling spirits, and forced them to do sentry duty like other soldiers, thus leaving them with no estimation or reputation in the army. But the old plan continued in force up to the evacuation of the fortress of Bacar (Bhakkar) and the beheadal of Prince Dārā, as farther on I shall relate.

For some time I dwelt in the house of Clodio, and when I had acquired the means I hired a separate house. Then came a man to me who said that he would put me in the way of gaining money. I inquired from him what it was he wanted. He told me he wanted nothing beyond permission to distil spirits under my protection and close to my house. He would give me ten rupees every day; thus I should be put to no expense; all I had to do was to assert that he was my servant. I agreed to the bargain, and out of regard for me no one said a word to him, for the Europeans in the service of Dārā had this privilege of distilling spirits and selling them without hindrance.

Finding myself with sufficient pay, and in good condition, I wrote to Mestre Jonh (Henry Young) at Sūrat, giving him notice of the king's orders—how he had ordered all the ambassador's property to be placed in the hands of the Governor of Sūrat, with directions to make it over to him. After some months he replied that he had then received delivery of everything.

When I left Venice I already knew sufficiently how to speak the Italian language, and, in addition, a little French. During this journey I learnt the Turkish and Persian languages. Finding myself established in India, I now set to work to learn the Indian tongue. Furthermore, as I was desirous of knowing about matters in the Mogul kingdom, I found an aged man of letters, who offered to read to me the "Royal Chronicles of the Mogul kings and princes." Therefore I am of opinion that the reader will be glad to listen to me, seeing that I have special information. I will speak of all the Mogul kings in my second book, which will close with the death of Aurangzeb's brothers, and therein will be seen what happened to me.

[Not long after entering Dārā's service, Manucci had

to follow his master to the wars. King Shāhjahān fell ill, and at the news of his illness three of his sons, Shāh Shujā', Murād Bakhsh, and Aurangzeb made preparations to seize the throne by force. Unable to take the field himself, Shāhjahān deputed Dārā to take his place.]

Finding himself in bodily weakness and desirous of pleasing Dārā, he transferred to him all his powers and dignities, and ordered everyone to yield him obedience. He wanted to try if, by this means, he could rid himself of all the ills from which he suffered, including the danger in which he stood of being captured by Aurangzeb, and dispossessed of his authority.

Some authors, recording what they have been told, say that Dārā seized his father and divested him of power by force; but I assert this to be a great untruth, for I know, and have tested it that Dārā was quite submissive. He did nothing without communicating it to his father. I might produce several proofs of what I say; but I will ask the reader to do me the favour of recollecting what I have said as to the letters written by Muhammad Amīn Khān and Shāistah Khān. On account of these Dārā wanted to have them decapitated, yet they were liberated by the order of Shāhjahān. If Dārā had, as others write, taken possession of his father and of his authority, he would have exercised this absolute power to order their heads to be cut off, as justice required.

Another case I will bring forward in proof of what I say. A few days before we took the field against Aurangzeb, the police seized a Genoese youth for having in his possession a bottle of wine, a thing not prohibited for Europeans. In order to petition for his release I went off to the magistrate, who at once placed me alongside the youth. I made a sign to my servant, who rushed off to tell my friends—artillerymen in Prince Dārā's service. These men came in a body, all of them armed, and, breaking down the doors of the prison, liberated us. The soldiers ran from the police-office, leaving the magistrate by himself in a state of astonishment at what was going on. Being aggrieved as I was, I thereupon went up to the magistrate and put a pistol to his breast; I did not slay him, but took compassion upon him on his humbling of himself. This affair was brought before Shāhjahān, who complained to Dārā of what his artillerymen had done. To satisfy the king, Dārā ordered the captain of artillery to administer a reproof to the Genoese. We all went in a body to the captain to lodge a complaint against the magistrate for the disgrace done to us, the king having accorded us the right to drink wine. Now, if Dārā had been as others say, no one would have had the audacity to displease his employés, nor to complain of them to Shāhjahān.

On finding that the King Shāhjahān had delivered himself with all his authority and his army into the hands of Prince Dārā, everybody seized their weapons; there was great uproar, each man acting on his own inclination. More than one hundred thousand horsemen assembled, and more than twenty thousand infantry. There were one hundred pieces of field artillery, every one of them carrying shot of from eight to twelve pounds; in addition, there was a twenty-pounder culverin, and over two hundred European artillerymen. There were no want of subordinates, of shopkeepers who furnish supplies for the sustenance of the whole realm and army, a large number of sarrāfos (*ṣarrāf*), who provide the cash required by the whole army; many majestic and well-armoured elephants, and five hundred camels. On each of the latter was a man seated atop with a swivel-gun, carrying a ball of from three to four ounces, which he loaded and fired without dismounting. There were also five hundred elephants with their howdahs, and in these sat two men with two guns like those upon the camels.

After all these preparations we issued from the city of Āgrah on the 14th of May, one thousand six hundred and fifty-six (correctly 1658). When on the march we covered the ground as far as the horizon, making a brave and splendid show. What disconcerted me was that no one would say that Dārā was sure of gaining the battle with all this grand array.

The greater number of the soldiers that Dārā had newly enlisted were not very warlike; they were butchers, barbers, blacksmiths, carpenters, tailors, and such-like. It is true that on their horses and with their arms they looked well at a review; but they had no heart, and knew nothing of war. If only Sulaimān Shukoh had arrived in time, there would have been no need of men like these, nor of Khalīlullah Khān. The wife of the latter had warned Dārā to put no reliance on her husband, nor trust to his soft speeches, for she knew him well, and, given the occasion, he would invariably engineer some treachery. Nor should he rely upon the thirty thousand Mogul troopers in his father's service.

Shāhjahān earnestly desired that Dārā should not offer battle until Sulaimān Shukoh had arrived. But Dārā's two brothers and enemies came on with such haste that they left him no chance of delaying. I have been assured that Aurangzeb professed such determination as to say that, if Taimūr-i-lang and all his descendants came against him, on no account would it be fitting for him to retreat. He was resolved to give battle, putting his faith in the traitors to be found in Dārā's camp.

When placed in the field, our army was so well distributed that it looked like a lovely city adorned with beautiful tents, flying innumerable flags of all colours and different shapes, each tent having its own flag and device so that it might be recognised. The prince Dārā went to take leave of the king, his father, and of Begam Ṣāḥib, his sister, who at that time were living in the fort of Āgrah. On beholding the son and brother so well beloved, they melted into floods of tears. The king began to speak, and thus addressed Dārā:

"My loved and cherished son! I have always been well inclined towards you as being my first-born son and full of good qualities—above all of the quality of obedience, which you have always displayed towards me. Your father hoped to see you become king peacefully, but none can fathom the secrets of the Lord Most High. My desire was to leave you in this fortress, and go forth myself against those rebels Aurangzeb and Murād Bakhsh, unworthy of the name of my sons or of your brothers. I had hoped to chastise the rebels and traitors who take the side of my enemies; but you have had compassion on my years and infirmities, and mean to expose your life for the peace of the kingdom, the freedom and the safety of your father. Not to dishearten you, I consent to your doing as you wish, but entreat you, my beloved son, to avoid a battle until the arrival of Sulṭān Sulaimān Shukoh your son. You will thus increase your chance of victory. I beg of you to curb your ardour. Being incapable of doing more, I pray that your life may be spared and that you may survive to become Emperor of all Hindūstān, and that our enemies may be slain. I place you in the hands of God, in whom we trust to give us the victory and make us triumph over rebels and traitors."

Having bade farewell to his father, Dārā soon appeared in the army; but the march could not be undertaken that day. Some of the war *matériel* was still wanting, nor did the astrologers judge the hour auspicious for a start. On the third day this huge army began its march. When Dārā was about to mount his magnificent elephant Fatejang (Fatḥ Jang)—that is to say "Victor in War"—he said these words: "Guerrib maf, magrur marg" (*Gharīb mu'āf, maghrūr marg*)—that is to say: "To the humble pardon, to the haughty death." The generals then present replied simultaneously " Hixa Alla" (Inshāllāh)—that is to say : " By the favour of God."

We began the march in such great order that it seemed as if the sea and land were united. Prince Dārā amidst his squadron appeared like a crystal tower, resplendent as a sun shining over all the land. Around him rode many squadrons of Rājput cavalry whose armour glittered from afar, and their lance heads with a tremulous motion sent forth rays of light. There were other squadrons of calvary armed with lances, in front of whom went many ferocious elephants clad in shining steel with chains on their trunks, their tusks encrusted with gold and silver, and broad cutlasses affixed thereto by rings. In advance was one with a handsome flag, and the driver, who guided the elephant, was armed with *armes blanches* (sword and shield).

A marvellous thing was it to behold the march, which moved over the heights and through the vales like the waves of a stormy sea. Thus we held on our way for four days, until we reached the bank of the River Chambal, where was a village called Dolpur (Dholpur). Our powerful army took up position on this ground, and entrenched the crossing, placing its pieces of artillery to cover the most exposed points.

We awaited the enemy, who was already near; he appeared afar off after three days. Being fully prepared, and in every way desirous of finding ourselves engaged in battle, we begged for leave to attack the enemy. But Dārā for two reasons would not consent. The first was that he was waiting for Sultān Sulaimān Shukoh and his force, who could not be very long in coming; even if they were delayed, he was sure the enemy would never risk a crossing at this place, which was well occupied and fortified. The second reason was the inadvisability of attacking the enemy in a situation full of hollows and rocks, and altogether a dangerous place.

At this time Aurangzeb persisted in his usual

stratagems and intrigues. After having encamped his army on the farther side, not far from the river, he called together his generals. He said to them that they must be prepared to deliver battle, and be every one ready with his force of cavalry. In making haste lay their chance of victory, and, full of confidence in their courage, he hoped in a brief space to be victorious. They could not postpone the battle, seeing the danger of Sultān Sulaimān Shukoh's arrival. A report of the above speech reached the army of Dārā, and was received with pleasure. Everybody made his preparations with the greatest eagerness, and expected every day that the enemy would come to attack us.

But Aurangzeb's secret plan was to win over Rajah Champet (Champat), to whom he sent valuable presents, proposing for him high rewards and making him liberal offers. He asked the rajah to allow him to pass through his territories in order to get across the river by another unknown ford, situated twelve leagues from us. These demands were conceded by Rajah Champat, hoping to avenge himself on Shāhjahān for the acts I have already told you of. Gained over by entreaties, and all unwitting of the misfortune that he had to undergo, the rajah accompanied Aurangzeb. The route was so difficult, the march so impeded by jungle and uneven ground, that Aurangzeb was unable to take with him the whole of his forces. He left his tents standing, and some of his men behind, by way of formality in order to conceal his design the more effectually. He crossed the river (as I was told) with over eight thousand horsemen, and though they were all much fatigued, he made himself master of the crossing on the thirtieth of May, 1656 (*i.e.* 1658).

This day was as full of joy for Aurangzeb as it was full of sadness for Dārā. The latter, receiving a report of the carrying out of the above design, fell into a great rage with Champat, who had given his word that in no case would he allow Aurangzeb to cross, and it was for this reason that Dārā had not blocked the ford in question. When the news came that Aurangzeb had actually crossed, Dārā was desirous of moving personally in pursuit of him.

He was, however, well advised by the General Hebraim Can (Ibrahīm Khan), son of Alimerda Can ('Alī Mardān Khan), to send instead, with the greatest expedition, twelve thousand horsemen to fall suddenly upon Aurangzeb and his soldiers, who were much fatigued, very scattered, and lying about on the river bank. But the traitor Khalīlullah Khān, having heard that Dārā had decided to make this attempt, came to him and said that it was inadvisable, it would not add to his credit or reputation. For, of a certainty, the name and fame of any victory would accrue to the commander, and not to his Highness. He ought not to listen to the advice of these boys, quite inexperienced in war, and it was a mistake to detach those twelve thousand cavalry from his division, for by so doing the victory which was now a certainty would become doubtful. The following day we marched in pursuit of Aurangzeb, but it was already too late. For during the night, and very early on the following morning, almost the whole remaining army of Aurangzeb came up, and, quitting the river, we arrived in an extensive plain.

It was the 1st of June of one thousand six hundred and fifty-six (*i.e.* 1658). We made use with great labour of the water in the ponds in the open fields, and the heat was stifling. Between the two armies there was not more than a league and a half's distance. During the time we were taking up ground for our army, the rest of Aurangzeb's force continued to join his ranks, but the whole of his artillery and baggage had not arrived. Having detailed information of everything in Aurangzeb's force, and knowing his men were exhausted, Dārā wanted to commence the action. But the traitors intervened on astrological grounds by saying that neither the day nor the hour was favourable. He must postpone the battle. He was already sure of the victory, because he had a good army, with valiant and high-spirited soldiers quite sufficiently numerous for the destruction of Aurangzeb, who in comparison to him was an invisible speck on this earth. All this they did solely that Aurangzeb might have time to take rest, to refresh his people, and secure the arrival of his guns.

The traitors had made an agreement with Aurangzeb that when he was ready to give battle he should warn them by three discharges of cannon, and thereupon they would make dispositions for delivering Dārā into his hands. Meanwhile Aurangzeb gave proof of how he understood recompensing those who helped him in his unjust undertaking. He caused his friend Champat to be sent for, who was waiting not far from his tents, in expectation of the many favours and presents promised to him. When he reached the presence, having no anticipation of what was about to happen to him, Aurangzeb instantly caused him to be bound, and carried to the route along which he designed to advance next morning to give battle; there he was to be offered up a sacrificial victim and beheaded. This command was executed.

On the 2nd of June (1658) Dārā received a letter from his father Shāhjahān, directing his retreat to Āgrah, there to entrench himself until the arrival of Sulaimān Shukoh. This could not be done, because if Dārā retreated, the enemy would without fail resume his advance with still greater spirit, while our troops would lose all confidence in the valour of their prince and commander. They would imagine if he retired that he had not the courage to attack. The greater part of our army, directly they saw such a movement, would inevitably transfer themselves to the enemy's side.

So far was Dārā from following the advice of his father that he had, on the contrary, made up his mind to deliver battle. In reply to his father, he wrote that he ought to take his ease and keep in good heart. He promised him that within three days he would drag Aurangzeb and Murād Bakhsh bound into his presence, when he might punish them as he saw fit. The truth is that he (Dārā) wished to fight on the 3rd of June, a Saturday. But the traitors, taking advantage of a shower of rain which fell in our camp, said it was not a good time to attack, for already the skies wept over his defeat as soon as they heard that he meant to fight. It would be much better to delay until the next day, which was known to be the first day, when God created light—a very auspicious day on which, without doubt, he would be victorious. All this they said because if Dārā had attacked the enemy on that day he would have gained a certain victory. For Aurangzeb had not then his ranks in proper order, nor had the agreed-on signal been given.

The presumption that I found in Dārā afflicted me, seeing him give credit to the words of traitors. But I consoled myself a good deal, being young, with the hope of getting some experience of war. On the whole I did not feel satisfied, finding that Dārā was not making the exertions required for the good ordering of such a huge army. He had not sufficient experience in matters of war, having been brought up among the dancing-women and buffoons of his father, and gave undue credit to the words of the traitors.

On the 3rd of June, at midnight, the enemy fired three pieces of artillery, the signal agreed upon with the traitors, showing them that Aurangzeb had now made his dispositions for giving battle at daybreak. We replied with three other shots. After one hour had elapsed Dārā emerged from the camp through the midst of our artillery, for which it was necessary to take down my tent to allow a passage for his exit with the few cavalry in his retinue.

A short time afterwards I mounted my horse and went forth out of curiosity to know what was going on, this being the first battle that I had been able to see. Trusting to my good horse, I went on, and halted on a height adjoining an uninhabited village; thence I saw, though it was still dark, many horsemen leave our army for that of Aurangzeb, and never return.

Almost at daybreak there came forth from the army of Aurangzeb several camels laden with bombs, escorted by some horsemen and many men on foot, who halted in the village and distributed themselves at considerable distances. As the light grew clearer I saw that Aurangzeb was advancing very leisurely with his whole army. It was formed into five divisions of cavalry.

In the first division, placed in the middle, was the strong and valiant Aurangzeb seated on a large elephant, accompanied by fifteen thousand horsemen well armed with lances, bows and arrows, and matchlocks. At his right hand he had his son, Sulṭān Muḥammad, and Mîrbaba (Mîr Bābā) his foster-brother, to whom on this occasion he gave the title of Badercan (Bahādur Khān) at the head of another fifteen thousand horsemen. The third division, on the right hand of Sulṭān Muḥammad, had also fifteen thousand horse under the command of Nezebetcan (Najābat Khān) and other generals. The fourth division was composed of another fifteen thousand well-armed cavalry, with whom was Prince Murād Bakhsh, seated on a lofty elephant, which rose like a tower in the midst of his squadrons. With him sat his little son.

The remainder of Aurangzeb's army consisted of one division of problematical value, made up of low-class men of unwarlike habits, in addition to baggage, carts, camels, and unloaded oxen; these had their place on the left of Murād Bakhsh. Behind followed all the artillery. As this army continued its advance in tranquillity, so I in the same manner retired until I saw that they had arrived close to the deserted village. Then the artillery was ordered to the front, behind them the musketeers, behind them again some camels carrying swivel guns (*trilhoens*). In their rear was the army, as I have above described. I answer for all this with all confidence.

I awaited the approach of our army in order to take my place. But seeing from afar that it did not stir, I went back close to it, where there were several scattered horsemen. There I halted to look at it, and consider our great army and its disposition. I noticed that while I had been away to look at the army of Aurangzeb, Dārā had arrayed his forces in the following order: The artillery was all in one row, and each carriage bore two scarlet pennons. This row of guns served as a wall to protect the musketeers behind it, to the number of twenty-five thousand men. These were supported by five hundred camels with swivel guns (*trilhoens*), to their rear stood the armour-clad elephants, and then the cavalry, twenty-eight thousand horsemen. Last of all was Dārā on his magnificent elephant, followed by numerous elephants carrying drums, trumpets, and all manner of music, forming his retinue.

In the division to the right of Dārā was Ramsing Rotella (Rām Singh, Rāṭhor) with his fifteen thousand Rājputs, all well-armed men of war. On their right was K͟halīlullah K͟hān with thirty thousand Moguls, whose orders were to encounter the miscellaneous division of which I spoke, this being his (K͟halīlullah K͟hān's) own pretext. On the left of Dārā was posted the valorous General Rustomcan Dacanj (Rustam K͟hān, Dakhinī) with fifteen thousand horse in all; at his left Raja Chartersilara (Chhatarsāl Rāe) with fifteen thousand horsemen, the greater part of them Rājputs. All this array made a lovely sight, both by the beauty of the arms and by the number of the standards and pennons of so many colours.

Be it known to the reader that these two armies were not ordered in the disposition obtaining in Europe. But one division was close to another as the trees of a pinewood, in the order that I have described.

I remained where I was in safety, there being no firing from either side. It was already eight o'clock of the day, when there came an order from our army that all the scattered horsemen must retire, because they wanted to discharge the artillery. Thereupon everyone withdrew into the army, and a poor Mogul cavalier riding behind me, not getting back in time, fell at the first fire of our artillery. Repeated orders poured in to keep up a continuous artillery fire, although the shot did no damage. They fell short of Aurangzeb's men, who were at a great distance from us. I was much amazed at their making us work thus for nothing. During the time that we were making this deafening din with our guns the enemy saluted us with nothing but a few bombs with tails, after the style of rockets.

After the first discharge Aurangzeb ordered one of his pieces of artillery to be fired in continuation of the signal to the traitors. After we had fired again several times he let off two pieces together. When we had fired ten times he replied with three pieces at once. This was the desired signal by which he was to let the traitors know that he was prepared to receive attack where he was, without moving towards Dārā. Then, leaving his division, Khalīlullah Khān came in search of Dārā. On reaching his presence he greeted him as victor, speaking thus: "May the victory be auspicious to the invincible Dārā. Without losing any of his men, solely by use of his artillery he has destroyed the greater part of the enemy, and little effort remains to gain a complete victory. It is not desirable to continue the artillery fire, but we must now advance and lay hold of the enemy."

Orders were given not to discharge the artillery any more, and the well-reputed General Rustam Khān was sent for in order to hear what he advised. When the latter heard the views of Khalīlullah Khān, he replied that it would be better to await the enemy and leave him to attack us, for he had come a great distance to seek us, and, according to usage, he could not avoid being the attacker. When he came on we could receive him with the fury and valour befitting the advantage that we had over him.

This advice was most prudent, but the cunning Khalīlullah Khān turned it into disparagement of Rustam Khān, saying: "I am greatly amazed that a captain so famous should tell us at such a juncture to show ourselves such cowards and of so little courage that after we have almost destroyed the enemy, we should yet be afraid to take the offensive." Dārā, without listening to other arguments, adopted the counsels of Khalīlullah Khān, and set his elephant in motion in order to attack the enemy with his heavy divisions. Orders were given to Rustam Khān to return to his division, and give evidence of his well-known valour. The artillery was ordered to be unchained to allow the troops to pass through the line.

Khalīlullah Khān, pleased at having accomplished his purpose of exposing Dārā to the risk of death, went with him half-way and then returned to his own command, the enemy being still at some distance. On this side, when Dārā started with his division against the enemy, everything fell into confusion. The barbers, butchers, and the rest turned right about face, abandoning the artillerymen and the guns. Many made for the baggage train to plunder it, which they did, breaking open the chests of silver and gold and carrying off what they could lay hands on. This resulted in many men being murdered while trying to rob their companions.

Dārā pursued his route courageously, making signs with his hands from the top of his elephant that all should hasten to take part in the victory. To this intent he ordered his drums to beat. I admired Dārā's high spirit, and I noticed that the enemy did not stir, contenting himself with a discharge of shells until Dārā had come quite close. Then all of a sudden the enemy discharged his cannon, musketry, and swivel pieces, which struck us and frightened numbers of our men, who scattered this way and that. Finding himself in imminent peril, Dārā ordered the guns to be dragged forward and the musket-men to advance, the *franquis* (Europeans) were also to join the movement. But it was no longer time, for all his men were in disarray, and everyone had taken his own road.

In spite of all this he (Dārā) did not lose heart, but waving his hands made signs to continue the advance. Then Rustam K͟hān and Chhatar Sāl Rāe, although they had suffered by the first discharge of the enemy, came up and collected as many fresh men as they could. Dārā did the same. Then with such vigour, courage, wrath, and violence did he attack his opponents that he broke through the guns and penetrated to their camp, putting to rout camels, infantry, and everything that was to be found in that direction.

Seeing the boldness of Dārā, the enemy sent as reinforcement a large division led by Secmir (Shek͟h Mīr), teacher of Aurangzeb, and other famous captains. This body made all haste, and at this point arose the hottest of the fighting on both sides. At length, coming to closer quarters, they took to their swords with the greatest vigour. Dārā continued to hold his ground, seated on his elephant, shouting and making signs with his hands. He advanced always with the greatest composure, until, unable to bear up against this stout resistance, the enemy was forced to retire.

I saw in this action, as in so many others where I was afterwards present, that the only soldiers who fought were those well to the front. Of those more to the rear, although holding their bared swords in their hands, the Moguls did nothing but shout "Boquox, boquox!" (*Ba-kush, ba-kush!*), and the Indians "Mar, mar!" (*Mār, mār!*)—that is to say, "Kill, kill!" If those in the front advanced, those behind followed the example, and if the former retired the others fled, a custom of Hindūstān quite contrary to that of Europe; and if they begin to take flight, by no method is it possible to stop them.

Owing to the great disorder of his people, caused by the valour of Dārā, Aurangzeb, who was not very far away, ran great risk of being taken. But he disregarded the danger, and ordered a large division of his best cavalry, which was close at hand, to take up the resistance to Dārā's advance. He tried to raise the courage of the few soldiers left to him by calling to the principal men, each by his name, saying: "Mardaney delavaram bahader vactas" (*Mardānī, dilāwarān-i-bahādur! waqt ast!*)—that is to say, "Men of power, valour, and courage! now is the time!" Then, raising his hands to heaven, he exclaimed: "Hia Codâ! hia Codâ!" (*Yā Khudā! Yā Khudā!*)—"O God! O God! in you is my trust! I will sooner die on this spot than give way." Placing his hands upon his morion, he ordered them to attach iron chains to the feet of his elephant as an attestation of his resolve. He pricked his elephant a little onward to reanimate the leaders who had gathered round him, all pledging him their word that they would yield their lives in his sight rather than recede one single step.

Dārā's design was to continue his advance until he had closed with Aurangzeb, and could attack him in person; but, owing to the difficulties of the ground and to the fatigue that overcame him, he made a short halt. This hindered his winning the day; for if he had kept his original rate of progress, and maintained the vigour of his onslaught, the victory was his. Aurangzeb could have made no resistance with the small force left round him, for with a few men it was not possible to repel his enemy's victorious fighters, full of bravery and strength.

But Aurangzeb's lucky star worked in his favour, for while Dārā was still halted news came to him that Chhatar Sāl Rāe had been routed and killed by Najābat Khān's force. Subsequently another still more unhappy report reached him (Dārā). Rustam Khān who fought against Sultān Muhammad and Bahādur

Khān, was also dead and his division in disorder. These leaders were killed by the traitors in their ranks, it being the more easy to kill them that they were riding on high elephants.

Learning that the troops of the two deceased generals were still fighting valorously, he (Dārā) turned off to reinforce those divisions, doing his work so effectually that he routed Sultān Muḥammad and Najābat Khān, and failed not at all in that which is expected of a valiant general. If that coward traitor, Khalīlullah Khān, had made the slightest effort in support of his Prince Dārā, there can be no doubt that this day would have seen the destruction of the rebels, and have become a consolation to Shāhjahān, a glory to Dārā, and a day of peace for all Hindūstān. For Shāh Shujā', although a valiant soldier, had not a large army, nor had he much sense, and it would have been possible to defeat him quickly, of which we will speak hereafter.

But it seems as if God meant to punish the sins and lasciviousness of Shāhjahān and the overweening pride of Hindūstān; for there came once more to Dārā a piece of news still more overwhelming—that is, the death of Rām Singh, Rāthor. This rajah attacked with such energy the Prince Murād Bakhsh that he penetrated the enemy's ranks and gave them much to do. He dispersed their vanguard with his brave Rājputs, captured their artillery, and, coming close up to Murād Bakhsh, stuck his elephant and its howdah full of arrows, and killed the *cornac*, or man who guides the elephant. Finally they planted three arrows in the face of Murād Bakhsh. He had as much as he could do to defend his life, to guide his elephant, and look after his restless infant son. The boy was so anxious to see what was going on that his father was forced to cover him with his shield and place one foot over his head.

There was no one on Aurangzeb's side who fought so well as this prince. Raging at this resistance, and finding it impossible to slay him, Rām Singh, Rāthor, and some of his Rājputs dismounted, and, like ravening dogs, leapt on the elephant, hoping to sever the girths by sword-cuts and lance-thrusts, and thus bring Murād Bakhsh to the ground. The latter, seizing the occasion, saw that he could make a good shot, and planted an arrow in the breast of Rām Singh, Rāṭhor, who forthwith fell to the ground. The elephant turned and seized him with its trunk, and, throwing him beneath his feet, finished him off. Thereupon the Rājputs, seeing their beloved captain was dead, increased in rage and fury, and battled more violently than ever.

Already a victor in three encounters, Dārā, when he heard this report, hastened with greater courage than ever to the reinforcement of the Rājputs against Murād Bakhsh. He felt certain that if this brother were put to death he could easily gain his purpose. But his evil fate would not concede to him the effecting of this, however great and glorious he held himself to be. There now came to pass a treason that had never been looked for, such as none had ever seen, none could ever have imagined. It was the cause of Dārā's total loss and ruin, although this did not appear at the time.

What happened was that the astute traitor Khalīlullah Khān, using the pretext of a good chance of seizing Aurangzeb, came to Dārā and acclaimed him as victor, and spoke to him thus: "I know well that I have been in many battles and campaigns, and beheld the mighty deeds of renowned warriors, yet never have I heard of a prince like your Highness, who, appearing for the first time in the battlefield, accomplished such valiant acts. One thing alone remains to display to the world your qualities—that is, the capture of Aurangzeb. I feel compassion for the fatigues your Highness has already undergone, but it would be wrong to lose such a good opportunity. Yonder stands Aurangzeb with a scanty following;

let us go at once and seize him, as can be done without any difficulty. Let your highness be pleased to descend from your elephant and mount your horse, and ride at the head of your own cavalry and the squadrons committed to my charge. We will go together to the attack. It was for this alone that I saved my division, seeing that up to now there was no necessity for my engaging."

Poor Dārā! Without fully considering what he was doing and what would follow when he was no longer to be seen on his elephant, towards which all turned their gaze, but relying on the soft words of K͟halīlullah K͟hān, by which he allowed himself to be persuaded and deceived, he took the advice, as it appeared to him that what had been said was very true. He alighted from his elephant, and this was as if he had quitted victory; for the soldiers and commanders, who in the midst of battle kept an eye on Dārā, not seeing him on his elephant, assumed that he must be already dead. For this reason they were thrown into great confusion.

I myself was in great astonishment and dismay, not knowing what to imagine, finding all in confusion, and Dārā no longer on his elephant; meanwhile the whole army was fleeing to the rear, like dark clouds blown by a high wind, seeking safety for their lives in the belief that Aurangzeb, although still at a good distance, was already upon us. Dārā, on beholding this great confusion and flight, fell into deep thought, and saw now the mistake he had made, and the plot laid for him by K͟halīlullah K͟hān. He repented him of the fault, but it was too late. Full of wrath and raging, he asked where was the traitor K͟halīlullah K͟hān. Let him be sought for and brought, for he meant to slay him. But the traitor was already afar off. His lord having dismounted from his elephant, and mounted his horse, he (K͟halīlullah K͟hān) rejoined his division, with the object of transferring himself and his soldiers to the side of Aurangzeb. The soldiers who followed him did not exceed five thousand horsemen; the rest of those under his command were soldiers of King Shāhjahān. But these latter fell into disorder like the others, finding themselves without a leader to direct them, owing to the treachery that had occurred.

These events of the battle which I have related occupied some three hours. The affair beginning at nine o'clock in the morning, it was near midday that the rout took place. A great many men and a still greater number of horses and other animals were killed. The reason of this was that our horses were much out of condition, and not used to the heavy work of a battle, while, on the contrary, Aurangzeb's horses were not overfed, and were used to work. Other causes were the great heat prevailing, the want of water, and the excessive dust. It seemed to me more died this way than by injury from weapons.

[Finding that the day was lost, and that it was impossible to rally his scattered army, Dārā took flight in the direction of Āgrah.]

The miserable and unfortunate Dārā, by a hurried flight, reached the gates of the Āgrah fortress at nine o'clock at night, and sought some repose. But he did not want to enter, fearing that Aurangzeb might invest it, and thus prevent his exit, when he would fall a prisoner, and be abandoned by everyone. At the same time he was greatly ashamed at appearing before his father. He remembered that Shāhjahān had wished to be present in the battle, but he had withheld consent, whereat he was now exceeding sorry. So far had he lost his wits that he knew not what he said or did.

He sent this message to Shāhjahān, his father, and his well-beloved sister, Begam Ṣāḥib: "What has now happened to me is what you foretold." He grieved them much, but as they loved him, in place of repining at his evil fate, and in spite of all differences, the good old man his father sent to him a faithful eunuch called Faim (Fahîm) to console him (Dārā), and assure him that he still cherished for him, and would for ever cherish, the same love and strong friendship that he had always had for him; he felt deeply the misfortune that had befallen him. But he must not despair. There was still the other great army under Sulaimān Shukoh; with it he could renew the attack on the rebels, and routing them inflict vengeance on them for their temerity.

At the same time Shāhjahān ordered to be sent to Dārā mules laden with gold coin. He suggested his proceeding to the city of Dihlī, and taking all the horses and elephants in the royal stables. Orders were sent to the governor of Dihlī to open the gates to Dārā, and to deliver to him the fortress, with all the treasures and other things within it. He was to be received with the same ceremonial and deference as if it were he (Shāhjahān) *in propriâ personâ*. For the execution of these orders trusty and well-known persons were sent in his suite, carrying letters to the above effect. He was advised to remain in Dihlī, and not proceed farther. He (Shāhjahān) gave his word of honour that he would do all he could to seize and chastise Aurangzeb. He would keep him (Dārā) informed of everything that happened.

The eunuch delivered this speech, but Dārā was to such an extent confused, enfeebled, and cast down, with his thoughts wandering and his mind full of tribulation, that he was unable to utter a word, and lay writhing on the ground. The eunuch tried all he could to console him on seeing him in this deep affliction, but he could not extract a single sensible word.

His sister, Begam Ṣāḥib, sent another faithful eunuch to him with some valuable jewels. She expressed her deep grief, telling him that she was even more discomfited than he; but she had not lost all hope of seeing him reign peacefully, that ever would she petition God in her prayers to look favourably on him. After this talk Dārā repaired hurriedly to his mansion, and ordered the removal of all the precious stones that could be carried off. At midnight he made a start, taking with him his three wives, his daughter, Jani Begom (Jānī Begam), his little son, Super Xacu (Sipihr Shukoh), and some chosen slave girls. On his departure for the city of Dihlī he was followed by some five hundred soldiers, for the most part slaves of his household. It was a great affliction to see such a down-come.

On arriving at the city of Dihlī he sent at once the orders of his father to the governor, requiring him to make over the fortress. But the governor, already averted by the letters of Aurangzeb, to whom he was well affected, declined to comply with Shāhjahān's orders. Thus the unhappy Dārā was forced, after seizing what horses there were in the royal stables, to resume his march, and make for Lāhor. Seeing our total defeat, I made in haste for the city of Āgrah, where I arrived at ten o'clock at night. The whole city was in an uproar, for a Portuguese called Antonio de Azevedo, who early in the battle had witnessed the plunder of the baggage, rode off at full speed. On arriving at the city of Āgrah, at two o'clock in the afternoon, his horse fell dead at his door. Thus the news spread that Dārā had lost the battle, and the confusion was increased by Dārā's own arrival. The curiosity of everyone was aroused to know how the defeat had happened, and men asked each passer-by about the safety of his master. This happened to me. An old woman asked me what had become of K̲h̲alīlullah K̲h̲ān. Owing to the rage I was in at his treachery, I replied at once that I was present when he was torn to pieces. The old woman was very disconsolate, and hastening her steps went off to give this news at his house. Much weeping and lamenting was caused thereby, they supposing it to be the truth, for I had entered into some details on purpose.

On learning that Dārā was resuming his journey and making for Dihlī, I decided that very instant upon rejoining him. But my steed was so worn out that he could hardly stand, just as were those of everyone who reached the city that night. I decided to take a rest for twenty-four hours, and after that to start and go in search of Dārā.

Aurangzeb showed no want of promptitude in carrying out his designs. Within twenty-four hours he dispatched Bahādur Khān with several troops of cavalry to occupy the road to and from Āgrah on the west. This was to hinder anyone following Dārā. As a result, the first men to take to the road before the day dawned, among them several Europeans, found free passage; but the rest, not knowing that Bahādur Khān was already in position, started on the journey, only to be plundered of all they carried and sent away with a good beating, coming back to the city.

Without knowing these facts, at nine o'clock in the morning I made a start, riding my horse, followed by a loaded camel and some servants. Issuing from the city, I saw several squadrons dispersed in the plain. As I imagined these to be our men, I decided to join them. Then I saw that a body of some five hundred horsemen with its commander was bearing down upon me. On its drawing near, the leader advanced from it, attended by two horsemen. When quite close he asked me lovingly where I was going. I replied without subterfuge that I was on my way to find my master Dārā. He took compassion on my youth and innocence, and said to me that if I followed his advice I should return home, for if I proceeded farther I ran great risk of losing my life. This captain was so generous that, to protect me, he escorted me safely to my house.

If he had not done this, there can be little doubt I should have been plundered by others posted on the road, or even by his own soldiers, who betrayed every desire to plunder me had he not prevented them. Seeing me into my house unharmed, he advised me not to leave it again. The government had already changed hands, and Aurangzeb was victor. For that time I had escaped, and I looked out for a safer opportunity to start in search of Dārā, for whom I had a great affection. If Aurangzeb had not barred the way, all Dārā's people would have gone on to rejoin him. But they could not then do it, as I have told you, for they came in tired out by their flight, and their horses quite exhausted.

I remained in the city of Āgrah, and observed the way in which Aurangzeb forwarded his designs. For on the eighth of the month of June, one thousand six hundred and fifty-six (correctly, 1658), four days after the battle, Aurangzeb and Murād Bakhsh arrived at Āgrah. They posted their army close to a garden called Zafarābād (Ja'farābād or Ẓafarābād) near the city, at a distance of two miles. Thence Aurangzeb sent his eunuch, called Fahīm, an able, astute, and loyal person, to visit his father, carrying a thousand beautiful protestations of love and submission. He professed to be much affected by what had passed, his excuse being that the ambitious and evil thoughts of Dārā had forced him into resorting to all these extremities. As for the rest, he was highly elated at the good news of his (Shāhjahān's) better health. He was now at the capital, ready to receive and obey his orders.

The eunuch Fahīm made no stint either of obeisances or of soft and humble speeches. He dwelt on the goodwill and excellent intentions of Aurangzeb. Nor, on the other hand, was Shāhjahān wanting in a plentiful display of loving satisfaction.

[There was much finessing, plots, and counterplots on both sides; but Aurangzeb had well-laid plans, and finally succeeded in occupying the fortress of Āgrah and in making his father a prisoner.]

Finding himself already practically with control

over all the nobles at court, and Shāhjahān securely lodged in prison, Aurangzeb appointed his maternal uncle Shāistah Khān, governor of the city of Āgrah. Taking out of the treasury whatever money he wanted, he and Murād Bakhsh started in pursuit of Dārā. The latter was already in Lāhor raising a new army, having lost all hope of aid from Sulaimān Shukoh.

On the day that the two armies quitted Āgrah, which was in the beginning of June, I disguised myself as a holy mendicant and joined their train, meaning to stick to the service of Dārā. The eunuch Shahbāz and the more intimate friends of Murād Bakhsh advised him to allow Aurangzeb to go after Dārā by himself, while he should conduct an investment of Āgrah and Dihlī with his army, which was already far larger than before. But, not perceiving the finessing and wiliness of Aurangzeb, he relied on the promises and oaths of fidelity which had been made to him upon the Alcoraõ (the *Qurān*). He neglected to listen to these faithful men, and allowed himself to be played with by that fabricator and deceiver.

[Before the armies reached Dihlī, Aurangzeb had carried out his intention of making his brother Murād Bakhsh a prisoner, and Manucci, anxious to rejoin his master, completed the last part of the journey alone.]

" Beholding all this [the capture of Murād Bakhsh] and hearing that Dārā had decided to raise a fresh army in the province of Lāhor, I started as a humble mendicant for the city of Dihlī. There I remained some fifteen days, awaiting the assembling of more travellers. For the villagers and thieves were plundering the highways, and created a good deal of tribulation to travellers, robbing them and slaying them. They were forced to do their stages with arms ready in their hands, while pursuing their way. Each night we took shelter in the *sarāes*, where we were able to take some rest in security. Every day we halted at noon to feed and rest the animals, and at two in the afternoon we resumed our march, until we reached another *sarāe* somewhere before sunset. Once on this journey we were resting at midday near a town called Panipat (Pānīpat), distant from Dihlī four days' journey. When the time came to start again, my cart-man could not be found, and the convoy set out. I knew not what to do, for after a good deal of effort I was unable to get hold of my cart-driver. By this trouble I was much put out, for I found that the oxen would not obey me, nor could I travel on foot, for fear of being attacked. The men of the place surrounded me, and wanted to rob me, which they did not do only because I had nothing. I was much perplexed. They advised me to continue my route, for during the night (as they assumed) someone would be able to kill me.

Meanwhile my cart-driver turned up; he came running in great haste from the halting-place. As soon as he got near me I fell upon him in a great rage and gave him a sound beating. I knew not the favour that had been accorded me by Divine Providence, which *in sui dispositione non falitur*, and even does us the most benefit when it seems the most against us. I started on my road, and the cart-man wanted to hurry, fancying that he could catch up the rest of the party, who were two hours ahead of us, and thereby enter into my good graces again. But I assured him we could never overtake them, anyhow, could not reach the *sarāe*. He had better drive on at a moderate pace. Still displeased with the cart-man, I inquired why he had been so heedless, knowing the perils existing on the road. He replied that, overcome by his necessities, he had gone some distance from the town, and then there had come on him heavy sleep, so that he had been unable to wake sooner; this was the cause of his delay.

During this conversation we had entered into a

wood, through which we had to pass. When within it I beheld with terror the greater number of our party heaped together, either decapitated or wounded, and all plundered and ruined; the few who survived were stripped naked. The cart-man, frightened to death at the spectacle, wanted to drive off with his cart across the jungle without attending the dead and wounded lying on the road. I told him to go slowly, that there was nothing to be afraid of, for the danger had passed (although I was a good deal frightened myself). I found one poor creature lying in the middle of the road with a spear thrust through him, who, raising his hands to heaven, prayed me to help him. Taking compassion on him, I stretched forth my hand to lift him into my cart, whereupon the driver pricked up his bullocks, and did not give me the chance of doing this deed of charity.

We went on our way, and coming forth from the wood, I noticed that the inhabitants of the village where we were to put up appeared before us. Aware of the great mishap that had occurred, when, in spite of all that, they saw a cart appear quietly from such a perilous spot, they were in the greatest amazement, and questioned me as to how I had saved my life. Then I replied that God knew how to deliver poor men from the hands of scoundrels. I continued my journey, always in the fear of thieves, until I reached the river called Bear (Biyās or Biāh), where I found an officer, Dautcan (Dā,ūd Khān), who, quitting Sulaimān Shukoh, had come to join Dārā through jungle and desert by a very difficult route, where he had been in fear of his life. This he did for the love he bore him (Dārā). The latter had entrusted him with sufficient artillery, cavalry, and infantry to bar the passage of the river to Aurangzeb.

I presented myself to him (Dā,ūd Khān), and as he recognised me he treated me with much honour, and granted me a passport for my onward journey. Without such no one could go on to the city of Lāhor.

There I arrived at four o'clock in the afternoon, when Prince Dārā was actually seated giving audience. Quitting the cart, I threw my small wallet across my shoulder, and taking in my hands my bow and seven arrows, I entered the palace. When my commander Barcandas Can (Barqandāz Khān) saw me, he advanced to greet me; and after embracing me with great affection, he led me joyfully to the presence of the prince just as I was. There I performed the usual obeisances, and he (Dārā) with exceeding gladness exclaimed in a loud voice: "Xabas! xabas!" (*Shābāsh! shābāsh!*)—that is to say, "Bravo! bravo!" His eyes brimming over with tears, he turned to his officers and said in a troubled tone: "See, you others, the fidelity of this European Farangī lad, who, although neither of my religion nor of my race, nor for long an eater of my salt, having only entered my service when these wars began, came after me with such loyalty through the midst of such dangers; while those maintained by me for so long, and getting immense payments, with base ingratitude and utter disloyalty abandoned me when I had need of them, just as you others have seen."

After this speech Dārā asked if other European Farangīs accompanied me. To this I answered that the hardships of the road hindered many from coming, but as they found a chance they would come. Dārā ordered a horse to be given to me, which was at once brought. Not liking the look of it, he directed them to give me another and better one. He increased my pay, making it, in place of eighty rupees, one hundred and fifty rupees every month. An order was issued for a present to me of five hundred rupees with a "serpao" (*sarāpā*). I put up at a house where several of my European friends were staying—they had got away from Agrah before it was invested—and with them I dwelt.

Aware that Aurangzeb was drawing nearer and nearer, and distrusting his officers, having a force insufficient for resistance, Dārā sent an order to withdraw the few men and guns posted at the river-crossing. He directed his powder-magazine to be blown up, which was speedily done. He then left Lāhor in the end of October one thousand six hundred and fifty-six (correctly 1658). He took with him the whole of his family, and at the head of eight thousand horsemen started for the city of Moltan (Multān), which lies on the bank of the River Rāvī, the same river as at Lāhor. The distance of that city (Multān) from Lāhor is ten days' journey.

I made up my mind not to march along with Dārā, owing to some business, but to leave on the third day. During the second day I passed before the door of the officer second in command of the artillery, a Turk by race, called Rumican' (Rūmī Khān), who was busy in the preparations and the enlistment of men; he had also some field-pieces, which he meant to take with him. As soon as he saw me he called me, and as I got near ordered me to dismount at once. He asked me where I was off to, and I answered that I was on my way to make preparations to start for the army. He told me to sit down, and said he also was starting that day; he would send to fetch my baggage, and I could go with him. I was suspicious, believing that he distrusted me, and I concluded that it would not suit me to march with him; for then it could be said that he had brought me by force, which would be to my discredit. So I answered him by praying his leave to go to my house to collect some cash and pay my debts, and put together my things; after that I would come back and join him. But the obstinate Turk would not listen to me nor give me leave, so it came to my deciding absolutely to kill him, if he would not allow me to go. For it was not right for me to be made to march by force. I was in Dārā's service, had a good reputation, and wished to rejoin without the slightest delay. Thus I told him that the favours I had received from Dārā left me under such an obligation that I would sooner lose my life than miss an occasion to prove my gratitude to my king. For Dārā I would sacrifice my person; and if he did not believe me, let him send twenty horsemen with me to my house, which was close by. I would then come back with them. Thus I spoke to him, having absolutely the intention of killing him, although I should lose my own life, if he refused. But God was good to me! For the Turk accepted this my ultimatum, and sent with me twenty horsemen with express orders to bring me back to his presence.

I got on my horse highly delighted, and went faster and faster, paying no heed to their telling me to go slowly. They urged on their horses to overtake me. This irritated me, so I turned in my seat with an angry face, and laying hold of my sword, so threatened them that they were afraid and drew back. They contented themselves by following me at a distance until I went in with a rush into the house of a friend, leaving the escort at the door. Directly I had got inside I seized a musket that was standing in a corner, and then went for them, discharging the piece to frighten them. Next, laying hold of my sword, I shouted: "Strike, strike!" though without much hope of success. But they, supposing that there were a number of us, scattered in all directions.

After the flight of these horsemen, I told my friend to get upon his horse and come along with me. For when the news should reach that officer, he would send a great many soldiers and capture us if we stayed. He would not listen, and leaving him in his house, I mounted on horseback and went outside the city until night came on. Then I came home peacefully. My poor friend had been carried off against his will, as I had prophesied. Next morning I removed such chattels as I could carry with me to the house of another friend. When I was about to bind my bundle on my horse's back, meaning to start on my journey to rejoin the army and Prince Dārā, there appeared one of the officers set over the *koṭwāl's pioens* (policemen), who was very drunk. This man had complete control over that officer of justice (the *koṭwāl*). He began to abuse me, and with harsh words ran down Dārā's followers. I dissembled and made use of all my patience, which conquers everything, chiefly because I saw that there would soon be a change in the government of the city through the departure of Dārā.

Rendered still more impertinent by my apparent quietude and patience, the officer went on with his insolence. In time he exhausted my patience, and in a rage I picked up a stone, and hurling it with the greatest force, hit him in the mouth, cutting his lips, and sending two teeth down his throat. He fell to the ground and spoke no more. I resumed the tying on of my bundle, and before I mounted gave the fellow several kicks, owing to the rage I was in.

Taking to my horse, I set out on my way, unaware that the man's servant had gone to tell his men. Having gone only a few paces, I perceived some thirty foot soldiers, all armed, coming hastily in search of me to take vengeance for the affront done to their officer. I wanted to turn back simply that I might rid myself of them. Then I reflected that I should only light upon others lying in wait for me. Fixing my turban more firmly, angry and resolute, sword in hand, I spurred my horse, on which I relied a good deal. I flung myself into their midst, and they, seeing my anger and resolve, were not bold enough to attack me, only having enough presence of mind to salute me and leave me a free passage. They followed me afar off, relying upon others who had been sent in pursuit. To these it happened as to the first lot, and they all followed me up to my issuing from the city. I then got rid of them and went on my way.

After three days I arrived in the army of Dārā, where I found the officer who had tried to carry me off by force from Lāhor. I told him I had come to lay a complaint against him before Dārā. He had been the cause of other Europeans not accompanying me, who subsequently had decided to remain where they were owing to the bad way he had treated me. The Turk, on hearing this, embraced me with the greatest submissiveness, and begged me to suppress my grievance for the sake of his good name.

We continued our marches until the early days of November, when we arrived at Multān, an ancient city where in old days, before the Portuguese were masters of the Eastern seas, there came many *cafillas* (*qāfilah*) of merchandise and spices and drugs of India. With us marched the great Dā‚ūd K͟hān, who, spurred by the loyalty and affection that he had to Dārā, would not abandon him, offering him through others to serve him faithfully, as he had done for many years. But Dārā did not trust him, led astray by the forged letters that Aurangzeb continued to write.

To impose on the people of Multān, Dārā made believe that he intended to stop in that city and enlist troops. He began to repair the houses in which formerly Aurangzeb lived when he governed that territory. He ordered them to send for the relations of a false prophet, then deceased, called Coia Bahaudim (K͟hwājah Bahā-ud-dīn)—that is to say, "Price of the Law"—one greatly venerated by the Mahomedans, who is buried in the middle of the city in a great dome covered with blue tiles, an ancient building. He earnestly entreated them to intercede for him with Muḥammad that he might favour him and give him the victory over Aurangzeb. They gave him their word that without fail they would supplicate Muḥammad; he might rest assured that his petitions would be considered, being as they were so just. During the following night they would so arrange that they should precede everyone and be the first to receive audience from Muḥammad, and thus comply with his Highness's desire.

The following day, very early, Dārā took care to have them called so as to know the result of their prayers. They appeared, as this sort of knave knows so well how to do, with downcast faces, and told him that all night long they had been in the presence of Muḥammad, but were unable to speak to him, because Aurangzeb was in conversation with him. But without fail they would the following night find an opening for his petitions. In order to gratify them, and bind them still more to his interests, Dārā made them a present of twenty-five thousand rupees and a covering of costly stuff to be spread on the tomb of the false prophet (*i.e.* Bahā-ud-dīn). But on their being sent for again the next morning, they came with the same answer, and it was the same on the third day.

When Dārā was informed that Aurangzeb had left Lāhor in pursuit, he lost faith in his prophets and held it best to withdraw from Multān. For this purpose he gave orders that all the boats, five hundred and seven in number, should be made ready for a voyage towards the fortress of Bhakkar. They were loaded with supplies of food requisite for a beleaguered citadel; they also put on board eight cannon carrying shot of from sixty to one hundred and twenty pounds' weight, besides light artillery, ammunition, and the necessary *matériel* of war. Each boat carried, more or less, a hundred tons of cargo.

While Dārā was thus preparing to resume his march, Aurangzeb was coming after him by long marches, moving on day and night without halting, at the head of the finest part of his army. These were enough to overcome the small force still attached to Dārā. Aurangzeb had left behind the rest of his army with orders to follow. Finding that he was pursued, Dārā was compelled to move. He ordered the boats to be started down the river, putting in command of them a valiant eunuch, Coia Vacent (Khwājah Basant)—that is to say, "Springtime." The prince left by the land route at the head of five thousand horsemen and five thousand infantry. Dārā's favoured general, Barqandāz Khān, went with him; most of the others deserted, as did those that he had taken on at Multān, carrying off the large sums of pay that he had disbursed to them.

Much to be marvelled at was the obstinate fidelity of Dā,ūd Khān. Keeping at a little distance from our troops, he continued to follow. He sent a clear message to Dārā that he might trust him; he wanted to accompany him whenever the occasion arose, and with his blood would seal the testimony of his loyalty. The prince should accept his advice, and not believe in the forged letters that had fallen into his hands. But Dārā, more and more suspicious, sent word to him that, if he were true to him, let him cease to follow him and go his own way. By this time Dā,ūd Khān saw that it was of no use to try to remain with his well-beloved prince, and sent an answer that he would obey orders on the condition that his dismissal was by writing.

It was not long before Dārā made over to him a paper in which it was stated: "I, Dārā, discharge Dā,ūd Khān, and command him to withdraw from my army, and accord him liberty to serve whom he pleases." What things may not be worked by a falsehood when accepted as true by a prince! Without reflecting on the evil that might accrue to him, the prince persisted in the unjust impression made upon him. Dā,ūd Khān received this writing at the city of Vehu (Ochu, perhaps Ūchh). Weeping like a child, so that it was pitiful to see him, he exclaimed: "It seems to me as if evil fortune dogged the steps of Dārā"; and therewith he departed.

Learning the news, Aurangzeb, when he arrived at the city of Multān, detached a force in pursuit of Dārā, with orders to capture him if they could; they were to pursue him wherever he went. Then he sent an affectionate letter to Dā,ūd Khān, tempting him with very high pay—an offer which was accepted on condition that he should not be ordered to take up arms against Dārā. This Aurangzeb accorded, and treated him with great consideration, and in that reign he held high appointments.

We continued our marches, suffering somewhat from failure of supplies, and several times from want of water. We passed through several rough woods, and arrived opposite the fortress of Bhakkar in the middle of the treacherous river of Sind, thus called after the union at this place, distant one hundred and thirty leagues from Multān city, of seven large rivers, which farther on I will tell you about. There we found the valiant eunuch Primavera occupied in the disembarkation of the big guns and the other munitions for the said fortress. At this time Dārā received word that Aurangzeb's troops, commanded by Bahādur Khān, sent in pursuit of us, had already arrived quite near. He saw that he could not resist such a strong force; he therefore ordered, with all possible haste, two thousand selected men—Pathans, Sayyids, Mughals, Rājputs—twenty-two Europeans of different nationalities, and other servants to occupy the said fortress. The command was given to the eunuch Primavera. The remainder of the army was ordered to cross with the same haste to the other side of the river, and seize all the boats to be found there, in order to hinder the enemy's crossing at that point.

When I knew of this order I presented myself before Dārā, and urgently besought him to take me along with him. With words of exceeding love and tenderness, he replied that he longed to take every one of us with him; but it was of the greatest importance to him to make sure of the said stronghold, and for this reason he left us in it, having such great reliance upon our valour and fidelity. I renewed my application, with protestations and entreaties added to tears, indications of the grief I felt at our separation, asking him to leave all the rest behind and take me along with him. Dārā, with a pleased face, repeated that it was desirable that we should all remain in the fortress, seeing that the place was of the greatest use to him against his enemies, that in it were goods which he held as dear as his own person; and, using other words of much affection, he sent me off.

I was overcome with tears and sighs at this parting, and, seeing the downcast state in which I was quitting the presence, he called me back. He then made me captain of the Europeans, and ordered them to give me five thousand rupees to divide among my men, and doubled my pay. It had been one hundred and fifty, and he made it three hundred rupees. He gave me his word that if God made him king he would create me a noble of his court, and reward my men, in whose loyalty he had much confidence. He added the present of a "serpao" (*serāpā*), and directed that I should receive a boat-load of Persian and Kābul wine. He recommended me earnestly to Primavera the eunuch, and told him to look well after me and my men. After shedding more tears, I left, and went into the fortress with the eunuch, while Dārā departed thence, taking all the boats. Hardly had he gone when we heard the drums of the enemy, and the report came in how Aurangzeb had left Multān for the Āgrah direction in the greatest haste, in the fear that Sulaimān Shukoh might come down from the mountains of Srīnagar.

After he had sent us away Dārā set out for the port of Sindī by land, ordering all the boats to assemble at that place for his departure. Having reached the vicinity of that port, he used all the boats found there to cross the river to the town of Sindī. When he got over, he ordered all the boats that could be found to be collected, so that by this means he might hinder the passage of the enemy then in his pursuit.

[Dārā finally reached Gujarāt, and took possession of the chief city, Aḥmadābād.]

While Dārā was renewing his strength in the province of Gujarāt, the enemy began a most vigorous investment of Bhakkar fort, where we were shut up along with the loyal and valiant eunuch Primavera. No one could get out, no one could enter. This fortress is in the middle of the mighty river Sindī (Indus), founded upon the live rock, stones from which could be used as flints for muskets. The fortress was nine hundred and seventy-five paces long, and five hundred and fifty-three broad. In the middle was a " cavalier " (tower) overlooking both banks of the river. On the east was a large town called Xaquer (Sakkar), and on the west another called Rorī; at a short distance from the fort, towards the north, was a little island known as Coia Quitan (Khwājah Khiḍr), where is a tomb held in great veneration by the Moors (*i.e.* Mahomedans).

We were very well fortified, provided with plenty of artillery and munitions of war, and had a considerable store of gold and silver, precious stones, and a great deal of baggage. In addition to this, Dārā left some ladies who had accompanied him, one wife of Sulaimān Shukoh, and two young sons much cherished by Dārā as being his grandsons. His plan was that if he did not succeed in the province of Gujarāt and suffered defeat, this fortress of Bhakkar would serve as a base to help him again.

After a few days of investment the enemy prepared two batteries mounted with cannon, left behind by Dārā in the foundry at Lāhor, he not being able to move them owing to the hurry with which we started, and the enemy leaving us no chance of putting them on the boats. With these they did us a good deal of damage. Be it known to the reader, that those seven rivers of whose junction I spoke did not touch the sides of the fortress for more than a pistol-shot on the west and two musket-shots on the east, because they flowed between rocks and hills. Thus the enemy gave us trouble enough; nor did we desist from doing our duty with our guns, dismounting his artillery, damaging the towns, and killing a number of men. Several times we made sallies under cover of our artillery, swarming into their trenches, killing and destroying all we found there. Once we captured four field pieces and a quantity of baggage lying close by them. Thus the traitor Khalīlullah Khān, at whose cost the investment was conducted, was forced to send more men against us. Regardless of these reinforcements, the commandant, Primavera, sent off before daybreak some boats with musketeers, who delivered attacks at various points and alarmed the enemy. They went on increasing the investing force until the place was evacuated, as farther on I shall relate.

When Aurangzeb received the news that Dārā was busy raising a new army in the province of Gujarāt, he did not turn aside to attack him. It was more urgent to hinder Shāh Shujā' from reaching Āgrah. But he was much concerned on learning that Sulaimān Shukoh, by favour of the Rajah of Srīnagar, was making ready to descend from the mountains; and aided by the said Rajah, at the head of a considerable force, hoped to avenge himself for what had happened to his father (Dārā) and himself. Aurangzeb, therefore, wrote a letter, giving many promises to the said Rajah, and also caused others to be written by different rajahs, chief among them being Rajah Jai Singh, asking the Srīnagar rajah to dissemble, and suggesting that by the use of certain arguments he should force the poor prince to remain quiet in those mountains.

In that fortress (*i.e.* Bhakkar) we remained, under continual assaults, defending ourselves boldly. In spite of all their efforts, the enemy were unable by force of arms to overcome us. Therefore they planned a means of getting the European artillerymen to withdraw from the fortress, and to this end they shot arrows to which letters were attached. These invited us to abandon the service of Dārā and evacuate the place. One of these arrows hit me on the shoulder when I was sitting in my bastion at eight o'clock at night. Withdrawing the arrow, I went with it at once, wounded as I was, to the eunuch. He gave me a robe (*sarāpā*) and some bottles of rose-water in recognition of my fidelity.

Since Aurangzeb had strongly enjoined on Khalīlullah Khān that he must reduce the place in one way or another, and as he saw that he could not do so by force of arms, he had recourse to many letters containing promises to our eunuch Primavera (Basant) that if he gave over the fortress his demands would be gratified. Enraged at length at the receipt of so many letters, the eunuch wrote to Khalīlullah Khān that if he would come in person he would enter into the desired agreement; he meant to surrender the place, as he perceived that Dārā's affairs were in a very bad way. Khalīlullah Khān received this letter with great delight, fancying he was about to accomplish great things for Aurangzeb, who was so keen on acquiring the place. He started from Lāhor with the remainder of his army to bring to a conclusion the anxiously desired surrender. On his arrival a truce was made between the two sides. Khalīlullah Khān wrote to the eunuch a letter full of civilities, displaying the great results to be gained by making over the stronghold, whereby he would be taken into favour by Aurangzeb; in fact, in so delivering it, he would find the only way to fortune.

Primavera the eunuch was quite rejoiced at the arrival of Khalīlullah Khān, and decided on giving him a reply. With this idea he sent for me, and ordered me to load with horns and old shoes the cannon nearest to the garden where Khalīlullah Khān had encamped. It was charged thus up to the very muzzle. The answer was after this wise: "I hold few words with you, for I am greatly amazed at you, and I hope to supply your want, having been all your life a pimp and used to shoe beatings from women. Herewith what you deserve, I offer you a present proportioned to your merits." The letter went on with more abuse, which I will not insert. Closing it he ordered it to be handed to Khalīlullah Khān. The eunuch watched for the arrival of the boat at the garden, which was not far from the fortress; and when it seemed that Khalīlullah Khān must be perusing the letter, he ordered us to fire off the cannon, and we covered Khalīlullah Khān's tent with the charge it contained.

The traitor was thereby much shamed and discomfited, not knowing how to hide the affront. The following night, when we were off our guard, he suddenly ordered a discharge of all his artillery and musketry, which was a complete surprise to us, and the shot fell all over the fortress. I assert without exaggeration that a pole on which we had a small flag was pierced by three balls. But our eunuch would not pass over such-like bravado, and the next night he suddenly ordered us to fire all our guns and musketry, and discharge a number of iron bombs to show that we had ample munitions of war. This took place at eight o'clock. To prove to him still better that we were not afraid, he ordered a number of vessels of artificial fire to be set alight, so that it was as clear as day. Thereupon Khalīlullah Khān, finding that he could not succeed, turned his face, discomfited, towards Lāhor, and left us invested as before.

Forty days after the departure of Khalīlullah Khān, we saw one morning a numerous force pass over the river from west to east at some distance from the fortress. Our artillery began to pound them as hard as it could. At this moment a horseman appeared on the river bank with a small white flag displayed. At once the eunuch gave an order for a small boat to fetch the horseman. On his entering the fortress he delivered a letter to the eunuch, and proclaimed loudly thus: "I demand on behalf of Aurangzeb that you surrender this stronghold, since we are carrying with us in this army the Prince Dārā, whom we have a prisoner." Hearing this sad and unexpected news, we were all cast down, and dropped our arms. The eunuch told the horseman he could not make over the place without the order of his prince, the Lord Dārā, from whom he had received charge. The messenger went away with this answer.

Before he had reached the farther bank, we saw coming seven boats full of armed men carrying a number of flags. Their officer was called Chegatcan (? Chaghatāe Khān), an Uzbak by race: he was highly elated, as if entering in triumph into his own house. I gave an order to my men to get their guns ready, and some pieces with grape (*varrer*, literally, "to sweep with a broom"). When they had already got near, we gave them a round from the artillery, which did a good deal of damage, both to the boats and to the men. After that they retreated, while our artillery went on firing.

Seeing how resolute we were, Bahādur Khān repaired to Prince Dārā, and requested him to order the eunuch to surrender the stronghold, since, the garrison being firm in their resistance, in all probability the whole of them would come to a miserable end within the fortress. On hearing this, Dārā had compassion upon his eunuch and upon us, and wrote a note with his own hand, stating: "Unfortunate in the one for whom you fought, I now request and require you to deliver up the place."

When the eunuch Primavera (Basant) saw the letter, he recognised the writing and began to weep bitterly. He wrote to Bahādur Khān that we demanded to come out with our baggage, and if he did not consent, we would fling the cannon and treasure into the river, and fight to the death with all desperation. Bahādur Khān sent back an assurance that we could leave with our baggage, but must make over the treasure, the princes, and all the *matériel* appertaining to the fortress. One condition was imposed: we must cross over to the west of the river, then eight days after he had marched we could take the road to Dihlī. He made this condition because he feared we might enter his camp, and do our utmost to rescue Dārā. After three days we issued from the fort in which we had endured so much. For, two days before the evacuation, I bought two calves for six hundred rupees, and paid one rupee for every ounce of butter. Without exaggerating, I bought one chicken for thirteen rupees.

The army of Bahādur Khān passed out of sight of Bhakkar with their princely prisoner.

Now I deal with our departure from Bhakkar. After surrendering the fortress we made over the treasure and the unhappy princes, the little sons of Sulaimān Shukoh, of whom nothing more was ever heard, and it seems as if, by order of Aurangzeb, they were got rid of within the fortress. After fifteen days the eunuch and all the people in the fort embarked in some boats, and we voyaged by the river to Multān against the stream, but with a favourable wind. In four-and-twenty days we reached the said city, then governed by Lascar Can (Lashkar Khān). He sent an invitation to our eunuch to honour him by dining at his house. But the eunuch replied that he would have liked it much, but the haste he was in did not allow of his accepting. He suspected some treachery, and it seems as if his heart gave him a presage of what was to befall him, as I shall relate.

At this city of Multān we provisioned ourselves for a start by land to the city of Dihlī, distant five-and-twenty days' journey. One day a Portuguese, by name Agostinho Dias, begged me to abandon the company of the eunuch, because he knew of a certainty that there existed an order of Aurangzeb for his seizure and execution. We quitted Multān, and in ten days reached the city of Lāhor, then governed by Khalīlullah Khān. Our eunuch settled himself in a house of his own, which was on the river bank. His men scattered in various directions, there not being enough room in the said house. We Europeans were at a distance of half a mile from Primavera (Basant).

On the third day after our arrival he (Basant) sent for me, but I did not go, as it was already evening. By another messenger he told me to come to him very early in the morning. At daybreak I mounted my horse, and on the road I met a former servant of mine called Delavar (Dilāwar), who asked me where I was going. I replied that I was going to the eunuch's house. At this he fell into a fright, and said that for God's sake I must not go. For everybody said that the eunuch would most certainly be killed on that day, and I could easily notice the changes in the city, the soldiers and troopers being posted at so many places. He demanded with much insistence that I should turn back; and reflecting a little, I remembered the advice of Agostinho Dias. In spite of this the love and gratitude I felt for the eunuch impelled me to go to his house without considering the danger.

Pricking on my steed, I shortly reached the house. Going within I sat down by K͟hojah Basant, finding him somewhat perturbed, and a few only in his company. He said to me softly that he had something to say to me. At this moment there appeared in the distance several bodies of horse with banners displayed. All of a sudden there came a horseman to the eunuch, and, addressing him politely, said: "K͟halīlullah K͟hān sends many compliments to Your Excellency, and intimates that he has received the king's order for Your Excellency to come forthwith into the city, to a house already prepared for you where you may remain in perfect safety!"

With equal civility the eunuch replied: "I am only a passer-by; I go to the royal presence, nor have I anything to do with the city; I return many thanks for K͟halīlullah K͟hān's kindness." The messenger started off with the reply, and the eunuch, seeing the troops that were appearing, became a little frightened.

He asked me if I could produce my men without delay. I replied that there must be some delay, and that they could not arrive in time, owing to their being so far away. At this point the soldiers present in the room, after whispering into each other's ears, rose one by one and went out. I remained seated along with ten persons, who were house servants, and, foreseeing the danger, I was anxious to leave, but the pride of a youth devoid of experience hindered me, and I wanted to see the end of it and what would happen.

Then came another message like the first, but more urgent, with this detail : that if he did not give heed to it, he ran in danger of his life. But the eunuch gave the same answer, and the infantry and cavalry continued to draw in nearer. During this time the eunuch was looking on calmly at all that was taking place outside, for the place where we were was a little elevated, with a view of the river sands. It had the shade of some great trees, and was enclosed all round with a low wall. On the bank of the river, near the wall and below our position, stood a relation of the eunuch Primavera (Basant) on horseback, lance in rest, waiting to give up his life if need arose.

When a third message came with greater urgency, begging the eunuch for God's sake to come into the fort in obedience to the king's orders, adding the intimation that it was his last warning, he answered not at all.

We saw the messenger start off at a run, and it was no joking matter, for the cavalry continued to advance, and drawing their swords shouted to the messenger, who heard not through the uproar that had already arisen. The house was encircled by a number of infantry, while on the river sands several squadrons rode from different directions, discharging arrows that fell like rain in the place where we were. The cavalier related to the eunuch, finding that the thing was serious, began to skirmish, pushing his horse at those squadrons, with his lance at the charge, until he got stuck in a marshy place full of mire, where, unable to move, he was killed by the arrows.

The infantry tried to scale the wall, but we defended ourselves, and prevented them from climbing over. Among others we killed the koṭwāl's son, whereat being enraged they set upon us with greater fury, and one resolute man leapt over behind the eunuch and at once cut off his head. Primavera (Basant) had been resisting vigorously on the other side. Many more scrambled over, and began to cut down the few of us found here and there. The man that cut off the eunuch's head and some others came against me with great rage, and, seeing that our defence was overcome, I went straight to them, and throwing my sword on the ground, stepped two paces to the front. Placing myself humbly before them, I lowered my head, and said: "Slay me, slay me," and shutting my eyes I awaited the blow. But finding it did not come, I lifted my head, and saw a soldier of the same troop of the enemy standing between us two. With hands extended he was begging on behalf of God that they should not kill me. But the other most angrily, his raised sword dripping with blood, ordered him to get out of the way. He who was pleading for me said: "First kill me, and spare this other." My assailant, seeing the determination of his fellow-soldier, went off to find someone else, and left me alone. He who saved me took me by the hand, and led me away, saying: "Come with me; I want to deliver you, and place you in safety." But I, knowing the instability of the Mahomedans, said to him that as he wanted to kill me he need practise no deception on me. As I was ready for my fate, there was no need to remove me from that place; but if he wanted to kill me he could do it where we were. Seeing what was in my mind, he sheathed his sword, and gave me his word not to hurt me, but at the cost of his life would prevent others doing so, and take me to a place of safety.

We came forth by a postern gate, where we saw some thirty men with swords . their hands, who came at me, saying: "Let us kill him; he, too, is of the eunuch's force." The man with me then laid one arm upon me, and, waving the other hand, demanded in the king's name that they should not kill me, nor lay hands on me. But they were keen to plunder me, and told him that he had become my advocate simply to strip me himself; but grieve him as it might they meant to kill me, and appropriate my clothes. Recognising their purpose and seeing them approach, I took off my turban there and then, and the rest of my vestments, being left with nothing but my under drawers and my shirt. I threw the clothes to them, and my defender conducted me a little farther; then he said I might go on in security, as I was now out of danger. But just as I imagined I was free there came towards me a soldier, a Hindū rustic, holding a drawn sword, who, with many abusive terms and threats, requested me to make over my shirt to him. Enraged at finding myself amidst so much persecution and so many affronts, I said that he might kill me if he liked, but that I would never give him the shirt.

Overwhelming him with abuse, I provided him with cause for dispatching me, but he did not want to damage the shirt, so he allowed me to live. In the end I decided to give up the shirt, so I took it off, in a rage, rather than lose my life. With my head sunk I went on my way, running considerable danger, although stripped naked, and full of grief and shame. I sought the house of one of my friends, a professing Mahomedan, whose name was Dulah (? Dulhā), a man of learning, from whom I had received much kindness. On my way a woman met me, and offered me a sheet with which to cover myself, saying that when I got home I could send it back to her. But, not willing to be indebted to her, I declined, and went on my way in the same pitiable state. When I was only a little distance from my friend's house I saw coming towards me the captain of infantry whose teeth I had broken with a stone. He recognised me, but took compassion on my plight, and lowering his head made no attempt to do me harm. Thence in a few more steps I got into the house of my friend Dulhā, to whom I recounted all that had happened to me. He welcomed me with great warmth, accorded me full rights of hospitality, and gave me clothes and food. I did not forget to render thanks to God for all His mercies, and for deliverance from so many perils.

This affair happened at eight o'clock in the day, and my servants removed my horse to where my men were, and gave them the melancholy news of my death. All my friends were much afflicted; and they sent off one of their number, called Ignacio Gomens, the one best liked by and most intimate with me, to the site of the affray to make a search for my body. They instructed him to bring it back so that they all jointly might inter me in some convenient spot, and commend my soul to God, seeing that there was no priest. Thus we were used to do when any of our friends died. All of them said, and were quite certain, that I must be dead. On arriving at the place of death Ignacio Gomens found eleven bodies with the eunuch's headless trunk. The head had been carried away to lay before Khalīlullah Khān, who was eager to satisfy his wrath and avenge himself for the indignity that had been done him. Ignacio Gomens came back, and reported what he had seen, and that my body was not forthcoming. My friends supposed that after my death the Mahomedans had, without a doubt, thrown me, a Christian, into the river. So they decided they would all go the next day in search of my body, and give it burial. But I, through God's favour, was still alive.

At six in the evening I left the house of my friend Dulhā, and took my road to the place where my followers were, with much quietness, rendering thanks to our Lord. On arriving close to them I knew them all, but they did not recognise me, although they looked at me. Then all of a sudden I gave a shout, whereupon they knew my voice, and came running with open arms towards me, unable to utter a word by reason of exceeding joy. They all began to weep with content, and after a rest I related in detail all that had happened to me on that day, and how God, out of His infinite compassion, had been my deliverer.

The following day we received a message from Khalīlullah Khān directing us to proceed to court to the king's presence, where we should be well received. By this we were made very contented. With us he sent a captain and thirty troopers, and in their train we reached in eight days the town of Cerend (Sihrind), which means "Head of India," as it divides the province of Lāhor from Hindūstān. Before our entry into the town we saw, in a field a little apart from the gate, some fifteen corpses. Asking whose they were, they replied, that they were those of Jīwan Khān and his relations and servants. After making over to Aurangzeb at Dihlī the Prince Dārā, they had received this reward. That same king gave orders to the governor of the fortress of Sihrind that when Jīwan Khān and his men should arrive on their way to their home, he should have them stoned in this field by all the populace, and thus both be rewarded and slain (a most fitting chastisement for his ingratitude). This gave us all great pleasure, and the Mahomedans themselves uttered a thousand curses over the corpse of Jīwan Khān.

From this town (Sihrind) we went on towards the court, and arrived at Dihlī in seven days, where we learnt that the king was much affected by the death of our eunuch, Primavera (Basant), his orders having been to seize, but not to kill him. But Khalīlullah Khān excused this excess, writing to the king that his death was necessary because it was known that he meant to go into the Srīnagar territory, where Prince Sulaimān Shukoh was, taking with him two thousand fighting men, hardy troops, and the best of the Europeans that Dārā had left in the fortress of Bhakkar. Without doubt if the eunuch had obtained free passage we should all have gone to find Prince Sulaimān Shukoh.

After three days we were presented to Aurangzeb. He was very anxious for us to enter his service, recognising the fidelity and valour with which we had served Dārā, and that among his own people he could not meet with such fidelity and stubbornness. Therefore, he now fixed four rupees a day for every European and for me five. My companions accepted his service, but I did not wish to do so, through the antipathy I had to him, and the point of honour I cherished, of not serving under the murderer of my master. I communicated my non-acceptance of employment. He caused me to be sent for once more, and asked why I did not accept service with him; did I want higher pay than he offered? But I replied to him that I would willingly enter his employ, but I longed to return to my native land, years having elapsed in absence from it; and thus he allowed me to leave.

PART II

[Although Manucci had refused to take service with Aurangzeb, he did not at once leave Dihlī, and we next find him acting the part of a physician.]

THE ENVOY FROM BALKH AND HIS SUITE (1661–1662)

IT happened that a relation of the envoy fell ill, and, imagining that I was a physician, as they suppose all Europeans to be, they called me to their house.

I knew a few secrets, but I did not give myself out as a physician, nor was I bold enough to teach myself medicine at the expense of others' lives. But seeing that these savages had sent for me to their house, I was anxious to see how they lived. I proceeded with great solemnity to the spot. When I had gone in I found the patient on a very dirty bed. I felt his pulse, but my thoughts were not given to the pulse, but to finding something I could seize on in the difficulty to effect a good recovery. Nevertheless I ascertained that he was in a high fever, and placing my hand upon his head, bathed in malodorous perspiration, I found it was burning hot, like a pot placed upon the fire. To induce him to believe that I was a great physician, I asked the patient's age, and then for a time I assumed a pensive attitude, as if I were seeking for the cause of the illness. Next, as is the fashion with doctors, I said some words making out the attack to be very grave. This was done in order not to lose my reputation and credit if he came to die.

All of them were in a state of admiration, saying among themselves that I was a great physician, and that the Franks had received from heaven the gift of being accomplished doctors. The principal envoy prayed me earnestly to put forth all my powers to cure this relation of his. I held out to him good hope of a cure, and, being unable to stay more in the place owing to the smell, I told them I was going home to prepare medicine, and that in the evening I would return once more.

I came out, and repaired to a friend of mine called Joaõ de Souza, a Portuguese, who was under an obligation to me, and recounted to him all that had passed. As he had considerable acquaintance with medicine, he was much astonished at such a report, and did not know what to prescribe for the patient. Still, he delivered to me some pills. For three days I went on with these, giving them to the sick man, who did not seem to me to be improving. But all the men assured me that he was recovering, whereat I rejoiced much. I seized the opening to still more cry up the medicine and dwell on the danger of the disease. Twice a day I visited the patient, once in the morning and once in the evening. Each time four horsemen arrived to escort me.

Almost every day that I went there I was obliged to dine with the envoy, and I thus had the chance of observing their mode of eating. Over fifty persons seated themselves together round the cloth; the food was flesh of camels and horses cooked with salt water, and some dishes of *pulão* of goat's flesh. The cloth, spread upon a carpet, was very dirty. To wait on us were two men with bare feet, who, walking upon the cloth, distributed the food, each with a big spoon in his hand.

It was disgusting to see how these Uzbak nobles ate, smearing their hands, lips, and faces with grease while eating, they having neither forks nor spoons. The only implements each had on him were three or four knives, large and small, which they usually carry hanging from their waist-belt. Mahomedans are accustomed to wash their hands after eating with pea-flour to remove grease, and most carefully clean their moustaches. But the Uzbak nobles do not stand on such ceremony. When they have done eating they lick their fingers, so as not to lose a grain of rice; they rub one hand against the other to warm the fat, and then pass both hands over face, moustaches, and beard. He is most lovely who is most greasy. They render thanks to God with "Alaham dilaha" (*Al-hamdu-l'illāhi*). Each man then begins to take tobacco, and remains for a time talking. The conversation hardly gets beyond the talk of fat, with complaints that in the Mogul territory they cannot get anything fat to eat, and that the *pulāos* are deficient in butter. As a salute to their repletion, they emit loud eructations, just like the bellowing of bulls.

Although against my will, I went on with my treatment of the sick man, and I found out by questioning the kind of food eaten by him when at home. He told me that, being a shepherd, he lived on camel's milk, and ate much cheese and curds made when milk turns sour. I ordered him to eat what he ate in his own country. Continuing with some tonic extract of coral, I restored him to health in five days, and the envoy was so pleased that he made me a present of nine melons and a quantity of dried fruit. He entreated me to continue in his house, and did all he could think of to persuade me to go with him, promising to procure for me from the King of Balkh lands and herds of horses and camels and flocks of sheep. He said I should be highly esteemed by the king and all the court.

I was very anxious to join his suite, as a means of seeing more of the world; but, as their habits did not please me, I made excuses many times that I should never get accustomed to their way of life.

Above all, I had seen once one of their Uzbak soldiers lay hold of a small knife and bleed his horse on the neck with great dexterity. Having drawn forty ounces of blood, he closed the wound with one finger and drank the blood with great gusto. After he was satisfied, he shared the rest with his companions, who came hurriedly, each trying to be first, like so many famished wolves. Afterwards the wound was tied up with a cloth, and the horse left to get well by itself. I asked why he drank his horse's blood. He replied that they were accustomed to it, because in their country, when plundering within an enemy's boundary, if provisions failed their soldiers sustained life with the blood of their horses; nor by this blood-letting did the horses lose their vigour. In addition to this, he told me it was their habit, when they captured any camel, horse, or sheep in an enemy's country, if they were unable to carry it off, to decapitate it, cut it into pieces, and place some between their saddle and their horse's back for consumption on the march whenever they were hungry.

THE ROYAL MARCH

On the seventh day, at three o'clock in the morning, the march began. First went the heavy artillery, which always marches in front, and is drawn up as an avenue through which to enter the next camp; with it went a handsome boat upon a large car, to ferry the royal person across any river when necessary; then followed the baggage. In this way, when morning broke, the camp was free, leaving only the cavalry and infantry, each in its appropriate position. With the rest, in addition to the other transport, went two hundred camels loaded with silver rupees, and each camel carrying four hundred and eighty pounds' weight of silver; one hundred camels loaded with gold coin, each carrying the same weight; and one hundred and fifty camels, loaded with nets used in hunting tigers.

The royal office of record was also there, for the original records always accompany the court; and this required eighty camels, thirty elephants, and twenty carts loaded with the registers and papers of account of the empire. In addition to these, there were fifty camels carrying water, each camel bearing two full metal vessels for the royal use. The princes of the blood royal marched in the same fashion, each according to his rank. Attending on the king are eight mules carrying small tents, which are used on the march when the king desires to rest, or to eat a little something, or for any particular necessity. Along with them are two mules carrying clothes, and one mule loaded with essences of various odoriferous flowers.

It is the custom of the court, when the king is to march the next day, that at ten o'clock of the night the royal kitchen should start. It consists of fifty camels loaded with supplies, and fifty well-fed cows to give milk. Also there are sent dainties in charge of cooks, from each one of whom the preparation of only one dish is required. For this department there is an official of standing, whose business it is to send in the dishes sealed up in bags of Malacca velvet, *et cetera*; and two hundred *culles* (*qulīs*), each with his basket of chinaware and other articles; further, there are fifty camels carrying one hundred cases packed with *sarāpā* (robes of honour); also thirty elephants loaded with special arms and jewels to be distributed among the generals, captains, *et cetera.* These arms are of the following kinds: swords, with their accoutrements, shields; various kinds of daggers, all worked in enamel and in gold, adorned with precious stones; plumes; also things to give to ladies, jewels to wear on the breast, and other varieties; also armlets of gold, mounted with pearls and diamonds. Again, there march close to the baggage one thousand labourers, with axes, mattocks, spades, and pick-axes to clear any difficult passage. Their commanders ride on horseback, carrying in their hands their badges of office, which are either an axe or a mattock in silver. On arriving at the place appointed for the royal halt, they put up their tents and place in position the heavy artillery. When the light artillery comes up, it is placed round the royal tents. Aurangzeb started at six o'clock of the day, seated on the throne presented to him by the Dutch, as I have stated. To carry this throne there were twelve men; in addition, there were three palanquins of different shapes, into which he could get when he pleased. There were also five elephants with different litters (*cherollas*) for his own use whenever he desired. Upon his issuing from his tents the light artillery began the march from its position round them. It was made up of one hundred field pieces, each drawn by two horses.

The following is the order of the king's march: At the time when he mounted the throne and issued from his tents all the warlike instruments of music were sounded. At the head came the son of the deceased Shekh Mīr with eight thousand cavaliers. In the right wing was Assenalican (Ḥasan 'Alī Khān), son of Alaberdican (Allahwirdī Khān). This is the Allahwirdī Khān who caused Prince Shāh Shujā' to get down from his elephant at the battle of Khajwah. Ḥasan 'Alī Khān commanded eight thousand horsemen; the left wing, consisting of eight thousand horsemen, was commanded by Muhammad Amīn Khān. In the rear of these two wings were the mounted huntsmen, each with his bird of prey (hawk) on his wrist. Immediately in front of the king went nine elephants with showy flags, behind these nine were other four, bearing green standards with a sun depicted on them. Behind these elephants were nine horses of state, all adorned and ready saddled, after these horses came two horsemen, one carrying a standard with Arabic letters on it, the other with a kettledrum, which he struck lightly from time to time as a warning that the king was approaching.

There was no want of men on foot, who advanced in ordered files on the one and the other side of the king; some displayed scarlet, others green, pennants; others, again, held in their hands their staves, with which they drove off the people when anyone made so bold as to draw near. There were on the right and left many horsemen with silver staves keeping the people back. Among the men on foot were some with perfumes, while others were continually watering the road.

By their side was an official provided with a description of the provinces, lands, and villages through which the king must pass, in order to explain at once if the king asked what land and whose province it was through which he was then passing. These men can give him an account of everything down to the petty villages, and the revenue obtained from the land.

Other men march with a rope in their hands, measuring the route in the following way: They begin at the royal tent upon the king's coming forth. The man in front who has the rope in his hand makes a mark on the ground, and when the man in the rear arrives at this mark he shouts out, and the first man makes a fresh mark, and counts "two." Thus they proceed throughout the march, counting "three," "four," and so on. Another man on foot holds a score in his hand, and keeps count. If perchance the king asks how far he has travelled, they reply at once, as they know how many of their ropes go to a league. There is another man on foot who has charge of the hourglass, and measures the time, and each time announces the number of hours with a mallet on a platter of bronze. Behind all these the king moves on his way quietly and very slowly.

So great is the dignity with the Mogul kings' travel, and the delicacy with which they are treated, that ahead of the column goes a camel carrying a white cloth, which is used to cover over any dead animal or human being found on the road. They place heaps of stones on the corners, so that the cloth may not be blown away by the wind. When he passes, the king stops and asks the why and wherefore.

Behind all these squadrons rode on horseback the princes Sulṭān Mu'aẓẓam and Sulṭān A'ẓam. After the king came ten horsemen, four with the royal matchlocks enclosed in cloth-of-gold bags; one bore his spear, one his sword, one his shield, one his dagger, one his bow, one the royal arrows and quiver; all of these in cloth-of-gold bags. After the weapons came the captain of the guard with his troops, then the three royal palanquins, and other palanquins for the princes, then, after the palanquins, twenty-four horsemen, eight with pipes, eight with trumpets, and eight with kettledrums. Behind these mounted musicians were the five royal elephants bearing litters (*cherollas*), also three elephants, one of which, that in the middle, bore three hands in silver upon a crossbar at the end of a pole, covered with its hood of Malacca (velvet). These signify "Observer of the Mahomedan faith." The other two bore hands in the same style which signify "Augmenter and Conservator of the faith." On the right of this middle one was another elephant which displayed a plate of copper (*lamina*) upon a staff with engraved letters in Arabic, meaning "God is One, and Muḥammad just." The other had a pair of scales, which means "a king dealing with justice." On the right (? left) hand was another elephant bearing a crocodile's head, with a body made of fine white cloth, which, when moved by the wind, looked like a real crocodile, signifying "Lord of the Rivers."

On the left went an elephant showing a spear, which means "the Conqueror"; to its left again, another with the head of a fish, having a body made of cloth, and when swaying in the wind this looked like a great fish, and it means "Lord of the seas." All these elephants were decorated with valuable housings and ornaments. They were followed by twelve more bearing large kettledrums, and other instruments made of refined metals not employed in Europe. They are of the nature of large dishes, which, being beaten one against another, make a great noise. These musical instruments are employed by Armenians, Syrians, and Maronites in Syria at church solemnities and at weddings; they are also used at such events by the Turks. After these musicians came Rajah Jai Singh with eight thousand horsemen, serving as rearguard. Be it known to the reader that each division of those spoken of had six highly adorned elephants, with rich trappings, displaying on brilliant flags the device of its commander.

At some distance from the foregoing came Roshan Ārā Begam upon a very large elephant in a litter called *pitambar*, which is a dome-roofed throne, very brilliant, made all of enamelled gold, and highly adorned. Behind her followed one hundred and fifty women, her servants, riding handsome horses, and covered from head to foot with their mantles of various colours, each with a cane in her hand. Before Roshan Ārā Begam's elephant marched four elephants with standards and a number of bold and aggressive men on foot to drive away everybody, noble or pauper, with blows from sticks and with pushes. Thus I wonder when I find someone writing in Europe, that he managed one day to get near enough to see a woman servant whisking away the flies from Roshan Ārā Begam, which is an impossibility. For the princesses and nobles' wives are shut up in such a manner that they cannot be seen, although they can observe the passers-by.

Behind Roshan Ārā Begam came her retinue, which consisted of several sour-faced eunuchs on horseback, with others on foot surrounding the litter; after these were three elephants with different kinds of litters covered in rich cloth. Still farther in the rear were many palanquins covered with different nettings of gold thread, in which travelled her chosen ladies. Following them were some sixty elephants with covered litters, carrying her other women. After Roshan Ārā Begam's retinue came three queens, wives of Aurangzeb, and other ladies each of the harem, each with her own special retinue. It would be very lengthy to recount all the details of this march, the Moguls being extremely choice in such matters, overlooking no detail that could minister to their glory.

It remains to state that ahead of all this innumerable throng there always moved, one day ahead at the least, the Grand Master of the Royal Household, with other engineers, to choose an appropriate site where the royal tents should be unloaded. For this purpose is always chosen some pleasant spot. The camp is divided in such a way that on the arrival of the army there may be no confusion. In the first instance they fix the site of the royal enclosure, which, by measurements I subsequently took several times, occupies five hundred paces in circumference. Behind the royal quarters is another gateway, where the women live, a place much respected. After this is arranged, they fix the position of the tents of the princes, the generals, and the nobles. This is so managed that between these tents and the royal tents there should be a wide space. The central space is encircled by scarlet cloths, having a height of three arm-lengths, and these serve as walls. Around these enclosing screens are posted the field pieces, in front of them is a ditch, and behind them are palisades of wood, made like network, which open and shut just like the ancient chairs of Venice. At the sides of the gateway, at a distance of one hundred and thirty paces, are two tents, holding each nine horses, most of them saddled. In front of the gateway is a large raised tent for the drummers and players of music.

Among the special royal tents are some where the

king gives audience; these are supported by small ornamented masts upon which are gilt knobs. No one else may make use of these knobs, only persons of the blood royal. On the top of a very high mast is a lighted lantern which serves as a guide to those who arrive late. The tents of the rajahs and nobles, although high, must not be so high as those of the king, otherwise they would run the risk of having their tents knocked down and being ruined themselves.

When the king comes out of his tent, to begin a march, the princes, nobles, and generals throng round to pay him court, each one bringing forward some short request, to which a brief answer is given. They accompany the king to the end of the camp in which they had halted for that day, then each departs to his proper place in his own division. Then the king joins the huntsmen, and announces whether he intends to go hunting or not. When he so wishes he leaves the army and is followed by only the men on foot and the soldiers of his guard. Everybody else continues the march very slowly. If he does not wish to hunt, the huntsmen move to their previously appointed places. When the advance tents come into sight, the musicians commence anew to play their instruments until the king has passed through the gateway of the tents. Then the small artillery is discharged, while the queens and ladies offer to the king congratulations on arrival, saying: "Manzel mobarec" (*Manzil mubārak*), which means "Happy be the journey."

It should be observed that, although the princesses and ladies start the last, they always arrive the first, having taken some shorter route. Ordinarily the women start after the baggage and move quickly. I knew that in this journey Roshan Ārā Begam did not take in her litter her maid-servant, but in the latter's place a youth dressed as a maid-servant. God knows what they were up to, in addition to drinking wine. The person who told me this was a friend of mine, a eunuch who loved wine. The same story was confirmed after the princess's death by several ladies of her suite.

[Manucci only marched three days with the army towards Kashmīr and then returned to Dihīl.]

This is why I do not write the whole of the king's journey to Kashmīr. I leave it to the reader's curiosity to read what Monsieur Bernier has written about that journey, although, if I am to speak the truth, he puts many things of his own into his Mogul history, and I could, through his chronology of the times, make it clear that he writes many things which did not occur —nor could they have occurred—in the way in which he relates them. Nor could he have been too well informed, for he did not live more than eight years at the Mogul court; it is so very large that there are an infinity of things to observe. Nor could he so observe, for he had no entrance to the court. As it seems to me, he relied for what he said upon the common people; and if there is any good thing in his books, it is due to the information given to him by Père Buzeo, also to what I gave him, having then no intention of writing anything. If I write now I do so at the demand of my friends, chiefly Monsieur François Martin, Director-General, and Monsieur Deslandes.

Thus I returned to Dihlī, where I stopped several days to take leave of my friends. Then I started for the city of Āgrah, where I came across the Jesuit Fathers. I remained there for a while in the enjoyment of the conversation of my old friends, with whom I had been in the fortress of Bhakkar. I did not care to take service with Aurangzeb, but they had accepted and were at this time artillerymen in the fort at Āgrah. They were urgent for me to enter the service; but finding that I would not listen to their words, they went and spoke to I'tibār Khān, fancying that he could persuade me. I'tibār Khān sent for me, and on visiting him I presented a cup of crystal. Receiving it with a pleased face, he ordered robes of honour to be given to me. He endeavoured to win me over, and urgently entreated me to remain in the fortress and enter the service. He would grant me any terms I demanded, and allot me the pay I received from Prince Dārā at Bhakkar. He would make me captain over the Christians (which was what they desired, remembering how well I had treated them at Bhakkar).

I tendered my excuses, and said in addition that I was most desirous to see different parts of the world; there was also the aversion that I had to Aurangzeb, and equally the face of I'tibār Khān displeased me—in fact, to speak properly, he looked like a baboon. To me it seemed that from one with a face like that no good deed could proceed. Nevertheless, I did not fail to go several times to court, as requested by I'tibār Khān, he imagining in this way to overcome little by little my resolve, and bring me to take employment. But each time I went to the audience served only to renew my determination not to stay in Āgrah.

Going thus several times into the fort, I noted the imprisonment of Shāhjahān was closer than can be expressed. There passed not a day, while I and others were in conversation with the governor, that there did not come under-eunuchs to whisper into his ear an account of all the words and acts of Shāhjahān, and even what passed among the wives, ladies, and slave-girls. Sometimes, smiling at what the eunuchs told him, he would make the company sharers in what was going on inside, adding some foul expressions in disparagement of Shāhjahān. Not content with this even, he sometimes allowed it to be seen that he treated him as a miserable slave. Once an under-eunuch came to tell him that Shāhjahān was in want of "papuz" (*pāposh*), which are slippers without heels, such as Mahomedans wear. He ordered several pairs to be brought, and the tradesmen produced several different kinds of *pāposh*, some of leather worth half a rupee, some of plain velvet, and some of velvet more or less embroidered. Some were worth as much as eight rupees, a very small thing for a great king like Shāhjahān, even when in prison. In spite of this the eunuch, immeasurably stingy, sent him shoes neither of eight rupees, nor of four, nor of two, but the common leather shoes. He smiled over it as if he had done some great deed; and it was a great deed, being after the nature of his friend Aurangzeb, who knew from this eunuch's physiognomy the vileness of his soul, and selected him to receive charge of his greatest enemy in the world, his father, so that by force of ill-treatment the wretched old man (Shāhjahān) might die.

I do not know how it was with the others who were present when this was done, but I certainly felt it much. I knew the dignity with which Shāhjahān had lived when he was free and Emperor of Hindūstān; it was doubly sad when one remembered that I'tibār Khān was formerly a slave of this same Shāhjahān, by whom he was given to Aurangzeb.

When the Jesuit Fathers saw that I did not want to remain in Āgrah, but was determined to go to Bengal, Father Henriques Roa (Heinrich Roth), a German rector of the college, earnestly entreated me to take with me two Portuguese friars, then living in his college. They were companions of others who had fled from the town of Chavel (Chaul), and he (Roth) did not wish to be accused of harbouring fugitives. Although I did not burden myself willingly with such merchandise—for I have always held that he who flees from a convent is capable of other misdeeds—nevertheless, to be agreeable to the Father Rector, I took with me the two friars, turning them into my servants. In twelve days we reached Allahābād.

I believe that the reader will be pleased to know that on the eastern side of this city is a fortress all of red stone. It was King Akbar who ordered it to be built; it is very handsome and very strong. For, in addition to art, Nature has also helped to make it strong: the River Ganges, flowing on the north or left side, directs its course towards the south until it reaches the fortress, while the River Jamnah, flowing on the east, at the right hand of the fort, forms a junction with the Ganges river beneath the walls. Besides these rivers there issues from the rock on which stand the fort and its outworks a petty stream with blue waters, which is called Tirt (Tîrth); it goes by a straight course, like a tongue, between the two rivers until it flows into them. Just as if the said two rivers held those waters in respect, on account of their birthplace, they allow them to pass down for a long distance without their colour being modified. Thus you can plainly see the waters of this streamlet flowing in the middle of the waters of the two rivers, Ganges and Jamnah.

I observed this very specially when during my stay one of my friends, named Aquim Momena (Ḥakîm Mumin), physician to Bahādur Khān, gave me a dinner upon the said fortification. As it was the first time I saw it, I showed my admiration of this work of Nature. For many gave me particular information, and told me that the Hindūs worship this River Tîrth, their story being that one of their gods opened with an arrow the spring from which the said river rises.

Every five years multitudes of Hindūs assemble and wash their bodies in the said stream. This yields a good revenue to the Mogul king, for every person who bathes in the river pays six and a quarter rupees. Such is the multitude of frequenters that in the crowding many are stifled. Nor on this account do the relations of the smothered persons make the usual lamentations. On the contrary, they boast that their relations died in a state of grace and holiness, all of which is included in the word *Tîrth.*

These three rivers flow beneath the city of Banāras (Benares), ninety leagues from Allahābād, pass near the city of Patana (Paṭnah), forty leagues distant from Benares, then, flowing onwards, water the shores of the small town of Muguer (Munger) at a distance of eighty leagues from Paṭnah, and, continuing their course, greet the town of Ragemahal (Rājmaḥal) at forty leagues from Munger. There they divide into two branches: one, keeping the name of Ganges, flows as far as Ugulim (Hūglī) in Bengal, and from Hūglī goes southward to the sea; the other branch, under the name of Jamnah, flows near the town of Daca (Ḍhākah), where it mingles with other great rivers.

We were some days in Allahābād, and the then governor was Bahādur Khān, who was absent on a campaign against some villagers who objected to pay their revenue without at least one fight, just as the villagers near Āgrah do. Leaving Allahābād, I took the road for Benares, by land, carrying with me a passport as is the practice with all travellers. The route was level and without hills, and in eight days we came to the city of Benares, where we remained several days. This city is small, but very ancient, and venerated by the Hindūs by reason of a temple there possessing a very ancient idol. Some years after my visit Aurangzeb sent orders for its destruction, when he undertook the knocking down of all temples.

In this city is made much cloth worked in gold and silver, which is distributed hence all over the Mogul realm, and is exported to many parts of the world. It is the fashion in Hindūstān to use this proverb: "Toracana Banarismo Rana" (*Thoṛā khānā, Banāras moṇ rahnā*)—that is: "Little to eat, but live in Benares"—suggesting that Benares is a nice place, with a good climate, productive land, and cheap food. Here I crossed the great river, showing the Allahābād passport, as is usual; and by land I arrived in four days at Paṭnah, a very large city with bazars, the greater part thatched and inhabited by many merchants; for here is prepared much white cloth of fine quality.

In this city were two factories—one of the English

and the other Dutch—seeing that here, besides cloth of cotton, much fine silk cloth is woven, and a huge quantity of saltpetre produced, which goes to be stored in Bengal, and is there loaded on ships for various parts of Europe. Bottles are also made, and cups of clay, finer than glass, lighter than paper, and highly scented; and these, as curiosities, are carried all over the world. When I was at Paṭnah I saw an Armenian friend of mine called Coja Safar (Khwājah Ṣafar), of Āgrah. He had a letter entitling him to receive from a *ṣarrāf* (money-changer) twenty-five thousand rupees. On his arrival he learned that the *ṣarrāf* had become bankrupt. The Armenian dissimulated. As all the merchants knew him, they brought him cloth, and he took delivery up to thirty thousand rupees' worth. He loaded up all this cloth for Sūrat, continuing himself at Paṭnah. When the time came for paying the merchants, he, in pursuance of the custom of the country, lighted two candles in the morning, as a sign that he had become bankrupt, he sat in his house with no turban on his head, a simple cloth bound round his head and loins, his seat an old bit of matting, and a dejected expression on his face.

A great tumult arose in the city, and the merchants thronged to learn the cause; there was a storm of questions, answers, and bad language. To all this he replied with a sad countenance, calmly, and without heat, by the word "Divalia" (*diwālā*), which means "bankrupt." No other response could they get. They carried him off to court; but on the quiet he had given the judge a bribe of five thousand rupees. At the hearing he (Ṣafar) produced the bill of exchange that he got at Āgrah upon the *ṣarrāf* of Paṭnah, and made the defence that this *sarrāf* was the cause that he, too, was a bankrupt. The judge decreed that the merchants must take the bill of exchange and procure payment for themselves, being fellow citizens of the *sarrāf*. It was unreasonable that a stranger should suffer in a foreign country. The Armenian, being thus absolved, made his way to Sūrat.

At this time Dautcan (Dā,ūd Khān) governed the city of Patnah. This is the man who was unwilling to forsake the service of Dārā, yet was forced to leave it because Dārā, in opposition to all reason, expelled him from the service when he marched out of Multān. The prince acted on unfounded suspicions, as I have recounted in the other part. I went to see him, and he was very delighted to see me, remembering that I had been something of a favourite with Dārā. He gave me a set of robes (*sarāpā*). He still retained much affection for the deceased prince, upbraiding the evil fortune that had pursued him. He said to me that if Prince Dārā were still alive he would never have taken service under Aurangzeb, and now that he had accepted employment he had been sent to govern Patnah. He was desirous for me to become his follower, making me great offers; but as I wished to continue my journey, I asked him to forgive me, as I had business in Bengal. He agreed to let me go on condition that I accepted from him a boat for making my journey by river to Bengal, as a mark of the affection he bore me.

I accepted the offer; and of the two horses I had I sold one, the other I embarked on the boat. Then I got into it, taking the two friars, with whom I was considerably incensed. We proceeded slowly, and, arriving near an island, while our meal was in preparation I landed with my boys to go shooting, there being an abundance of game in these islands, all of them uninhabited. Having shot sufficient for supper and breakfast, I returned to the boat, and every evening we slept close to the bank.

One day during this voyage the boatman told me not to put any trust in the friars, for they were not my friends—on the contrary, they had several times wanted to resume the journey while I was out on an island shooting; but the boatman would never consent, knowing that Dā,ūd Khān would wreak vengeance on him for daring so to act. I knew quite well that the friars were capable of doing this, for the more I tried to please them, the more insolent they became. They did not recognise the benefit I was doing them, for no other reason than their being men of religious profession, recommended by the Father Rector of the Jesuits in Āgrah. I wanted to find out whether really they spoke thus to the boatman, and I learnt after some days that they again did as before. Thus I was compelled to show myself in a rage, and I said to them that, if they did not mend their impertinent ways, I would abandon them on some island, and leave them to the disposal of Time and the wild beasts. I hoped that they would not thereafter venture to incur my displeasure. All men of wisdom know that, with certain characters, it is necessary to be resolute before you can make them abate their rage, and thus was it requisite to do on this occasion to make them thoroughly uneasy.

Finally I reached Rājmaḥal, the former court residence of Prince Shāh Shuja', where I delayed a few days to see the ruins of the city, the dilapidated palaces, the great fallen mansions, the neglected groves and gardens. At this time the city was ruled by Mirzā Jānī, who had been the captain of Shāh Shujā's artillery in the severe battle of Khajwah. Upon the defeat of that prince, Mīr Jumlah, who was viceroy of Bengal, aware of the prudence and valour of Mirzā Jānī, made him governor of this city.

From Rājmaḥal I continued my journey on the river to the city of Daca (Ḍhākah), which was reached in fifteen days from leaving Rājmaḥal. The city of Ḍhākah is the metropolis of the whole province of Bengal, where a viceroy always resides who wields the greatest power, although when I reached it Mīr Jumlah, the then viceroy, was not there, he having gone to make war on Assam, a campaign of which I will speak later on. The city of Ḍhākah, without being strong or large, has many inhabitants. Most of its houses are made of straw. At this period there were two factories, one English and the other Dutch; there were many Christians, white and black Portuguese, with a church served by a friar called Agostinho.

Here I made the acquaintance of an Englishman named Thomas Plata (? Platt), a courteous man, who had from Mīr Jumlah five hundred rupees a month. He was master of the riverside, and employed in building boats and making ammunition for river fighting. This Englishman carried me off to his house, and I received from him many favours; I shall have something to say about him after the death of Mīr Jumlah through something that then happened to him. After some days I embarked once more, accompanied by the friars, traversing the great river of Ḍhākah, on my way to Hūglī. Having discovered that I had little time to spare, and that there was a shorter and a safer route to Hūglī, we therefore quitted the main stream and passed by a way between forests, which are called the Forests of Sunderi (Sundarbanṣ).

In forty days we got through the forest and reached the waters of Hūglī, not far from the sea. The friars made for the harbour of Balasor, where they wanted to beg for alms. I disembarked at Hūglī and went to see the Father Prior of St. Augustin's, named Frey Iraõ Bautista. Here I found the chief inhabitants of Hūglī, all of them rich Portuguese, for in those days they alone were allowed to deal in salt throughout the province of Bengal. The Father asked me at once if there had come with me two fugitive friars. I replied that two Fathers had come, but they were not fugitives —on the contrary, they were religious persons much to be esteemed; that they had come to gather alms for their convent and were gone to Balasor. Thus did I repay the troubles they had caused me on the journey. But they did not equally return them to me the good I had done them, as I shall relate. The Father Prior placed trust in my words, and made ready two cells to receive the friars on their arrival, which came to pass a few days afterwards, when they were well received.

Some days after my arrival the Jesuit Fathers came to visit me, and in course of conversation they said to me that they had a tiny church, and that only built of straw. They desired to construct one of stone, but the governor objected, although they were ready to pay him five thousand rupees. The governor was Mirzagol (? Mirzā Gūl or Mughal), an old man of Persian race, who had been in Shāh Shujā's service when he fought the famous battle of Khajwah against Aurangzeb. He afterwards entered the service of Aurangzeb, and Mīr Jumlah, who knew his prudence, made him governor of Hūglī. This governor was determined that the Jesuit Fathers should not build a church, and he issued orders that no one should work at such an edifice under penalty of losing a hand.

The Fathers begged me most earnestly to speak to Mirzā Gūl on this matter. To be of service to the Fathers, I paid a visit to the governor, when we had a talk over the events in the recent wars, so that he took a fancy to me. He said to me that if he could be of use to me in any way he would do it willingly. Seeing an opening for carrying out the project of the Fathers, who were with me, I explained to him, after many polite words, that I should be content if he would allow the Fathers to build a church. This was the greatest favour that he could do me. Then I presented to him their petition, which he granted on the spot.

When they learnt this, the Portuguese were all amazed that I, with a few words, had secured what they could not obtain for five thousand rupees. This thing caused them to seek every mode of keeping me in Hūglī, they supposing that, as I had managed so easily such a difficult affair, I would prove of benefit to the Portuguese should I take up my residence there. They found that I was not willing; on the contrary, I wanted to go back to the Mogul territory to practise the science of medicine, of which I had begun to learn the elements, and was continuing my studies. I knew from experience that Frank physicians are held in esteem by the Mahomedans. They then thought to detain me by a marriage to a young lady, with the promise of thirty thousand rupees and two *pataxos* loaded with salt, making the whole one hundred thousand rupees, also a house furnished with everything necessary for a newly-married couple.

I was really anxious that this contract should be carried through; all the same, I made a show of not caring a rap, pretending, on the contrary, that I was absolutely determined to return to the Mogul country. The Jesuit Fathers were never tired of trying to get a "Yes" from me, but though desirous in my heart of assenting, I made a show of refusal, so that they might not fancy they were conferring any benefit on me, nor, if afterwards there chanced to be any quarrel, could they throw in my face the benefit they had done me.

The friends with whom I had travelled from Āgrah to Bengal were anxious on this occasion to repay me for the kindness I had done them in taking them as my companions. They came to interview me, and by a long argument tried to draw from my purse three thousand rupees. They said if I gave them the three thousand rupees they had the power of arranging a very profitable marriage for me. They supposed that at the time I knew nothing of this proposed marriage, and thus they came confidently hoping to suck three thousand rupees out of me. With an unmoved face I gave them my thanks, saying that I had no wish to marry. Worn out by talking, they had to quit my dwelling without the rupees.

They (the friars) waited until a day on which my proposed father-in-law had prepared a luncheon, and intended to come with the Jesuit Fathers and other friends of his to carry me with them to this feast. He meant to obtain my acquiescence during the meal. All of a sudden they (the two friars) appeared in the company. Everybody was pleased, looking on the friars as my friends; and they were invited to come also to my house to fetch me, and settle about the wedding. Those two men, who sought nothing but my harm, began to give vent to the rage that they had against me at not having been able to extract the three thousand rupees from me. They expressed their surprise that a rich man, having only one daughter, the heiress of much wealth, should seek for her the ill-fortune of being married to a foreign youth, one of little ability. On the other hand, there were many Portuguese of good sense, of good family, well-established merchants in Hūglī, who were willing to marry the girl; if others were consenting to this union they could not concur in such an injury being inflicted on the girl.

Everybody was amazed at this kind of talk from the friars, they all supposing them to be my friends, as I had vouched for them; and their words found acceptance in the minds of many present. The two knew that someone would come and tell me what had happened, therefore they cunningly took the initiative, and came within the same hour to visit me. They said Huglī was not a good place for me; it were better to quit it at once. The Father Prior of the Augustinians was, they said, very vexed with me for obtaining permission for the Jesuit Fathers to build their church. He had sworn that when he came across me he would thrust some insult upon me.

As soon as they had left my house I took pen and

ink, and wrote a letter to the said Father Prior, asking the cause of his displeasure. For it did not seem to me sufficient cause to be vexed because a stranger had assisted in getting God glorified. Nevertheless, if I had offended I would come to him for my penance. But it did not seem to me right that he should show such signs of displeasure as recounted to me by such-and-such priests. He replied to me that he had no grievance about my gaining the permission for the Jesuit Fathers, but it was because they had promised him one hundred and fifty rupees if the negotiation succeeded, and now were unwilling to keep their word. Meanwhile there appeared the foster brother of her who was to be my wife; he was my great friend, and he told me all that occurred. The story was confirmed by other friends who had been present during the telling of falsehoods about me by the two friars.

I came out of my house, and went to the Father Prior of the Augustinians, where I made known what the friars were, for I now saw they were full of guile. I told him, as was the truth, that they collected alms not for the convent, but for themselves. They had tried to levy from my purse three thousand rupees; but, as I did not wish to give them this money, they invented falsehoods about me. They supposed I wanted to get married, whereas the thought of it had never entered my head. The Father Prior approved of what I said, and extracted from the hands of the fugitives the alms collected, writing to the convent of the said friars at Goa as to what he had done. He gave orders in his convent of the Augustinians for the preparation of a satisfactory account of the money. The said Father Prior made complaint to me for my not having denounced them as absconders. I replied that under the impression that they intended to do better deeds than those they had committed in the Mogul country I judged myself under an obligation to screen my neighbour's faults, but finding that they were acting worse than before I held it now opportune to declare the truth.

Certain friends were very anxious for me to remain in Hūglī to renew the proposals of marriage. But being quite ready for a start I declined to listen to anyone. Two days after the above-mentioned event I quitted Hūglī by land. Some imagined that I was not really going, for before I had reached Cassim Bazar (Qāsim Bāzār) they sent me couriers calling on me to return, saying that already the plot of my enemies had been discovered, and my father-in-law was anxiously awaiting me to give me his daughter as my bride. I paid no heed to such letters and promises, for I had by that time made up my mind to go once more to Dihlī.

I reached Qāsim Bāzār, at three days' journey from Hūglī, and here I saw that they make much high-quality piece-goods, and much white cloth. There are in this village, which is near the Ganges, three factories of the French, English, and Dutch. From Qāsim Bāzār I took the road to Rājmaḥal, and there waited to see a Hindū woman burnt, although I had already seen many. She had poisoned her husband by reason of her love for a musician, hoping to get married afterwards to this lover. But on the husband's death the musician refused to marry her. Thus finding herself deprived of a husband, and her reputation gone, she resolved to be burnt. A great crowd collected to look on; among them appeared the musician, hoping to receive from her something by way of memorial. It is usual for women who go to be burnt to distribute betel-leaf or jewels. The place was a large pit. As she was circumambulating this pit she came close to the young musician, and, taking from her neck a gold chain she had on as an ornament, she flung it round the young man's neck, and taking him forcibly into her arms jumped into the pit. Everyone was taken aback at this, not anticipating such a thing. Thus did she and the youth together expiate their sin and the murder of the husband.

From Rājmahal I made once more for Paṭnah, where I halted several days, spending a jolly time with some English and Dutch friends. I then started for Allahābād, and from Allahābād I went to Āgrah, where was King Shāhjahān, still kept with the same rigour as ordered by King Aurangzeb, who was then in Kashmīr. The routes I traversed are much frequented, full of villages and *sarāes*, food being good and cheap.

Some time after my arrival in Āgrah there came to my house a Dutch surgeon named Jacob, a fugitive from the harbour of Goa, having killed a man when the Dutch blockaded the entrance to that place. His visit was most opportune. For the governor of the city, who suffered from a fistula, had sent for me to see if I could cure him. None of the Europeans living in the fort knew the proper treatment, nor was there any Mahomedan surgeon who would venture to deal with the case. I asked Jacob, who was unable to speak Moors, and was a poor, miserable creature, whether he had the courage to treat such a complaint. He replied in the affirmative, and so I went with him to the governor, and in a short time we cured him, when he gave us a considerable sum for our trouble, besides the presents sent to me during the time we were attending him. Thus little by little I began to turn myself into a physician, although I did not make bold to announce myself as such.

During my stay in Āgrah I went one day to make an excursion into the country on horseback, in the company of a young Armenian. We came where a Hindū woman had begun to move round her pyre, which was already blazing; she rested her eyes on us, as if she appealed to us for help. The Armenian asked if I would join him in saving the woman from death. I said I would. Seizing our swords, and our servants doing the same, we charged our horses into the midst of the crowd looking on, shouting "Mata, mata!" ("Kill, kill!"), whereat the Brahmans, being frightened, all took to flight and left the woman unguarded. The Armenian laid hold of her, and making her mount behind him, carried her off. Subsequently, having had her baptized, he married her. When I passed through Sūrat I found her living there with her son, and she returned me many thanks for the benefit done to her. When the king returned from Kashmīr, the Brahmans went to complain that the soldiers did not allow women to be burnt, in accordance with their customs. The king issued an order that in all lands under Mogul control never again should the officials allow a woman to be burnt. This order endures to this day.

The king having arrived at Dihlī from Kashmīr, I went several times to make my bow to Rajah Jai Singh, who took a fancy to me, and in the end requested me to teach him how to play Hombre, as I had already done to his son Queretsing (Kīrat Singh). Several times we played together, and we two won from the said Rajah some sums of money. At this time Rajah Jai Singh said he had need of me. He wanted me to join him in this most important enterprise, and he would make me commander of his artillery. For this purpose I must search for Europeans I knew and who were good soldiers. Afterwards he would entrust other business to me. Meanwhile he fixed my pay at ten rupees a day. I could not resist his proposal, and I had great trust in his word, nor did I like to offend him at such a time. For I had not yet the boldness to announce myself as a physician. He gave me a rich *sarāpā* (set of robes), and a good horse, with sufficient money for my equipment.

Everything having been arranged, we quitted Dihlī with a strong force. Aurangzeb ordered Mahābat Khān to return to the government of Gujarāt, and

Bahādur Khān, the king's foster-brother, was ordered to return to court. At this time happened an amusing affair. Bahādur Khān, as the king's foster-brother, had been lifted from an obscure position to that of a general. He had become very high and mighty and vain-glorious. Everyone arriving from court was asked eagerly as to the king's health, not calling him by his title, but speaking of him as his brother; thus he used to say: "How is my brother?" Mahābat Khān decided to teach him a lesson. On reaching Gujarāt, he took his seat in his tent and arranged with his foster-brother that when Bahādur Khān was there he should, richly clad, and with an aigrette of gold stuck in his turban, gallop past on a fine horse, acting the braggart, as if on his way to his own quarters. Bahādur Khān wondered at this performance, and asked who was that mighty warrior. Mahābat Khān did not use the man's name, but, assuming an innocent air, he said briefly: "These foster-brothers are shameless creatures, and have no tact in what they do. They fancy that being our brothers by milk, they are equal members of our house!" Bahādur Khān quite saw the hit, but pretended not to. Nor by this was he turned from his line of conduct. For the proverb is a true one: "However many stratagems a man possesses, they sooner or later ruin him."

Two things happened to me during this march. The first was that, being dressed in the costume of the country, I fastened my gown or *cabaya* (*qabā*) on the right side as is the fashion of Mahomedans. The Hindūs fasten theirs on the left. I also went with my beard shaved, wearing only moustaches like the Rājpūts, but without pearls hanging from my ears as they have. The Rājpūt officers wondered at this get-up, neither Rājpūt nor Mahomedan. They asked me what religion I belonged to. I replied that I was of the Christian religion. Once more they asked me if I were a Mohamedan Christian or a Hindū Christian—

for they recognise no other religions than these in Hindūstān. I seized the opportunity to tell them a little about our faith.

The other matter was that one day Rajah Jai Singh asked me whether in Europe there were armies, wars, and squadrons. I replied to him that the bravery with which the Farangīs fought, of which I was an example, sufficed to show him that we in Europe knew what war and fighting meant. We were accustomed to fight in two ways: one by sea, the other by land. That upon the sea took place thus:

A number of planks are joined together by rails in the form of a large enclosed house, with many cannon in tiers. Entering into the said house, the soldiers attach huge cloths to masts, and, driven by the winds, these serve to put the said house in motion. The course is regulated by a large plank fixed on the house, and capable of movement from one side to another. In this way, with good matchlocks, pistols, and swords, and a sufficient supply of food, of powder, and of ball, they set out in search of their enemies. When they encounter one, the fight begins with the firing of cannon, which breaks the masts or makes holes in the said houses, allowing entrance to the water. But those who are within assemble and with skill plug the hole. For this they always have materials ready.

Meanwhile some attend to the vessel, and others fight without intermission. The dead bodies are thrown into the sea, so that they may not hinder the fight. Nor are there surgeons wanting to aid the wounded, who are carried to a room specially set apart. As their courage grows hotter, they bring the vessels nearer, emptying all their matchlocks and pistols, until at length, the fight waxing still fiercer, they grapple one with the other; then the sword-blows scatter streams of blood, reddening the sea. There being no mode of flight for the fighters, it is therefore necessary to conquer or die. Sometimes it happens that the captain who is losing, resolving not to be overcome, orders all his cannon and other pieces to be double-shotted. He then sets fire to the ship's magazine of powder; thus he destroys himself along with the others. The rajah wondered at such a mode of warfare, and it seemed to him very hard and cruel that a man, if he did not want to defend himself, could not even run away.

The other mode of fighting was on land. There the foot soldiers were separated from the squadrons of horse, and all had their matchlocks and swords. Those who were mounted had good carbines, pistols, and swords. When I was giving this account, finding some pikes or spears there, I exhibited how the spearmen stood in front of the companies to hinder the cavalry from getting in and throwing into disorder the well-ordered ranks of the infantry. Thus the battle would commence with great order and discipline, the cavalry helping wherever it was necessary to repress an onslaught of the enemy. Many a thing did we tell him of our fighting in the open country. Upon this he set to laughing, assuming us to have no horses in our country, and thus we could know nothing of fighting on horseback.

For this reason we agreed, I and Luis Beiçaõ, a French surgeon, Guilherme (William), an Englishman, and Domingo de Saã, a Portuguese, who had formerly been a cavalry soldier in Portugal, to give the next morning during the march, and in the rajah's presence, a demonstration of our mode of fighting on horseback. We rode out with our carbines, two pistols in our holsters, and two in our waistbelts, and carrying our swords. We rode two and two, and began to career about, our horses being excellent. Then first of all we skirmished with the carbine, and after some circling and recircling, letting off our pistols we made pretence of flight and pursuit. Then, turning round and making a half-circle, the fugitive attacked the pursuer and let off his pistol. Thus we went on till all our charges were fired off—of course without bullets. Then laying hand upon our swords, we made gestures as if giving sword-cuts, which the others parried.

The rajah, who was on his elephant, halted, and when our display was finished we rode up and made our bow. He asked what meant these excursions and alarms. I replied that purposely we had done this to let him see that we knew how to fight on horseback in the European way. He asked me several times if really they fought like that in Europe. I answered that this was only a small specimen. We would show him sport when it came to reality, observing the same order; and if there were on the field dead men or horses we should ride over them as if riding on a carpet, and make no account of them. He praised our way of fighting, saying he thought it a sound mode of warfare, and he should like to form a troop of European cavalry if I could obtain them. I answered that it was not easy to get so many men in Hindūstān who had been trained in our wars. He then gave us our leave with a good present, and thenceforth thought more of European nations, who, if it were not for their drinking habits, would be held in high estimation, and could aid our kings to carry out some project in those lands.

While this embassy (to Persia) was in progress, we were marching onwards to the city of Aurangābād, on reaching which we joined Shāh 'Ālam. Sending for me, Rajah Jai Singh ordered me to go as envoy to the three rajahs—that is to say, Rāmanagar (Rāmnagar), Pentt (Pent), and Chottia (Chiūtia), who are petty rajahs among the Hindūs, and the Portuguese call them kings of the Colles (? Kolīs). It was through their lands that Shivā Jī passed on his way to attack Sūrat. Rajah Jai Singh gave me a set of robes and a horse, and sent with me thirty troopers and infantry, also a considerable sum for expenses. My orders were to go to these rajahs, and tell them they must give their word not to take the side of Shivā Jī, nor allow him passage. He (Jai Singh) must declare war against them in the name of the Mogul emperor, if they did not take up arms against Shivā Jī and embrace the cause of Aurangzeb. As security for their promise they must come in themselves, or send their sons to attend on the court, where they would be assigned pay and rank befitting their condition.

I took my departure on this deputat on, and the first person I visited was the Rajah of Rāmanagar, whose territories lie amidst frightful hills and gloomy forests. I was well received by this rajah, who invited me to take a rest while he deliberated on what he thought it was best to do. I amused myself meanwhile going out to shoot and fish; nor did the rajah fail in providing pastimes in the nature of plays and games. Meanwhile he was corresponding with the other two rajahs, whether they thought it suited them to take the Mogul side against Shivā Jī. I was not backward in making promises and using threats, according as I considered it appropriate. Sometimes I put myself into a passion and demanded an answer, else I would be off. In the end the rajah chose the side of Aurangzeb, giving me a horse and a sword. He made over to me his son in confirmation of his word.

I then went to the second rajah, where I was received in a friendly manner, and treated just as I had been at the first place. He petitioned for time, feigning that he had not had time to write to the others. Here I received many honours according to their custom—dances, plays, and the chase. Finally he too gave me a horse and a sword, and delivered to me his son to be conducted to court. But this tall and robust young man died on the journey, by reason of the great heat of the sun, which inflamed his blood He would not agree to be bled, as I counselled, he not trusting me.

Next I proceeded to the third rajah, who showed himself recalcitrant. But finding I was determined, he set to work to conciliate me. Not having any sons, he made over to me his brother to be taken to court with me; he then bestowed on me a sword and a horse, and bade me farewell. It happened that at this time he was fighting the Portuguese of Damaõ (Damān), so I arranged matters and persuaded them to make peace.

Here two things happened to me that I wish to recount, so that inquiring persons may learn that these people are much given to sorcery. I had a handsome horse that Rajah Jai Singh had given me. The Rajah of Chottia (Chiūtia), took a fancy to this horse, and requested me to sell it to him; he would pay me one thousand rupees. I was not willing; but when it was time for my departure the horse had lost the use of its legs, and was unable to move. I waited for eight days without any good, when the rajah sent me word that, though the horse was damaged, he would still give me one thousand rupees. In a rage I started from the place, telling my people that if within twenty-four hours the horse could not move, to cut his throat and bring the hide to me. Finding me so resolute, the rajah sent me one thousand two hundred rupees, beseeching me not to order the horse's throat to be cut, but to content myself with the present, and he would keep the horse in remembrance of me. I contented myself with taking the twelve hundred rupees, knowing quite well that if I did not, I should lose both horse and rupees.

Another affair happened to me on this return journey to the camp with the hostages. It was thus: One of my servants passing through a field of radishes, stretched out his hand to pluck one out of the ground, when his hand adhered in such a fashion to the radish that he could not take it away. It was necessary to find the owner of the field to get him liberated. This was done, and after taking something as a bribe, and giving him a beating, the owner recited some words and the man was freed. I could never sufficiently state to what an extent the Hindūs and Mahomedans in India are in the habit of practising witchcraft. I quite well know that if I were to recount that they can even make a cock crow in the belly of the man who stole and ate it, no credit would be given to me. Nevertheless, the truth is that many a time I heard the crowing in different cases, and of such instances I was told over and over again.

A few days after my arrival Shivā Jī gave himself up and came into our camp. Since I went at night to converse and play (cards) with the rajah whenever he so desired, it happened one night during this period that we were having a game, the rajah, his Brahman, and I, when in came Shivā Jī. We all rose up, and Shivā Jī, seeing me, a youth well favoured of body, whom he had not beheld on other occasions, asked Rajah Jai Singh of what country I was the rajah. Jai Singh replied that I was a Farangī rajah. He wondered at such an answer, and said that he also had in his service many Farangīs, but they were not of this style. Rajah Jai Singh wanted to do me honour, and responded that as a rule Nature made a distinction between the great and the humble, and I being a rajah, she had given me a mind and a body very different from those of others. I rose to my feet as a mark of recognition for the compliment, and made the appropriate obeisance. This was the opening which afforded me occasion many times to converse with Shivā Jī, since I possessed, like anyone else in the camp, the Persian and Hindūstān languages. I gave him information about the greatness of European kings, he being of opinion that there was not in Europe any other king than the King of Portugal. I also talked to him about our religion.

During this advance and retreat there was with our army the Father Damiaõ Vieira, a Portuguese expelled by the Jesuit Fathers. The cause of his appearance was that during our stay below the fortress of Punagar (? Pūnā-gaṛh) the Hindūs of Chāwal came to complain to Rajah Jai Singh that the Portuguese were seizing forcibly the sons of the Hindūs and making them Christians. This made the rajah angry, for he was zealous in the Hindū faith, and he made preparations to send a force against Chāwal.

On becoming aware of this I gave notice, there and then, to Ignacio Sermento at Bassain. He was chief of the northern territory of the Portuguese, which extends to Damaõ (Damān). I requested him to send someone as envoy with some presents, and I would arrange matters. He sent this padre, with a young Mahomedan in his suite. He brought this youth expressly to get from him half of what he might acquire, as being well acquainted with the territories of Chāwal. He was clever enough to secure the rajah's taking this young man into his service, and thus they shared the pay in a brotherly manner. I spoke to the rajah and pointed out to him that there was no occasion for the Hindūs of Chāwal to complain, since what the Portuguese were doing had gone on certainly for a hundred years, nor did they make Christians of anyone but orphans who had no relations forthcoming.

The padre was not content with having accomplished his mission with somewhat of honour, but he must needs enter on warlike proposals. He promised the rajah that he would so manage that the viceroy of Goa should give aid to the Moguls, in the acquisition of Bījāpur. Over and over again I told the padre that it was not a good thing to enter into such matters, that he had much better withdraw to Goa. For the King of Bījāpur was a better neighbour to the Portuguese than the King of the Moguls would ever be. The latter having conquered Bījāpur, would next try to take Goa. The padre was not pleased with my views, and complained to the rajah, so that the rajah said to me one day, without giving a reason, that I should avoid meeting the padre. After the business had been settled, I received from the Portuguese a certificate signed by Ignacio Sermento, wherein he swore on the

Holy Evangelists that I had done great service to the Crown of Portugal.

We got to Bījāpur as I said, and there we beheld the miracles that the padre had promised us. We were to take Bījāpur with the greatest ease, whereas it all but happened that Sharzah Khān broke all our heads. Therefore, finding, after we had retreated, that we were going into quarters, I began to long for a life among Christians; and I was disgusted at the conduct of the padre, who continued to live on in the army. I asked the rajah for leave to resign, as I wanted to return to my country, and I put forward as excuse that I wanted to get married. They never refuse anyone leave when it is with that object. The rajah asked his Brahman and the astrologers, with whom these princes are always well provided, if he should ever see me again. They replied that we should never meet again. He believed that I was doomed to die, but he reckoned badly, for while I got back to the Mogul country, he was left dead far from home.

On my taking leave he gave me a set of robes, and something by way of a present. Upon quitting the army I went into a village belonging to the Portuguese called Camba (Kāmbe) close to Galiani (Kaliyānī) and Beundi (Bhiwandī) in the country of Shivā Jī. In this village are made many things of wood—handsome chairs, sideboards, bedsteads, and different playthings. Here I stayed for several days, at the request of a friend of mine, who was the owner of the village, and he kept me in his house until he had stolen some gold coins I had. Thence I made for Bassaim (Bassain, Wasai), a Portuguese town, there to pass Lent, and I lived outside the town. I was very near losing my life here. A gentleman (*fidalgo*) asked me about some *fidalgos* of the Mello family, then living in the Mogul country, who had been banished for putting to death two brothers named Medonças (? Mendoza), brothers-in-law of the questioner, on the accusation of treason to the Portuguese Crown. I had no idea that he was an enemy of these fugitives, and I replied that they were men of worth and honoured gentlemen. This sufficed to set him plotting against me, and he sent out men to assassinate me. But it was God's pleasure that, when coming out of the town on my horse, I should meet some gentlemen, who requested me to put my horse to speed, which I did most vigorously. With a pleasantry I took my leave of them, and spurred my horse into a gallop, though it was already tired out; getting my sword out of its scabbard, it was as much as I could do to get hold of it, seeing that my horse would hardly let me.

But here we must admire God's providence, who had resolved on saving me. Here was I galloping my horse, sword in hand, when I came up with four men at a corner round which I had to pass. They stood there waiting for me with naked swords ready to slay me. But guessing that I had been already warned, and was coming at them, resolved to fight to the death, they were in fear and allowed me to pass without hindrance. I was subsequently informed that he who had laid this plot for me was the *fidalgo* to whom I had praised the Mellos. Thus fearing that he would lose no occasion of executing his evil intent, I left for Goa, and there I arrived in the month of May, one thousand six hundred and sixty-six (1666). Of the place itself I shall have much to say presently, but the reader must first permit me to say something about my own stay there.

I did not obtain there what I sought, for I found myself in a place where treachery is great and prevalent, where there is little fear of God and no concern for strangers. Not that I can complain myself of ill-treatment, for the viceroy desired to honour me with the command of a war-galley; but since I had many necessary expenses, and I was not rich enough to take upon myself the payment of the soldiers and sailors from my own pocket, I declined.

My advice to the viceroy was that he should take great care not to let the Mogul become master of Bījāpur, for, on finding an opportunity, he would use all his strength to take Goa, as was his usual practice.

As I had need of money for expenses, I went several times to the General Ignacio Sermento, to ask for the three hundred rupees which he continued to owe me for certain articles that he had asked me to send him when I was in the Mogul country. Never could I succeed in getting what was due. At length, when he was about to start for his government of Mozambique, I begged him to make me a gift of the three hundred rupees—at any rate, under the name of alms. As a foreigner, I had no remedy against him, and when he heard me ask for charity he ordered the sum to be paid me. Thus is it the custom of certain of these gentlemen to pay their debts after wearying out their creditors. I was very fortunate. Others, in place of collecting the money they have lent, have lost a limb, or even their life. I do not want to talk of that, for those who are curious may ask the Portuguese themselves; there are among them men of sincerity, as there are in other nations; such men can tell them more than I dare to write about the Portuguese of India.

I stopped in Goa a year and three months. It is a place with a climate suited to men from forty up to old age, but it is very unhealthy for young men. Thus, a few months after my arrival, I fell ill, and could never recover my health. Therefore I retired to the convent of the Italian Carmelite priests, where I was well received and attended to for six months, during which I continued unwell.

The viceroy, when I arrived, was Antonio de Mello de Castro, who died afterwards a prisoner in Portugal, through good works of thieving, *et cetera*, of which he had been guilty in India. To replace him came Joaõ

Nunes da Cunha ; and this new governor, as soon as he arrived, undertook a great expedition. He kept his object secret, and it would have resulted in great honour to the Portuguese if those who were envious of his earning this glory had not impeded its execution. There came from Masqaṭ, a fortress on the Arabian coast formerly belonging to the Portuguese, which by their negligence they lost, when it passed into the hands of an Arabian prince—there came, I say, from this fortress to Goa a Portuguese named Andre da Andrada, who was commander of artillery there, and passed for a Mahomedan. This man pledged his word to the new viceroy to deliver over the fortress if a strong fleet appeared before it by sea, and to secure that end he would spike the guns.

The viceroy took up the proposal, and hired a strong fleet of good ships and frigates for this service. But he let no one know what he meant to do, and from this secrecy the Dutch dreaded some sudden blow to them, as they could not find out what such preparations were meant for. By the distribution of copious bribes in all directions they won over several of the officers. The viceroy, being desirous of equipping his ships well, ordered the embarkation by force of every valid man, compelled the better class of Portuguese from the northern parts to come to Goa, and directed that no one should be allowed to quit the place. Thus, when the ships were well fitted out, he made over sealed instructions to the captains with the order not to open them until arrival at a certain latitude.

Thus the fleet set sail without anyone knowing its destination. But the bribed pilots and captains sailed hither and thither with the ships without overcoming the contrary winds until they reached the appointed latitude, where the letters of instruction were opened ; and some of them managed secretly to tamper with the water-casks, so that all the water was lost. The fault was put upon the viceroy, who, in his desire for haste, had not given time to prepare the ships properly. Thus there put into port only one frigate, which, in obedience to orders, anchored at Bandar Congo, on the Arabian coast, a Portuguese territory that now belongs to the King of Persia. There it waited some time for its companions, until it was obliged to return to Goa to avoid capture by those of Masqaṭ, who profited by the treason.

At the time of this expedition I was anxious to quit Goa, but I could not do it in lay clothing. I therefore left in the garb of a Carmelite monk until I got beyond the district of Goa and had entered the territory of Bījāpur, of which Shivā Jī had already taken possession. There I returned to my ordinary costume, and placed myself under the guidance of Divine Providence. I prayed God to deliver me from many perils, above all from robbers; for, a little time before my arrival, they had at a certain place murdered fifteen persons. Nor did they murder me as I passed by, but when they might have done it they saw me to be poor and a foreigner. A few paces farther on I met a traveller near some cattle sheds, who was escaping in haste, and he warned me to press onwards because the people following us were robbers; but, weakened by illness, I could not keep up with the pace of the man who was acting as my guide in a country I did not know. I passed several *chungams*, which are places where they collect money from people passing. The severity they exercise upon travellers is great, depriving them of the smallest piece of money to be found on them, with no tenderness for the poor, taking from them in default of money their shirts, coats, and sheets.

Having come to the boundary of the Bījāpur territory near the river Bimbra (Bhīmā), I stopped for the night in a village called Pandarapur (Pandharpur), and on my arrival I took up my quarters in a public *bāzār*, as is the custom of travellers, and deposited myself in an open shop. Some people passing said my waist-cloth was crammed with pearls. I answered that I was only a poor traveller. God was good to me that night! For at midnight the robbers entered the village, and the first thing they did was to come to the shop where I had put up. As they began by throwing stones, I sought refuge inside, dragging with me a servant boy whom I had with me, to prevent his being killed. They did not venture inside, but shouted to me to fling out whatever I had, thrusting with their spears and cutting with their swords at the door. I assured them that I could fling nothing out, for I was a poor man, having nothing with me. Such was the terror that throttled me that I could not utter a word, for I remembered what had been said to me that evening, that I had a waist-belt full of pearls, and I believed that they had come resolved to take my life; therefore I threw out two chains, each of which might be worth some fifty rupees. They made off, robbing the *bāzār* and killing people, so that there was great tribulation in the village.

Not considering myself safe in that shop, I sallied forth, and traversing the streets I reached a house where I halted, and finding the door open I ascended some steps and reached a terraced roof. Here I fancied myself in security. But the owner of the house, who had heard the outcry in the village, came out of his room with sword and shield. On seeing me, he ordered me roughly to make my way downstairs. I told him I was a foreigner who had fled from the *bāzār*, where the thieves had robbed me, and to save my life had taken refuge there, finding the door open. This did not persuade him to let me remain, but he insisted on my departing. I was content that he even let me go unharmed, for on hearing his first talk I feared much he was about to finish what the robbers had begun.

I now went to the steps of a temple, where many persons had taken shelter out of the way of the arrows flying about the streets and the sword-blows being distributed in all directions. Nor was it without some trouble that I got in even there. Next a Brahman refused to let me stop, thrusting me forth by force. But God repaid him for his want of charity, for while he was interfering with me, there came an arrow and hit him on the leg, and I was rid of him. The thieves withdrew, and I, too, found a refuge again in the *bāzār*, but not in the same shop, for I feared greatly they might come there once again. I spent the night in the discomfort that everyone can imagine. At dawn, feeling much afflicted, I chewed a clove, washing it down with a little warm water, whereupon I vomited several clots of thickened blood, and felt relieved.

I continued my journey up to the crossing on the river (? the Bhīma). Although it is wide, there were no boats; I crossed seated on a small bedstead attached to the tops of four pots. I then reached Paranda (Parendā) in the Mogul territory, where I came across my friends of the fortress of Bhakkar. They took compassion on my poverty, regaled me, succoured me with money, clothes, and a mount, on which I resumed my travels and arrived at Aurangābād.

Travelling is a teacher of many things, and he who wanders without learning anything can only be said to have the head of an ass. The horse given me by Manoel Ribeiro at Parendā had only arrived a few days before from Dihlī, a journey of forty-six days, and it was thus much out of condition. It happened one day that my servant opened his bag in which he had a nutmeg, and by carelessness he left this nut on the ground, and the horse ate it. Next day on mounting, I noticed that he was much more lively in his gait. I did not know the cause of this freshness, then I remembered that he had eaten a nut the night before, and I concluded that must be the cause. Nor was I wrong, for on giving him each day one nut, he became ever more ready and clever.

After my arrival in Aurangābād I lived retīred. This was the time at which, as I have related, Shāh 'Ālam was busy trying to get hold of Shivā Jī, and I was informed of the friar's death in the way I have recounted. I went on through Burhānpur, where I found several friends among the servants of Jai Singh, all disconsolate at the death of that great general. I felt his death very much, although I had no intention of re-entering his service, for I wanted to start as a doctor. Thence I went on to Āgrah, where I visited the Jesuit Fathers, and reported to them what was going on at Goa. I did not stay long, but passed on to Dihlī. Thereupon, on learning of my arrival, there was no fail of women who proposed marriage to me and sent me cloth, and money, and banquets of food. One of them sent me fifty gold coins and a horse, and handsome stuff to make me clothes. I went to see Kīrat Singh, the younger son of Rajah Jai Singh, who in remembrance of the great affection his father held me in, and which he continued to give me, gave me a set of robes, two horses, and five rupees every day, and a handsome house to live in. By this means, those envious of my good fortune, who had expected to see me under the necessity of applying to them for my expenses, knowing that I was out of service, were in amazement at seeing me well dressed, owning horses, and keeping servants. Any foreigner who is out of employment can only subsist in a miserable fashion in that country.

I lived in Dilhī one year in splendid style, having honourable means of making money. Then, by the king's order, Kīrat Singh went to Kābul, and I determined to move to Lāhor and give myself out as a doctor. I could not start this at Dihlī, where there were already some Europeans, while in Lāhor there was none.

On reaching Lāhor I found that Muhammad Amīn Khān was governor, Aurangzeb having kept his promise to make him viceroy. As soon as I arrived

I put up in the *sarāe* with my grand carpets and my petty establishment, until I could find a house. I hired one belonging to Barqandāz Khān, my commander in Dārā's time, and I instructed my servants to inform everyone that I was a Farangī doctor. Through this many came to talk with me, and in return I had no want of words, God having given me a sufficiently mercurial temperament. Thus it began to be noised about in Lāhor that a Frank doctor had arrived, a man of fine manners, eloquent speech, and great experience. I rejoiced at such a reputation, but my heart beat fast, for then I had had no experience. It pleased God our Sovereign Lord to open the door to me with a case furnished to me by His Divine Providence.

There came to me in the house where I had settled an old woman, who told me that the wife of the *qāẓī* was very ill, and given up by all the Persian and Indian physicians. She requested the favour of my proceeding to the *qāẓī's* house to see the woman, and decide whether there was any cure, for all the doctors had said that if anyone cured her they would burn all their books and profess themselves disciples of him who cured her. I put several questions about the illness of the woman; I told the messenger to return home, and I would follow, saying that although the complaint seemed mortal, I would see if there was any remedy.

I mounted my horse and rode to the *qāẓī's* house, followed by my servants. Entering the house, I felt the patient's pulse. The attack was growing more and more severe, and no pulse could be felt, nor could I find out the seat of the disease. I trusted more to several secret experiments I knew, and to my questions. I racked my brains to think of something I could give the patient that might do her good. I asked her if she had been relieved, and they told me that for days she did not know what thing a motion was. This sufficed for me to start my treatment, and I told the old woman that the only thing was to administer a clyster. The old woman and the patient's son were much opposed to this, the Mahomedans having objections to this treatment. But the patient was already speechless. I said: "*Agar zarūrat bāyad, rawā bakhshad,*" that is: "Necessity has no law," which are words of the Qurān. Thus they gave in to my resorting to this treatment, and I told the old woman to come to my house in a few hours, and I would give her all that was required for the application.

I came forth from this house leaving an excellent impression from my many questions and my copious flow of talk. But now came the moment when our Nicolao Manuchy found himself in a difficulty. For I knew not what ingredients I must employ, nor to what implements I must have recourse for this wonderful operation. After much searching of heart, I remembered that the enemas administered to me at Goa were concocted of mallows, wild endive, and some other herbs, with a trifle of bran, black sugar, salt, olive oil, and *Canna fistula.* I sent out for these things, and made a concoction. But the greatest difficulty was to get the instrument. For this I sent and got a cow's udder, and for the tube I took a piece of cane from a *huqqah* snake, through which the Mahomedans draw their tobacco. I managed to put these together in a manner that would serve. I placed the concoction into the udder, and fastened the tube to it. Then the old woman came, and to her I made over the injection, teaching her how she was to deal with it. I enjoined on her to come and inform me when the operation had been performed.

I declared to her that if in a period of three hours the enema did not take effect, the patient had no hope of life. It was advisable for me to make this assertion, since should the patient die, I could say that I had foretold the result as inevitable. This was necessary to keep my reputation intact. Off went the old woman, and my heart began to beat hard, not knowing what effect the medicine might have. Soon I heard a knocking at my door as by one in haste. My anxiety was redoubled. It might be the news of the patient's death, through which I should lose the reputation that I was in search of. For the Mahomedans easily assign one a reputation, and as easily take it away. A happy cure at the start suffices to give the greatest credit, even if the cure be a mere accident. On the contrary, if there is a failure in the first case, even when the doctor is exceedingly learned and experienced, it suffices to prevent him ever being esteemed.

I sent to have the door opened, when the old woman fell at my feet and gave me blessings, telling me that the patient had already begun to mend. Thus she urgently prayed me to visit the *qāẓī's* house to see the patient and continue the cure. Proud and elated by this news, I told her how necessary it was to confide in experienced physicians, that if I had not given her this medicament composed of ingredients known alone to me the patient was bound to die. I went and found that the patient had already begun to speak and recognise everyone who was present. She was very different from what she had been for some days, for they told me that she knew no one and could not speak. I thought it advisable to discharge nature further, so I gave her a light medicine, continuing it daily, until the system was well cleansed. Then, with chicken-broth and *bezoar* stone, I began to strengthen the patient in such a way that in a few days she was restored to perfect health.

This case became notorious among the principal men in Lāhor, for this wife was much loved by her husband the *qāẓī*, so that he had called in all the physicians to treat her disease. Thus there began to be talk of the Farangī doctor who was capable of resuscitating the dead. This caused me to be called in by many sick persons; and by adhering to certain books I had, I succeeded by God's favour in almost every case in which I was sent for.

My fame reached the court of Muḥammad Amīn K̲h̲ān, governor of the city and viceroy of the province of Lāhor. He sent for me, and, after a long conversation on the subject of diseases and good health, he wanted to make me take service with him, offering me little pay, but great liberty. But I knew the style of man—very haughty, far from genial, just like the character of his father, Mīr Jumlah. So that I said that as to becoming his servant I objected; still I should not fail to appear at the palace whenever necessary, either for himself or for those of his family. He was a little put out by my answer, but I paid no attention to that, for I was already on friendly terms with the chief people in the city, and by God's blessing my practice was successful. Thus I knew of a certainty that, in spite of Muḥammad Amīn K̲h̲ān's desire to do me an injury, he would never dare. He would not give such an opening to the other nobles to make complaint of him at the court of Dihlī. On the other hand, although he was much aggrieved at my not frequenting his audiences, he betrayed no anger, for he saw I was of use for attending his wives and sons. There happened to me a terrible business at the time of his departure from Lāhor for Kābul (1670–71).

This was the year in which Muḥammad Amīn K̲h̲ān gave me a lot of annoyance, for, having been ordered by the king to Kābul, as governor in place of Mahābat K̲h̲ān, he wanted to take me with him by force. I made my excuses, saying I did not wish to leave Lāhor.

He left with his retinue, and finding that neither by promises nor by threats could I be made to follow him, he ordered me to be carried off by force. Thus I travelled with him for three days as far as Little

Gūjarāt, crossing the river of Lāhor and the river Chināb. He acted thus not only from his desire to keep me, but also because his wife so willed it. She went the length of unveiling before me her daughter's face (a most unusual thing among them), and said to me that if I would not go for her sake, at the least I might for her daughter's, whom I had brought back to health when she was very ill. I had come thus far, but never forsook the project I intended to carry out; for he who serves by compulsion can never be satisfied. Thus, the marches being at night on account of the heat, I turned back without saying a word to anyone except an Englishman, whom I told I was going to the town of Little Gūjarāt to buy some medicines, and if Muḥammad Amīn Khān should ask him about me, he was to give that answer.

That nobleman had given an order, that no one was to be allowed to cross to the other side of the river, permitting nothing to remain on our side except the ferry boat, for conveying the couriers to and from the court; but I so took my measures that this boat was forced to carry me across, for, as I approached, I sent my servants to take possession of the boat and keep it until I arrived. I came up and ordered the boatmen to convey me across, pretending I was a courier from Mahābat Khān to the court. As soon as I had passed the river it began to dawn, and I met a body of Muḥammad Amīn Khān's people. When they asked me where I was going, I answered angrily that Mirzā 'Abdullah being unwell the prince had sent me to treat him. Thus I got past them. I reached Lāhor by fast travelling before he could overtake me on the way.

But Muḥammad Amīn Khān planned a piece of treachery for my destruction. This consisted in writing to Gitar, commander of the fort and provisional governor, to his own agent (? *wakīl*), to the *koṭwāl*, and to the *qāẓī*, requiring them to forward me to his camp. If I refused, they were to charge me with having stolen from him five lakhs of rupees. They knew quite well it was a false accusation, but Muḥammad Amīn K̲h̲ān being a great man, they did not hesitate to do everything possible to have me seized. But I was not asleep, and I was tolerably versed in Mahomedan tricks, for they stick at nothing to gain success in their desires. Therefore I did not stay inside Lāhor at my house, but hid myself in the gardens, moving about from one place to another in disguise. This went on for forty days, and proclamation was made, that anyone knowing where I was hid and discovering me, would be highly rewarded, and whoever concealed me in his house would be compelled to pay the five lakhs of rupees robbed by me from Muḥammad Amīn K̲h̲ān.

At this time Fidā,e K̲h̲ān, who was to succeed Muḥammad Amīn K̲h̲ān as governor, was approaching. He was his predecessor's enemy. In advance of his own arrival he sent two hundred cavalry, conveying letters to the provisional governor, the *kotwāl*, and the *qāẓī*, telling them to carry on the government in his name until he should arrive. At each court of justice was posted one of Fidā,e K̲h̲ān's troopers to act as witness, and verify everything that took place. When I knew this I came boldly into Lāhor, and had an interview with the trooper who attended the *koṭwāl's* court, also with the man posted at the deputy governor's, telling them my story. Both men pledged me their word that they would help me, but I told them not to take action until they saw me being taken away by force to Muḥammad Amīn K̲h̲ān. Secure of their aid if anything happened to me, I returned to my house. The *koṭwāl* and the other officials were in fear of Muḥammad Amīn K̲h̲ān, so the *koṭwāl* sent for me and locked me up in prison, and three times on three different days he asked me in public audience whether I would willingly go to Muḥammad Amīn K̲h̲ān or not. On my saying resolutely that I would not go, he said that as Muḥammad Amīn K̲h̲ān had accounts to go into with me, I must be forced to go. My reply was that I had no sort of account with him, nor knew I aught about his jewels, for I was no official of his household, but only a Frank surgeon to whom jewels would not be made over. Seeing me thus firm, he too spoke resolutely, at the instigation of Muḥammad Amīn Khān's *wakīl*, declaring that I must absolutely go.

They had already removed me from the audience, and were making me mount into a carriage prepared for that purpose, when the trooper whom I had already made my friend, announced openly, that if they wished to send me they might, but hereafter Fidā,e Khān would have something to say to them, he having given special instructions for Hakīm Niccolao, the Frank, to be looked after, he being his (Fidā,e Khān's) private doctor. He called on everyone to bear witness, how he had made requisition on his master's behalf. Upon hearing this the *koṭwāl* got into a fright and sent for me once more, and said to me in a loud voice that the trooper had made requisition on behalf of Fidā,e Khān, but the law demanded that at the very least I should produce bail for my person, so as to be able afterwards to justify itself against a claim by Muḥammad Amīn Khān.

Sureties were not wanting who, knowing the truth, were willing to bind themselves for me. But neither the *koṭwāl* nor the *wakīl* would accept them as bail, warning them that in this way they would have to defend themselves from Muḥammad Amīn Khān, a violent and powerful man. Thus it came to pass, that all of them were afraid to do what they wished, until at last a Hindū turned up, who, in defiance of Muhammad Amīn Khān, became surety, I giving him an indemnity, and thus I was free.

Meanwhile Mirzā Ṣāliḥ, the son of Fidā,e Khān, arrived. I visited him and paid my respects, having beforehand had some good words said to him about me, for I was tolerably well known in Lahor. In this way, when Fidā,e Khān himself subsequently arrived, he (Mirzā Ṣāliḥ) presented me to his father, by whom I was well received. I presented to him a box full of an electuary. He sent for the *koṭwāl*, and told him to take good care that no one interfered with me, and he also gave me his word to be favourable to me. This, of a truth, he was as long as he lived, and that too in things of great importance.

Aurangzeb has Mahābat Khān Poisoned

He (Aurangzeb) ordered, as I have said, that poison should be given to him secretly; and, since he was on his way to Lāhor, they told the king there was in that city a Frank physician who might cure him. For this reason there came to me a letter without any name, which stated that in no way must I afford aid to Mahābat Khān. He who brought me the letter, a man unknown to me, took me by the hand, and, pressing it, said I must pay great heed to the letter, and not to act to the contrary, and then off he went.

Knowing that Mahābat Khān was on his way, and being on friendly terms, I sent out to him a present of some good spirits, that I had prepared myself. His doctor, who had the order to give him the poison, seized the opportunity for my ruin and his own preservation. On the day that the Nawāb drank my wine he gave him the poison in an elixir, such as the Mahomedans are accustomed to take. Mahābat Khān found himself troubled with sharp pains, and suspected that there must be poison in my spirits, and that I had acted thus at the instigation of Fidā,e Khān, his enemy. He sent to fetch me in the greatest haste, just as I was ready to go out for a stroll. At once I suspected something. I jumped on my horse and went off to him, he being eighteen leagues away.

Entering the tent, I found everyone in astonishment, for they had the idea that I would never come, being, as they asserted, the culprit. He ordered the tent to be prepared for me, and a good supper, sending to entertain me several of his nephews, great friends of mine; also a captain called Mīrak Aṭā-ullah. This man was to spy upon me, and see if I spoke with any sign of fear or surprise; but, as I was quite innocent, I spoke in my usual manner. Next morning I went to see Mahābat Khān again, and I asked him if he had tested the spirits that I had sent, and he said he had. Thereupon I prayed the favour of his giving me a drink of it. They brought me the bottle from which he had drank. I drank, and after I had done so I gave some to his nephews, who praised the liquor. I did this to let him be satisfied that it was not my liquor that had made him bad, but some other thing. I remained with him in talk a long time, and he observed that the spirits did neither me nor his nephews any harm. He then invited me to treat him. I made excuse, saying that he was provided with his own doctor, a very wise man, and that I was not acquainted with that disease. Thus I remained with him nineteen days, and he detained me to find out if the spirits we drank did any harm, either to me or his nephews. He was obliged to let me go without being able to find from me whether he had poison in his inside or not. At my departure he conferred on me a set of robes, and sent the same captain with twenty horsemen to escort me, so that his men, who thought me the cause of his illness, should not harm me. He died a few days afterwards of fetid discharges, a sign that his bowels were ulcerated.

Hardly had I reached Lāhor when a terrible affair happened. This was that the holy man of Balkh, to whom Aurangzeb had married the daughter of Murād Bakhsh, went mad. I was treating him as such. But Fidā,e Khān, being away at Peshāwar, Amānat Khān was in his place. He listened to the proposals of the sorcerers, who said that the holy man was possessed by a demon, and not mad. I was obliged to abandon the treatment, Amānat Khān being aggrieved that I had taken on myself to treat a royal connection without first of all consulting him. My answer was that, being by profession a medical man, I went to the house of anyone who sent for me, without making any distinctions; but since he did not approve of my continuing the treatment, I would that very hour quit the house and the patient.

It happened that a few days afterwards, the sorcerers assuring him that the man was now sane and had no longer a demon in his inside, they allowed him to go for a walk with the princess and her ladies. Having a dagger in his waist-belt, he drew it, and, seizing the princess, stabbed her beneath the ribs towards the side. When the ladies and the eunuchs, on hearing her cries, ran to the spot, he killed one woman with the same dagger, and wounded another in the arm. After this he jumped into the reservoir, playing (*bailando*) with the dagger, and other obscenities. Then they carried away the princess in a palanquin as speedily as possible to the palace, and a eunuch came careering on horseback to my house. I was urged to make all haste; I knew not why or wherefore. I sent an order to harness my carriage for us both to go together. But I could not extract from his mouth where it was necessary to go, until at last he told me to carry with me the remedies for the treatment of a wound that the holy man had inflicted on the princess. I protested that I could not go without the permission of the governor, because the princess was of royal blood, nor could I treat her without the king's orders. He paid no heed to those words, and most urgently entreated me not to delay, for the princess was in danger of death. He then told me the whole story.

We started in the carriage, and he made out I was drunk, ordering the carriage to be driven with all speed, stopping for neither hucksters' stalls nor people. Everybody was amazed to see a Frank, who usually went by rather quietly, rush past so desperately. We reached the palace, and, on being told the facts as to the wound, I feared a lesion of the bowels. However, continuing my inquiries, I found that the wounds were not mortal. I did my utmost to get an examination before I began the treatment; but the Mahomedans are very touchy in the matter of allowing their women to be seen, or even touched, by the hand; above all, the lady being of royal blood, it could not be done without express permission from the king. Thus an examination was impossible. But I ordered them to describe the wound, and I had the dagger brought, and I saw that it was only by God's grace that it had not cut the bowels. I made my tents and plasters, mixing in them a balsam which I made; and, since the persons in the service of these great people are intelligent, I instructed them as to what they had to do. By God's help the treatment succeeded, and in eleven days I healed her completely.

When for the first time I applied the medicine I went to the governor and reported the facts. This was to prevent his expressing surprise afterwards, on hearing such news, and becoming frightened that the king would remark on the want of care with which he had guarded a man who had been declared mad. He entreated me earnestly to make my best efforts to cure the princess. Meanwhile he wrote to the king about the case, and told him that a demon had entered the body of the holy man, and the princess had been mortally wounded with a dagger. But a Frank doctor named Ḥakīm Niccolao had attended her, and held out hopes that she would be well in a short time. This event brought me to the notice of many nobles who were in the camp. For on the matter becoming public, my friends wrote to their acquaintances, and the princess herself, as soon as she was well, wrote to the king that I had perfectly restored her, and she gave me a handsome present.

Another case occurred which made me famous throughout the kingdom. It was as follows: Fidā,e Khān ordered the beheadal of a powerful rebel, who plundered in all directions in the king's territories; he was brother-in-law of the *qāẓī* of Lāhor. His name was Theka Araham (? Thīkā,Arāin) and he was extremely fat. I thought it was a good chance of laying in a stock of human fat, procuring it from the man and his companion, who also was very obese. I spoke to Fidā,e K͟hān, pointing out the necessity I was under of having this medicament. As the opportunity was favourable, would he give orders to remove the fat from these two condemned men? He then ordered the *koṭwāl* to have this done, and in compliance with the order, men were sent to carry out the operation. I thus acquired eighteen *sirs*—that is, five hundred and four ounces purified.

This matter caused great talk in the city, and the *qāẓī*, assembling many of the learned, sent men to complain to the king against Fidā,e K͟hān, for protecting a Frank. On his behalf he had committed the sacrilege of removing the fat of a Mahomedan, a man who read the Qurān and yet had been thus afflicted. According to the strict law the Frank deserved to be burnt, but as Fidā,e K͟hān declined to listen to argument, they were forced to come to His Majesty to present a complaint and demand justice.

I was warned of the plot, and spoke to Fidā,e K͟hān about the *qāẓī's* intentions. He sent at once a messenger to court, to report that the population of Lāhor were restless, and if there came any complaint about the beheaded man, Thīkā,Arāin, it must not be listened to, for the *qāẓī* and others had been his supporters. This was enough to secure that on the arrival of the complaint at court, where many had clad themselves in mourning to present the petition, the king should send them away after saying very little, with the remark: "Caziey zemi, bessare zemi" (*Qaẓāyā-i-zamīn bar-sar-i-zamīn*). This means: "Cases about land are settled on the land itself." Thus I was left unharmed for that once, and freed from a great persecution that would have cost me my life.

God was pleased to deliver me once more after

several months. For there came a relation of the beheaded man expressly to kill me. By a lucky chance he came when I was prescribing for the sick, distributing medicine, adding alms for those in want. He came into my *dīwān* with his sword and shield, leaving his spear and horse at my door. Without any salutation he sat down in front of me and watched my movements, the humanity with which I spoke to the sick, and the liberality with which I succoured the needy. Nor did I fail from time to time to observe the face of this new guest, without knowing either who he was or what he wanted. I wondered at his wrathful countenance, his head-shakings, and other signs of a man in anger. Having got rid of my patients, I asked him more than once if he wanted anything in which I could be of use, but he returned no answer. At length there being no one else left, he asked me if I knew the cause of his coming. I replied I did not. He said he had come resolved to kill me because I had removed the fat from his uncle. But finding that in my hands it was being well employed, he felt satisfied at making my acquaintance. He rose to his feet, refusing to eat, or take betel, or listen to my words. He could have killed me quite safely, but God was pleased to change his intentions, in reward for the little or much that I managed to do for the poor who were in ill-health.

The *qāẓī* did not find it so easy to forget his anger against me. Fidā,e K͟hān did not stay much longer in Lāhor. He (the *qāẓī*) then sent someone for me, and on my presenting myself he was very affectionate, but did all he knew to trip me up in my talk. He began a conversation about the fat of his brother-in-law, asking me if ever I gave such fat to be taken for a medicine, and for what complaints it was used. I answered, in ignorance of his maliciousness, that fat was not administered by the mouth, but served simply to make ointments in nervous disorders. It was lucky that I answered thus, for if I had said that the fat was also given by the mouth, it would have been enough to afford him an opening for planning a fresh persecution against me, and ordering me to be tortured.

It appeared to him most barbarous to prescribe human fat to be taken, imagining I did this to make mock of the Mahomedans, by getting one man to eat the fat of another. After this, I fell into conversation with him and discovered his malice, and saw the kindness God had done me in making me reply as above. For it was this which had delivered me from death. But he who came to catch me got caught himself. On his demanding of me some remedy for a cough he had, I told him of various drugs; among other things I said that, as he was an old man, human "myrrh" would be good. He answered that he had already taken it, but it had done him not the least good. Upon this, with a smile, I said openly to him, that to me it did not seem much of a thing to give human fat through the mouth by way of medicine, when at the same time he had no scruple in eating human flesh and fat. For that is what is meant by human "myrrh." He also could not help laughing, and told me that such medicines were to be taken secretly only, so that no one knew.

This persecution was bad enough, but without a doubt the Christians persecuted me worse than the Mahomedans. It arose from their envy at seeing me with name and fame, whereas at the place where I had settled down I had done no harm to any one of them. God alone knows how many times they tried to murder me, and they sent men to steal my books, on which I relied. Finding their projects had no success, they made up their minds to do openly what they had failed to do in hiding. To this end they sent four Europeans of various nations to murder me. Two came into the house as friends and began to talk to me; another who was to do the deed stood in the doorway, shouting hoarsely a thousand abusive terms at my servants; and the last sat on his horse with his pistols ready, to back up what was going on at the door. Hearing this row I came out, begging the disturber to hold his tongue; he might come in if he wanted to, but if he did not come in, let him go his way. When he heard this he fired his pistol, which was already at full-cock, when one of my servants, grappling with him, took the pistol from his hand. He drew his sword to defend himself from the servants, who had begun settling his business for him with thick sticks, applying them without remorse to him and his servants until they fled. Then I recognised that it was planned treachery and ordered one of my servants, with a drawn bow, to see that the one on horseback should not move his hand in the direction of his pistols; if he moved, an arrow was at once to be let fly at him. Thus terrorised, he was afraid to stir or to assist his companion who was getting his beating. I told the others with their bows and arrows to watch, without a word, over the two men in the house. Meanwhile, I ordered a good thrashing to be given to the insolent fellow. While drawing his sword to defend himself from the servants he cut his hand, and one of my servants seized him round the body so violently that he was brought to the ground. But he would not let his sword be taken away; I therefore ordered them to give it to him well until he let go the sword. Seeing that he still clung to it, one of the men planted one foot on his chest, and so crushed it that he had to give up the sword. Thereupon I told them to bind him and carry him to the magistrate. But the man on horseback dismounted, and earnestly begged me not to pass this affront upon a white man. His petition was his undoing. I told him to fall at his protector's feet. He declined, but my servants by thumps and holding his neck got him to his knees.

Then I left all the four, and rode off at once to Fidā,e K͟hān, who at the time this happened was in

Lāhor. He recognised that I had good reason for anything that I had done, and sent men to escort my assailants to the other side of the river Chināb, and on the road he who was the leader died. I will state here that my enemies seized this occasion at the time that the Europeans of the army were on their way to the attack on the Pathāns, since being war-time no one would be able to know afterwards who had made the attempt. But God, who seemed to cherish a special desire for my protection, would not permit my death at the hands of those who wished to do so on the quiet by entering my house in the guise of friends. They did not succeed in this or other treacheries, but my enemies managed to give me poison, from which I escaped, although I felt its effects for some years.

So great was the name that I had of being fortunate with the cases that I undertook that they came from many places distant from Lāhor to call me in to visit patients. This was of great profit to me, even to the extent that many wanted me in marriage. If I had been of little wisdom I should have had no want of marriage proposals of exceptional quality among the Mahomedans. But, thanks to God, although I left home a mere youth, there remained ever graven on my memory the good teaching of my parents.

But I cannot resist telling of one case that happened to me with a well-connected widow woman, the daughter of Dīndār Khān, Paṭhān. On one occasion I had treated one of her sisters at Qasūr, twenty leagues from Lāhor. This lady was present, and took such a fancy to me that she wanted to marry me. She herself spoke to me about it, and told me she would make her own arrangements for flight. At first I paid no heed to these things, still, seeing the woman so determined, and she being rich, well proportioned, and intelligent, I began to entertain the idea of carrying her off to Europe as she desired.

The agreement was that she should give sufficient

money to buy a big ship, on which would be placed the bulk of her wealth. Then she would pretend that she had vowed a pilgrimage to Mekka, would obtain permission for this, and leave home. When she was on her voyage, and had left the port of Sūrat, I with my ship was to fall upon the vessel going to Mekka, and carry her off with me to Europe. The agreement was in process of execution, but she was not sufficiently prudent. She roused suspicions of her affection for me by forwarding message upon message by an old woman in her service. But the special cause for the non-execution of the agreement was a Portuguese called Joaõ Rodrigues de Abreu. After having done him many favours, and proved him sufficiently faithful, I confided our plans to him, intending to take him along with me. But he did not act in correspondence to my friendship, for he went off and told Misrī Khān, who was a suitor for marriage with the same woman.

Discovering thus the agreement we had made, and the friendship of the said widow, which she had declared by sending me messages with valuable presents, Misrī Khān, through fear of Fidā,e Khān and other nobles who were very fond of me, was content not to do me any harm, or send men to murder me, but only wrote me a letter in which he said that he knew quite well why Jānī Bībī, the widow's maidservant, came so often to my house, but he saw quite well that what I was doing would in the end cost me my life. I pretended I did not understand the letter, and replied that Jānī Bībī came and went as if she were my mother. If it displeased him that she came to my house he had only to tell her not to go again. By this means I found out we were already discovered. When Jānī Bībī came I asked her to inform her mistress that it was no longer safe to come, and she must conceal everything or she would cause my death. On finding that her project could not succeed, the widow married Misrī Khān, but only lived for eight days after her marriage. If I had been like many

Europeans in the Mogul country and Hindūstān, I should have accepted the money that she wanted to give me for buying the ship, then taken flight for Europe, disregarding the marriage and all my promises. I did not act thus, not for fear of discovery, but because I had always professed to be an honest man, and thus I did not allow myself to fall into this temptation. The only thing that weighed upon me was that, through the treachery of that Portuguese, the lady continued to be a Mahomedan when she desired to become a Christian.

The fame I had acquired as a good surgeon and physician was the cause, among other things, that I was importuned by the eunuch Daulat, a man of staid habits, rich, and well known. This eunuch was in the employ of 'Ali Mardān Khān, he who made over the fortress of Qandahār to the King Shāhjahān. When his master died, in the year one thousand six hundred and fifty-two, this eunuch of his carried his bones to Persia to be buried in the tomb of his forefathers. The fact became known to Shāh 'Abbās, at that time King of Persia, who ordered the arrest of the eunuch Daulat. 'Ali Mardān Khān's remains he directed to be burnt, and the eunuch's nose and ears to be cut off. He was then to be expelled from the country. The king held it an act of presumption to bring the bones of a traitor to the kingdom of which in his lifetime he was a declared enemy.

The wretched Daulat retired full of shame to Lāhor, and kept close within his house. Knowing the work I had done, he several times requested me by some art or ingenuity to make his nostrils and ears grow again, an impossible thing. But he imagined that Christians could do impossible things with elixirs. Therefore he besought and entreated me that I would do to him this favour, and he would give me anything I asked. I answered that now there was no remedy, the wounds being old, for if they had been fresh something might have been done. This reply of mine only inspired greater hopes, and he asked me to renew the sores by making new wounds. Then I was to cut off the best-shaped nose and the finest ears from one or other of his slaves, and apply them to his face. He embraced me, he styled me Galen, Bū Alī (*i.e.* Avicenna), Aristotle, and Plato; he begged me to do him this favour, and make him happy all the rest of his life.

The slaves then present were in a great state of mind lest I should accept the eunuch's proposal, and gazed at me with mournful faces, as if entreating me not to comply with the request. I was laughing inwardly at them, contrasting the eagerness of Daulat with the fright of the slaves. But as a final answer I stated that even if I did what he asked, and cut off the noses and ears of the slaves, it would be of no avail, for being another's flesh it would never unite, the only result being to disfigure his slaves without any benefit to him. Finding there was no remedy, and being a facetious fellow, he said in joke: "I know not what sins I have committed to be made an out-and-out eunuch twice over, first in my inferior part, and secondly in my upper half. Now there is nothing more to deprive me of, nor do I fear anything but losing my head itself." This saying served us often afterwards as a subject of conversation.

Not only was I famed as a doctor, but it was rumoured that I possessed the power of expelling demons from the bodies of the possessed. This idea spread because I was a man capable of conversation, in which I showed my nimbleness of wit whenever an occasion presented itself. Once some Mahomedans were at my house consulting me about their complaints, when night came on. I did not want to lose the chance of over-aweing them, and letting them see that I had the power of giving orders to the devil. In the middle of our talk I began to speak as if to some demon, telling him to hold his tongue and not interrupt my talk, and let me serve these gentlemen, for it was already late. Then

I resumed my conversation with the Mahomedans. But now they had only half their souls left in their bodies, and spoke in trembling tones. I made use of their terror for my own amusement, and raising my voice still more I shouted at him whom I assumed to be present, lying invisible in some corner. I resumed my talk to the Mahomedans, and this I did four or five times, each time showing myself more provoked and fierce. At length I threatened the demon with expulsion from the house, and rising to my feet, angrily laid hold of a coarse glass bottle in which I had a little spirits of wine, and going near the candle set light to it, and uttered a lot of abuse to the supposed unquiet spirit. Then approaching the window, I made a noise with the bottle like a pistol-shot. I returned the bottle to its place and said to the demon that I objected to his coming any more into my house. I then turned again to the Mahomedans, and resumed the conversation. They were unable to speak a word out of fright, and prayed for permission to leave, they would come back another time. But the special joke was that they were afraid to go out, dreading that the demon might attack them in the street. I reassured them by saying that the demon stood in fear of me, and would not do such a thing, for I had the means of punishing him. It would suffice, while going to their houses, for them to say *en route* that they came from the Doctor Ṣāḥib. A grand medicine certainly, and a great exorcism for a make-believe phantasm!

But this was not enough to induce them to venture out; whereby I was forced to send with them one of my servants, who as they progressed was to mutter: "Duhāī Ḥakīm Jī"—that is: "On the part of the Doctor Ṣāḥib." Under these conditions I got rid of all those Mahomedans. Being credulous in matters of sorcery, they began to bruit abroad in all directions that the Frank doctor had the power of expelling demons, including dominion over them. This was enough to make many come, and among them they brought before me many women who pretended to be possessed (as is their habit when they want to leave their houses to carry out their tricks, and meet their lovers), and it was hoped that I could deal with them. The usual treatment was bullying, tricks, emetics, clysters, which caused much amazement, the actual cautery, and evil-smelling fumigation with filthy things. Nor did I desist until the patients were worn out and said that now the devil had fled. In this manner I restored many to their senses, with great increase of reputation, and still greater diversion for myself. It may be that some reader will not put faith in me, but Europeans who are acquainted with the Mogul country, and my character in India, know that I was capable of many practical jokes of this sort. What is certain is that I very seldom lost my temper, and knew how to divert myself in proper time and place with harmless amusements.

Having acquired a sufficient capital, I became desirous of withdrawing from the Mogul country and living once more amongst Christians. This I could not effect by moving to Goa, for the mode of life of those gentlemen did not suit me. I resolved to retire to a village called Bandora, which is under the Jesuit Fathers, who do not allow any of the Portuguese to live in it, beyond a few of their own faction. For as soon as a white man appears they put a spy on him, who follows him constantly. On no account will they allow such a man to sleep in the village. Nevertheless, as they knew that I was not a troublesome man, they were content to allow me to become a resident. In the village dwelt many merchants of different nations, it being a place of trade. One could live there in security through the efforts of the fathers in defending themselves from the thieves, who traversed the ocean in such numbers that it was necessary for many vessels together to leave port, for the Malavares (? Mālabāris) and Sanganes (? Sanjānīs) infest this coast.

The news spread that I meant to leave Lāhor, and I

was forced to affect that the report was false, for they would never have let me go away, neither the nobles nor the lower orders, for I had great repute and was much thought of. To keep me they placed spies upon me to hinder my departure. But I carried out my intention in such a way as to mislead the spies; I left at night without letting anyone know. Thus I was able to proceed on my journey, for I left my heavy luggage behind, and everything in my house in its usual order. I reached Sihrind without interference, and from Sihrind, passing outside Dihlī, I rested in Āgrah. From Āgrah I went to Sūrat, where I came across the woman I spoke of earlier, she who married the Armenian. From Sūrat I went on to Damāõ, then through the territories of the Portuguese, where the Fathers of the society (*i.e.* the Jesuits) did me many kindnesses, and at length I arrived at Bandora.

Here I was advised by some people to buy a ship, and thus not to leave my capital without fructifying. They proposed to me for taking charge of the ship a certain Ignacio de Taide, a Portuguese, who lived with the reputation of being a good Christian. To him I made over my ship and its cargo, which in all cost me the sum of fourteen thousand rupees. This caused others to confide to him considerable sums of money, seeing that I had faith in him. My orders to him were not to stray from the convoy. But having other views of his own, he went with the convoy only for a certain time. After that he began to fall behind, and, abandoning the ship, disappeared, for he had raised large sums on *Respondentia* bonds; he now started the story that the pirates had seized the ship. In that case he would not be obliged to pay the money that he borrowed. By this means I was left devoid of capital, having nothing left but a little money for daily expenses. This necessitated my asking payment from Diogo de Mello de Sampayo, son of Luis de Mello de Sampayo, called the Roncador (the Bully), of whom I have spoken, he who fought so valorously at Damāõ. I asked him to do me the favour of returning the two hundred rupees with which I had helped him in his necessity, out of which he had only repaid twenty. But all I received was the answer that he had given me the twenty rupees in charity; as for the money he owed me, I might collect it from the Mogul, who was indebted to him in a large amount.

Finding myself without means and very ill, I made up my mind to return, on recovering my health, to the Mogul country, and try my fortune once more. Thus when I had got well, I left Bandora with a friar in my charge, whose name out of respect I will not disclose, and Antonio Machado, a man well known for his bravado and talk, which led to his murder at Goa. God alone knows what I endured with this fellow-traveller, who, looking on the Mahomedans of Hindūstān as being the same as the Portuguese, tried to carry everything off by bravado. He ignored the fact that Hindūstāni Mahomedans are very touchy, and possess sense and judgment like any other nation. If I wanted to write here the foolish acts done on the road by these two men, my story would become a very long one.

On arrival in Āgrah, I left behind me the friar, who stayed on account of some business. The other man wished to come with me as far as Dihlī; then he attempted by force to take up his quarters in my house. But I declined, and he was forced to search for a home elsewhere. He encountered all that I had prognosticated, for I was fairly well acquainted with the Mogul country. It wanted very little more for this man to have brought the Fathers of the society (the Jesuits) to perdition; for, in his desperation, having nothing to eat, he tried to denounce them to the *qāẓī* of Āgrah. He said that the only object of the Fathers' stay in the Mogul realm was to buy Qurāns and transmit them to Europe. There on a fixed day in each year a festival took place, when they burnt the image of Muḥammad. This was quite enough to have caused the Fathers to be burnt alive; and, seeing themselves in such danger, they collected as an alms the sum of five hundred rupees (for him), and were thus delivered from a great peril. For, being a man of little understanding, he was capable of doing such a silly thing. He wandered hither and thither, and then quitted Mogul territory, I giving him his expenses to take him as far as Sūrat.

On my reaching Dihlī several nobles took notice of my arrival, and called me in. The chief of these was the Master of the Ceremonies to Prince Shāh 'Ālam, whose wife was very ill, and given up by the other doctors. My treatment of her renewed my reputation, which during my absence of a year had somewhat diminished. But the Persian doctors in the household of Shāh 'Ālam did not approve of my continuing at court after having cured the said woman whose case they had given up. This caused me to decide on a return to Lāhor, for I saw that the court was not for me.

With this intention I left secretly, but the princess, wife of Shāh 'Ālam, who had learnt of the benefit I had effected in the case of the wife of the Master of the Ceremonies, brought to mind the cases I had cured at Lāhor, when her parents were there. I had also treated her in secret for a small abscess she had in her ear. Accordingly she besought the prince one night to take me into his service, allotting to me noble's pay. Not to discontent the princess, whom he loved much, the prince fixed for me three hundred rupees a month, and gave me in addition the title of *manṣabdār*—that is to say, of a noble. This was a singular favour, the Mahomedans not being accustomed to grant such honours to Christians; furthermore, such physicians and surgeons remain subordinate to, and under the orders of, the head physician. But I was a privileged person, for I agreed to serve on no other condition than that I must be left free, nor must anyone give me orders.

Thus I took service with Shāh 'Ālam, although my Christian enemies did all they knew to prevent the prince's accepting me. And thus, unwilling as I was to serve Aurangzeb, I was the servant of his son, beginning my service in the year one thousand six hundred and seventy-eight. (See further pp. 199-213, 277 and following.)

It was at this time (some years later) that out of disgust I resolved to live no longer among Mahomedans, now that I had put together a sufficient sum. Nor did Shāh 'Ālam pay me at all punctually. I therefore decided to return to Goa, where I had some money in the hands of the Theatine Fathers, meaning to leave eventually for Europe. For this reason I asked several times for my discharge, which he (Shāh 'Ālam) always refused me, till at length I told him that my private affairs needed my presence at Sūrat, and he must give me leave for at least two months. He consented to do this, and I went to Sūrat; there Senhor Francisco Martin, at this day General of the Royal Company of France, gave me an armed sloop to carry me as far as Damān in Portuguese territory. Thence I went to Goa, and lived in the gardens. When Aurangzeb's letter reached the viceroy he had me sent for to translate it into Portuguese. On hearing the proposals, I gave him advice as to what he should do. For this war could not be of any benefit to the Portuguese, seeing that the Mogul would never be content to leave the Portuguese to themselves, after he had destroyed Sambhā Jī. In spite of this the viceroy engaged in the war against that prince, and thereby all but lost Goa.

Sambhā Jī learnt the above news, and Akbar, who was living in that prince's territory, not far from Goa, was anxious to show his gratitude for the honour Sambhā Jī had shown him. He also sought occasion to prepare for the flight which he designed to make into Persia, and wanted to ask the viceroy to provide him with a ship for that purpose. He sent an envoy to the viceroy, forwarding at the same time some rubies and diamonds for sale. He prayed as a favour that permission might be granted him to build a ship on the river of Goa, for his flight into Persia, he being persecuted by his father Aurangzeb.

He really wanted to build the ship, but also hoped to land, a few at a time, a large number of men, and then all of a sudden to seize Goa. Knowing as I did the tricks of the Mahomedans, I advised the viceroy to take great care, and find out how many men were disembarked, for they might cause damage to Goa before his Excellency could prevent them; and truly Sambhā Jī's intention was to get a number of men into the island. Then he meant to come in person to attack, after the men already landed in the island had occupied the best positions. Thus would he manage to accomplish his purpose. The viceroy gave heed to my words, and he noticed that the next day a great number of men came from Sambhā Jī's territory for work at the ship, but not so many withdrew at night. Orders were therefore given that all must withdraw, and that the next day as many as came in the morning must go back at night.

Nor did the viceroy content himself with giving Akbar leave to build his ship; he also made ready some presents to be sent to him. I held my tongue till I saw that these things were already prepared, when, out of the affection I bore to my fellow-Christians, I went to the viceroy. I said to him that to me it seemed that His Excellency was not acting with sufficient caution. He intended to write to the Mogul (Aurangzeb), agreeing at his request to make war on Sambhā Jī; while by these presents he acted as if he thought that great king to be of small account; for, not content with allowing Akbar to build a ship, he was sending him presents. By this the Mogul would be angered, and would seek an opening for some attempt against Goa, because of the favour shown to his rebellious son. The viceroy was pleased to listen, and came to a stop, and did not send the presents. Meanwhile the ship was finished, and Akbar had it removed to the port of Vingorla, twelve leagues distant from Goa, and in the territory of Sambhā Jī.

Finding that by using the chance afforded by the matter of the ship he could not carry out his design, Sambhā Jī sent to the viceroy tutored spies, who told him that in the fortress of Pondā were great treasures. His object was to get the viceroy to leave Goa with a large force for the conquest of that fortress. Then he meant to cut off the Portuguese retreat and prevent their return, in this way making himself master of Goa. The facts became known to a French trader, then in Rājāpur, and he wrote to me to warn the viceroy of Sambhā Jī's purpose. He was coming down with his army.

I told His Excellency, but he would not heed my words. He issued forth with eight hundred white soldiers and eight thousand Canarese. He crossed with them to the other side of the river, and began his campaign. With him went five pieces of heavy artillery. The men inside Pondā defended themselves until the arrival of Sambhā Jī along with Akbar's men. They attacked with great fury the viceroy's army, and gave him as much to do as he could manage. His best troops were killed, and if he had not used wooden obstructions with which to impede the onset of the cavalry, he would never have been able to get back to Goa, nor could he have made any defence. The rainy weather impeded the discharge of his matchlocks; thus coming on still closer, a trooper among the Rājpūts dealt His Excellency a sword-blow on the ribs. Retreating slowly, he reached the river bank with great difficulty, and once more entered Goa. He recognised, although too late, that he had been misled. Great grief was caused in the city by the fruitless loss of so many lives.

In the interval Goa was governed by the archbishop Dom Manoel de Souza de Menezes. There came a boat sent by the general of Aurangzeb's fleet, which was on the watch to prevent Akbar leaving Vingorla in the ship he had built. It brought a message for the viceroy, urging him to make a valiant fight of it, and before very long he (Aurangzeb) would arrive to his assistance. But the archbishop would not listen to the envoy, and gave the answer that he must go and deal direct with the viceroy. I knew this because I translated the letters, and I did not wish to forsake the viceroy at such a time, so that he might have no cause of complaint against me. I therefore demanded permission of his lordship, and with great difficulty he granted me a boat to travel in. We in Goa did not then know the miserable plight of the viceroy.

I left, but the archbishop, I know not why, sent an order to the guards posted on the river to seize me. Thus, while I disbursed my coin to aid and serve the Christians against the power of the Mogul, they made me out to be a traitor. They persuaded the archbishop that I was taking with me five hundred Shivājīs (*i.e.* Mahrattahs) to cut off the viceroy's retreat and prevent him returning to Goa. For this reason he directed my arrest. The captains of the guard knew quite well I was innocent, for when I reached them I had no one with me but a servant. In spite of this, as the orders were absolute, they civilly made me a prisoner without communicating to me their orders. I made pretence of not recognising that the way they were treating me betrayed suspicion of my acts. At this time I saw the arrival of several boat-loads of dead and wounded, a proof that Sambhā Jī had defeated the viceroy.

But if I took as a joke this treatment of me by the archbishop, it was not really such. Nor did the envoy look upon the manner in which he had been received as any joke; for, wishing to make him out greater than he was, they placed him in danger of losing his head. They began to spread a rumour that he was not an envoy, but the very Sambha Jī himself. This story was so much accepted that men were already in search of him to slay him. Such is the power of fear when it enters into people who are otherwise of good sense! When I saw what their purpose was, I did my very best that they should not kill him, but only arrest him. I assured them that he was not Sambhā Jī, but a Mogul, as he really was. For, if they had killed him, I, too, ran a very great risk of losing my life, and that for nothing else than trying to help his Excellency at the time the said envoy arrived.

It pleased God that at last the viceroy should arrive, and he, too, was at first persuaded that the man was Sambhā Jī in person. But after I had spoken with him, I assured him that, even if he were really Sambhā Jī in person, no violence could be done by him, for I would keep close to him when the letters were presented. Thus I conducted the envoy into the presence of the viceroy, who was already in a fright.

Then, taking myself the letters from the envoy's hands, I presented them to His Excellency. Thereupon he recognised the great mistake which had held the whole island in perturbation. He (the envoy) had with him only two servants.

But let us now return to Sambhā Jī. He had missed his blow when he had fought the viceroy, for if he had only occupied the river bank it would have been easy for him to slaughter everybody, and equally easy to take Goa. All the same, he did not despair of success in his attempt; for, after the defeat of the viceroy, he took possession of the lands of Salseite (Salsette) and Bardes, between which lies the island of Goa, and, after stiff fighting, tried to disembark men on the island (of Goa). But the Portuguese resisted valiantly, above all, the Augustinian Fathers, who were at a crossing against which Sambhā Jī made his principal efforts.

Thus, finding he had not carried out what he

wanted to do, and seeing that by force of arms he should not conquer, he adopted the way customary in Hindūstān—that of deceit. He therefore made Akbar act as mediator and send in a letter to the viceroy. In it he said that, being on the point of leaving for Persia, as a friend of both sides, he wanted to restore peace and amity between Sambhā Jī and the Portuguese. With this object would they send a trusty person capable of dealing with such a negotiation? He would bring it to a conclusion to the satisfaction of both parties.

The viceroy selected me for this business. On my side I recognised that I was a foreigner, so I took along with me one priest and one layman, both Portuguese, to bear testimony to my acts and words. I made declaration to the viceroy that they would never conduct me to Akbar, but to Sambhā Jī instead. I questioned the viceroy as to what I should do in that case. He said to me that under no circumstances did he wish me to approach Sambhā Jī. With this point determined on, I quitted Goa.

Hardly had I arrived in Sambhā Jī's territory when they wanted to carry me to him and not to Akbar. Thereupon I declared I would not go, that I would sooner lose my head than act against the orders I had received. Akbar learnt this, and dispatched Durgā Dās, as representing his person during the negotiations with Sambhā Jī. On these conditions I, too, attended, or else they would have carried me there by force.

We reached the presence of Sambhā Jī, who received me with great politeness. During the conversation he made bitter complaint of the viceroy's declaring war against him in spite of the King of Portugal's orders. The king had ordered him to maintain peace with his neighbours. Many other things against the viceroy did he say to me during this talk. It was on this occasion that he told me that with his own sword he had decapitated his chief captains, owing to their disaffection. He showed me the sword.

Finally, he gave me my leave to go, adding that, seeing the viceroy would not send him an envoy, he meant to be the first and send one to him and so let him see how much he desired to uphold peace between the Portuguese.

Taking one of his officers by the hand, he said to me: "This is the man I mean to send; he is the key of my treasure-house." Then, laying hold of my hand also, he made the man over to me, and said he was doing him (the viceroy) much honour, for the man was his chief favourite. He sent me away, handing me two handkerchiefs of gold thread, and in the evening the envoy came to visit me. He set forth his pretensions, which were that he should land in the isle with one thousand, or at least five hundred men as his guard, taking also seven horses (as he said) to show his rank. We hammered away for a long time at this subject, he beseeching me earnestly to secure this honourable treatment for him from the viceroy. But I displayed total indifference, saying it lay with the viceroy to concede to him or not what he asked, at the same time I would lay his requests before His Excellency. But horses were not necessary, the fortress being quite near, nor could the horses climb to it.

The reader must be made aware here of what the envoy's intentions were. The first was to get with this large number of men into Goa, where there was not a large enough garrison to defend all the posts. Coming, thus attended, to pay his court to the viceroy, it would be very easy to carry out their object. For they would enter with the fixed intention of assassinating the viceroy, and consequently would come wearing concealed chain-mail. Having succeeded, some of them would jump on the horses, and, careering about, would strike terror into the inhabitants, and throw everything into disorder. Thus Sambhā Jī would have time to land his force without any difficulty and capture defenceless Goa.

I returned to Goa and reported to the viceroy what was going on, and of the probable intentions of Sambhā Jī. For the time being he should not, I thought, give audience in the royal hall, but in the fortress of Dangī (Dangim), which was quite close to the sea. Strong guards should be posted so as to hinder the envoy from carrying out his plans. Although there was some difficulty in doing what I said, nevertheless, acknowledging that I had some acquaintance with the tricks of people in Hindūstān, the viceroy did as I advised. Thus I went back to tell the ambassador that he might come. I took with me no more than three boats, so that too many people might not come. But so many crowded in that our boat was in great danger of going to the bottom. I complained to the envoy of this carelessness, and he grew angry, for he saw that with so small a number he would not be able to carry out his project. He wanted to give up coming. But, encouraging him, I brought him to the above-mentioned fortress. Matters were disposed in such a way that not more than seven persons were able to enter with him. These were received by the viceroy with great pomp.

The envoy's design was unmasked during the audience, for he made no statement about terms of peace, stating that his coming was for nothing more than to know if the Portuguese gentlemen really desired to make peace or not, and whether they would pay tribute to his prince. The viceroy replied that he wanted peace, but would not pay any tribute. The envoy answered that he would take this reply to his prince, and then took his leave far from well contented, not having been able to make himself a name by a piece of treachery (*i.e.* assassination), for amongst them this mode of going to work is a proof of great valour.

Although peace negotiations were going on, there

was no suspension of arms, for continuously Sambhā Jī went on fighting at Goa with great vigour. In the course of these contests, as there were not many troops in the island, there was reason to fear that Sambhā Jī might land his soldiers there. The viceroy therefore sought someone who would go to the Mogul fleet, then off Vingorla, to request the admiral to sail with his ships till he was within sight of Goa. Thus some fear would be instilled into Sambhā Jī's men then in Salsette and Bardes. For all they could do, they could not find any person willing to take upon himself to risk his life for the public benefit. Then, knowing the heartiness with which I had laboured to the utmost of my power, he asked me if I would perform this benefit on behalf of a city which found itself in such a sorry plight.

I gave a favourable reply, and, as I was leaving Goa, Dom Rodrigo da Costa, in command of the fleet, declared that I was on my way to destruction. God was pleased to show the care He had over my person, for one morning in the dark I found myself with my boat in the midst of thirty-seven *galliots* belonging to Sambhā Jī. As soon as we discovered that the fleet was not that of the Moguls, but of Sambhā Jī, we were very apprehensive, and already the master of the vessel and several seamen wanted to jump into the sea. But I laid hold of my matchlock and frightened them, saying that the first who moved was a dead man. If they set to work to row with all their strength, I would give them five hundred *xerafins* (*ashrafī*, a gold coin) on arrival in Goa. This was in addition to several pieces of gold that I distributed among them on the spot. As the man who guided the helm was very skilful, we feigned to be part of that fleet until we forged ahead of all the *galliots*. Then putting on a spurt we drew away from our enemies, who began a chase in the hope of capturing us.

Keeping on our course, we arrived at the Mogul

fleet, and I carried out my instructions. But the commander replied that he could not come away from Vingorla for fear that Prince Akbar might escape. Thus it turned out that I put my life to danger without doing any good. Nevertheless, I went back to Goa by another route, and there I reported the Mogul fleet to be already on its way to give assistance against Sambhā Jī. This I did that all might recover heart and resolution, and continue the war with greater courage.

Sambhā Jī's soldiers took the island of Santo Estevao, and were very near to Goa. They gave so much trouble to the city that the viceroy resolved to send an embassy to the said prince to see if he could obtain a peace, and I was obliged to go a second time to Sambhā Jī. But on my arrival I found a spy, then in his service, who gave me a faithful report of the latest news. He told me that the army of Shāh 'Ālam was already quite close. This was enough to decide me not to pursue my negotiations; therefore I determined to retrace my steps, and to advise the viceroy that the deliverance of Goa was at hand with the aid of Shāh 'Ālam. I stayed in Goa afterwards to visit that prince and negotiate as soon as he arrived. In my place they sent to Sambhā Jī Manoel Saraiva and an Augustinian Father. But the fighting still went on with great energy. Well was it for the Portuguese that Sambhā Jī never knew exactly how few men there were in the island. If he had known, he could have carried out his scheme in its entirety.

I do not know if it was from carelessness or from real want of soldiers that the vessels which were on guard had not more than seven or eight men to each vessel. I know the fact because one night the viceroy invited me to go with him in his boat on his rounds to see if the officers were doing their duty. We found them nearly all asleep, and instead of challenging us, it was necessary for us to accost them, to find out if there was anyone in the vessel or not. Not aware that it was the viceroy who was passing, they gave us ill-conditioned replies, and we ascertained that there was not a single officer in the ships. But what was my astonishment, on reaching the fort opposite the bar at the entrance of the river, to find that we had to beat at a door for a long time, making much noise without getting any response. Finally came a soldier, who replied to us by stating that there were only eleven men. Yet this fort was of the greatest importance, and Sambhā Jī had only to take it to get possession of Goa without any further difficulty.

The viceroy was angry at getting such a reply, and asked why the men of the garrison had not answered. The soldier said they could not answer, for there was no one, only a boy who tended the goats. These were the preparations that we found in the ships and at that fort at a time when Sambhā Jī was doing all he could to capture a city that had ever remained the glory of the Portuguese! From this the reader may judge how little these gentlemen thought of the courage of veteran soldiers such as those of Sambhā Jī, or else, over-confident in themselves, they imagined that their mere name would bar the way to the enemy, or it may be that in reality there were no troops available. In any case, those they had in their service could not have cared much whether they lived under the rule of the Portugal king or that of Sambhā Jī.

Aurangzeb received the reply of the Goa viceroy, in which he promised to allow free passage up the river to his fleet coming from Sūrat with supplies for the army of his son, Shāh 'Ālam. The king ordered that prince to march with forty-five thousand horsemen in the direction of Goa, traversing the kingdom of Bījāpur. His instructions were to capture the island of Goa by treachery, thus becoming able thereafter to invade easily the territories of Sambhā Jī.

On this march Shāh 'Ālam took several of Sambhā Jī's forts, and arrived in time to deliver the island from the hands of that prince. It was already in great danger. Sambhā Jī made every possible exertion to take it before Shāh 'Ālam arrived, but it did not happen according to his desire. Thus, on the arrival of the Mogul fleet, he was obliged to decamp, but before he disappeared he ordered the mortars in Santo Estevao to be charged, with the idea of bursting them, seeing that he could not carry them away. But in this he did not succeed, for only one of them burst; then spiking the rest he fled.

As soon as Shāh 'Ālam arrived he sent an envoy to the viceroy as far as the river bank. On learning this, His Excellency ordered me to go and speak to this envoy, who was the brother of Sec Mahamed (Shekh Muḥammad). I went to the spot, and while afar off, I saluted him in the European fashion. But he, remaining seated in his palanquin, paid little or no heed to me, and, ignoring the politeness customary in India, which is to raise the hand to the head, he placed it on his breast, as usual among the Persians. This made me angry, and I declined to advance any farther. His example was not followed by the slaves and servants of Shāh 'Ālam; they knew how anxious their master was to retain me at his court. They all bowed to me with great respect.

I did not neglect to say in a loud voice what seemed to me necessary against such a messenger, and turning my back, cheerfully accosted my friends. All the same, I did not lose the words said by the envoy. They amounted to nothing more than that the Portuguese were under great obligations to Shāh 'Ālam, and they ought to commence at once to count out the millions they would have to give for having been delivered from Sambhā Jī. Then spies went off to Shāh 'Ālam and told him that the viceroy had sent me to treat with the ambassador, and that the latter had failed to render me due honour.

The prince was much put out, and in that man's place sent my friend Miraxam (Mīr A'ẓam) with orders to conciliate me in every way. On his reaching the river bank I advanced to meet him, but he, having received different instructions from the first man, rose to his feet when he saw me, and coming towards me, embraced me. He told me the prince's orders were that he was to do whatever I might suggest, as he had no knowledge of the viceroy. Then he delivered me a letter sent to me by the prince. In it he begged me to come to him, as he greatly desired to speak to me, and he trusted I would not refuse, having eaten the salt of his house.

I did not wish to take him (the envoy) into Goa, so I escorted him to a little island called Ilha de Manoel de Mota. There I regaled him during the night. On the day following I conducted him to the viceroy, who was in the fortress of Santiago, near the mainland. There he presented Shāh 'Ālam's letter. It began by requesting that Ḥakīm Niculao, his old servant, should be sent to him. As soon as he arrived they would arrange things to the satisfaction of both sides. Next it stated how, in conformity with the letter of the viceroy sent to the great Aurangzeb, permission was given for the entry into the river of the ships carrying supplies for the army sent against Sambhā Jī. Yet the fleet in question had not arrived. Fulfilment of the promise was now requested.

The viceroy replied that he would certainly carry out what he had promised, but the route taken must be by the other river, that of Bardes, not by that of Goa. But the envoy persisted in his demand, that they wanted to pass through the river of Goa, as had been promised to His Majesty. Finally the viceroy answered that I would go to his Highness, and that there matters would be settled.

During the discussion the king's fleet, which was at the harbour mouth, continued to advance. When a report of this reached the viceroy, I said to Dom Rodrigo da Costa that now was the time for a display of courage and energy. Therefore, without any delay, the fleet ought to be fired upon. He hurried to the spot, where he found that, by the carelessness of the commandant of Aguada, some five-and-twenty *galliots* had already entered and were close to the Fort of the Kings. When arrived he ordered at once the discharge of three loaded cannon, to intimidate them, and cause their retirement. They replied that they were friends, and had come under the protection of the viceroy's promise; they should therefore stop firing, as that was not the way to receive friends.

When the Aguada fort became aware that the Fort of the Kings declined to allow a passage, it too fired several times, in order to prevent the remainder of the fleet which was following from completing its purpose. Thus was Goa saved this time, for without a doubt it would have been lost had the fleet entered. The twenty-five *galliots* which were already inside took refuge behind the Fort of the Kings in a river which is called Nelur. Here they remained until the receipt of fresh orders from Shāh 'Ālam. They plundered along the shore, and carried off any goods and women or girls found there.

At nightfall I issued from Goa with the envoy in order to go to the encampment of Shāh 'Alam. When we disembarked, the spies informed us that the enemy were in sight. Mīr A'ẓam feared some harm to my person, and ordered twenty horsemen to accompany me as far as the camp. He stopped behind with thirty horsemen. In this way I reached the camp, where, being known, many greeted me with loud voices. I cannot express the affection with which they came to embrace me.

If the reader could only know the manner in which I had behaved to all the officials and ministers, he would not be surprised that they received me with as much love as if I had been one of their relations.

I proceeded to the prince's tents, and there the eunuchs, who knew how eagerly the prince and princess were looking for me, came forward to receive me. The chief eunuch told me that Shāh 'Alam had ordered that at whatever hour I might arrive he should forthwith be informed; he had also directed the whole army to be in readiness the next morning. For if I did not arrive he meant to send his troops across the river by swimming it. I said to the man that the prince should not be roused; it was already midnight and I could wait, nor was it right that a tired prince should be woke on account of one of his servants.

When the prince got up next morning, they reported my arrival. He was more anxious for this than for the taking of Goa, and was now content. He issued orders for his soldiers to return to their quarters, as he no longer meant to take any action. Next, he sent word inside to the princesses and princes that I had come, and called them all together with great glee, and ordered a letter to be written to his mother Nabab Baegi (Nawāb Bāe Jī) telling how he had now caught me. For this queen had complained bitterly about his giving me leave of absence. She called me within the *pardah*, where I first made my bow as a European, and then did obeisance in court fashion.

She was much amused at seeing me in European costume, my beard shaved off, and wearing a peruke. As the princess had not been used to seeing me in such a get-up, she asked me what drugs I took to return to youth. Then, jokingly, I gave her my reasons, and let her understand that I did not wish to serve any more, because the officials did not carry out the promises made me by His Highness. The prince replied that I ought not to trouble myself about this; I had only to apply to him on the occurrence of any difficulty, and without fail he would ensure me any satisfaction I could desire. Laughing at the liberty I was taking, I told him that I could no more rely on His Highness than on the rest, for many times he had broken his promises. Then he brought forward his heir, Sulṭān Mazudin (Mu'izz-ud-dīn), as security, and added one hundred rupees a month to my former pay. He ordered my pay to be disbursed for the whole time of my absence from his court. In addition he promised to maintain four horses to carry my baggage, and eight men to carry my palanquin, with my food daily sent from his table.

After this we entered upon a conversation over the differences with the viceroy. As I was obliged, in my capacity of envoy from the viceroy, to take the part of the Portuguese gentlemen, I said to His Highness that the viceroy could not on any conditions allow the royal fleet to come through the river of Goa, such being the orders of the King of Portugal. If His Excellency disobeyed such orders, his head would be in great danger.

Shāh 'Ālam persisted that at least the *galliots* already in the river, behind the Fort of the Kings, should continue their course. He assigned as reason that, other ships being allowed to pass, they might just as well allow the said *galliots* to go up, since they were already inside. I retorted that other ships allowed to pass were merchantmen, as to which there was no prohibition. But in respect to His Highness's ships and those of other crowns, there was a rigorous order not to let them pass. If the viceroy in his letter to Aurangzeb had promised a passage, that must be understood not of the Goa river, but of the lands belonging to the Portuguese. He did not decline to comply, but offered a passage through other rivers. To show better to His Highness that the viceroy maintained friendship with His Highness and with his father, he would provide men to guide the vessels to any port His Highness wished.

This proposal so much approved itself to Shāh 'Ālam, that he was willing to order the *galliots* already inside to go out again. He sent me with people to carry this order to the captain-general of the fleet; and I left with him other men to act as guides in conducting him by land to the mouth of the river Bardes.

To conclude the story: before giving me my leave, he sent me an exquisite *sarāpā* (set of robes) and a horse. I was made to promise that I would return to him next day at two o'clock in the afternoon. I took with me the men carrying to the captain-general of the fleet the orders to turn back and proceed to meet the prince by way of the Bardes river.

I went to Goa, and recounted to the viceroy what had happened. He was considerably gratified at the way I had arranged matters, and at deliverance from the peril he had been in of losing the island. I urged him to give the ambassadors their dismissal, with the presents he meant to send to His Highness. In the morning I did my very best to be sent off early, in order to fulfil my promise to reach His Highness at two o'clock in the afternoon. But His Excellency wanted me to carry a letter to the prince, and kept me waiting longer than was necessary. For this reason, the prince finding I did not arrive at the appointed hour, ordered Bardes to be plundered and thereby force the viceroy to send me at once.

His Highness had ordered that as soon as ever they perceived me approaching they were to stop plundering. The sentries who recognised me shouted and ran about to make the soldiers give over, but that did not help the poor wretches already stripped bare. I reached the prince, and was well received; but I made somewhat of a remonstrance at the irregularity of the soldiers plundering Bardes when we were friends. The prince smiled, and said to me: "It would have been still worse for them had you not appeared." There we halted several days until the supplies for the army had been landed. It is impossible for me to detail the gifts I received from all the court, and even from the princesses and sons of Shāh 'Ālam. The latter was aware that I was serving him reluctantly, and thus instigated these others to propitiate me.

We went to Vingorla, and the prince captured that place easily, seeing that nearly everybody took to flight. The fleet continued to accompany us. After a few days the Portuguese ambassadors arrived; they were João Antunes Portugal and Manoel de Santo Pinto. They brought some showy presents and lengths of ornamented China cloth, some lovely branches of coral, and six small pieces of artillery, with other objects, the whole being worth a good amount.

They were well received, and *sarāpā* (sets of robes) were ordered for each of them, in addition to two thousand rupees. For the viceroy there were given a caparisoned horse, a dagger mounted with precious stones, a little bottle of essence of roses, and an honourable *formao* (*farmān*, or rescript?).

It should be noted here that at the presentation of these ambassadors I did not act as interpreter, but some other European. In reading out the conditions he succeeded in doing a piece of bad work for the Portuguese. For in one paragraph the viceroy desired Shāh 'Ālam either to give him eight hundred horses, or permit him to buy them in the camp. The European stated as the viceroy's proposal that, if the prince gave him eight hundred horses he would consider himself a subject. This was as much as to say that he would place Goa in the prince's hands. When I heard this I prayed the royal scribe to stop writing, for the interpreter did not understand the viceroy's proposal. All he said was that being in want of eight hundred horses to continue the campaign against Sambhā Jī he asked for these eight hundred horses; and should His Highness decline to give them he prayed leave to buy them in the camp. The interpreter was angered, but I judged it necessary on such an occasion to speak up, to defend truth, and to protect Goa from a pretext under cover of which Aurangzeb would proceed to occupy that island.

In the evening of the same day I encountered Shekh Muḥammad at the entrance of the prince's tents. He is the man who had gone first as envoy from Aurangzeb to the viceroy, and had promised

Aurangzeb to make over Goa to Shāh 'Ālam. He complained to me, telling me it was not for me to intervene in the royal affairs, nor was it my business to act as agent for the Portuguese. In time we began to raise our voices, so that the prince heard the altercation, and asked the cause, and who were the men making so much noise. Then they told him how Ḥakīm Niculão and Shekh Muḥammad were shouting at each other over the pending negotiations. The prince, who did not want any violence, sent word to Shekh Muḥammad to go away, and not open his mouth on such affairs. As for me, he called me inside, reassured me, and gave me his word that he would not touch the Portuguese. Of a certainty had he listened to Shekh Muḥammad he must have taken Goa, for that man was very familiar with the ground, being a native of those parts.

Manoel de Santo Pinto then returned to the viceroy, and reported to him the above two affairs. On this account the viceroy sent me, through him, the proposition that I should either accept the knighthood of Sant' Iago, or a village yielding annually a thousand *xerafins* (*ashrafī*). I did not want to accept one or the other, but Manoel de Santo Pinto pressed the accepting of one of the offers, as it would affront the viceroy if I refused. I therefore accepted the knighthood of Sant' Iago, which he forthwith conferred on me, together with the letters patent, in which he set forth the two particular services aforesaid which I rendered the crown of Portugal, as may be seen from the following copy of that patent:

"Dom Pedro, by the Grace of God, Prince of Portugal and of the Algarves, on this and that side of the sea in Africa, of Guinea, and of the conquered commercial navigation of Ethiopia, Arabia, Persia, and India, *et cetera*; as regent and successor, and ruler of the said realms and lordships, and governor and perpetual administrator, as I am, of the Mastership and Knighthood of the three Military orders:

"Be it known to all beholding this Patent, that having regard to the services done by Niculão Manuchy in our Indian dominions on various occasions arising in our service; by translating the letters written by the Mogul King to the Count, our viceroy in the said Dominions, and by being present during the conferences with his ambassador, Shekh Muḥammad, upon the matters under negotiation; subsequently, upon the approach of the prince Muḥammad Mu'aẓẓam, Shāh 'Ālam, eldest son of the said King, with his army, to the vicinity of the said Dominions, by accompanying the envoy that the said Count, our viceroy, sent to the said Prince, and by going more than once to the said army on various matters of great importance appertaining to the said Dominions. Wherein the said Niculão Manuchy conducted himself with great fidelity and zeal in our service; from which we anticipate he will act in the same way from now henceforth.

"For all these reasons he is worthy of every honour and favour, and to prove to the said Prince the esteem in which we hold his person, We hold it expedient to make a grant to the said Niculão Manuchi of the vestment of the order of Saõ Tiago, which he can wear on his breast like a true knight, for which he will be recognised and respected as such, enjoying all the honours and privileges thereto appertaining.

"Wherefore I order that this Patent now issued be made over to him, that it be carried out and observed in its entirety as therein set forth, and that it be sealed with the seal bearing the Royal Arms of the Crown of Portugal. Our Lord the Prince issues it through Francisco de Tavora, Count of Alvor, one of his Councillors of State, Viceroy and Captain-General of India, executed by the Custodian Souza Moreira in Goa the twenty and ninth of January of one thousand six hundred and eighty-four.

"Ordered to be recorded.

"*The Secretary*,
"LUIS GONSALVES COTA.

(Seal.) "COUNT OF ALVOR.

"LUIS GONSALVES COTA.

"Patent by which Your Highness is pleased to grant to Niculão Manuchi the vestment of the Order of Saõ Thiago, to be borne on his breast as a true knight enjoying all the honours and privileges pertaining thereto, as is above declared.

"Verified by Your Highness.

"Registered in the Book of Grants in the State Secretariat on page twenty-nine.

"LUIS GONSALVES COTA."

I did not wish to continue in the service of Shāh 'Ālam, for I did not feel happy living among Mahomedans. I saw that these campaigns would not soon come to an end, and thus I would be forced to wander here and there and everywhere with the prince's camp. I took my measures for flight, as was my intention. The first thing I did was to pray the ambassador from the Portuguese to wait for me with his *galliot* (armed boat). For when the prince started to march with his army I meant to get back to Goa with him (the envoy). He gave me his word that he would await me. Then I resolved to return the two thousand rupees given me by Shāh 'Ālam to enable me to march with the army. I did not want it said of me that Hakīm Niculão fled after having received two thousand rupees. So I took them to Sulṭān Mu'izz-ud-dīn, Shāh 'Ālam's heir, and asked him to consent to holding the said two thousand rupees, as I had no place to put them. He ordered hīs eunuch to take charge of them.

I waited until the prince had set out, and then I made off, hoping to catch up the ambassador and his boat. But he had gone off to feast himself in the Dutch Factory, and thus the attempt failed. When the prince knew of it he fell into a great rage at my attempted flight, and ordered his foster-brother, Mīr Muḥammad, to whose charge he had committed me, to go off in search of me, and not to come back to his presence until he brought me with him. He sent an order to the commander of the fleet to proceed in search of me and carry me off by force or persuasion. For he declared unconditionally that he meant to keep me in his service.

But he knew that I was no lover of violence, so he sent to the seashore a caparisoned horse for me to ride, and an elephant along with five hundred horsemen to escort me. This was all to do me great honour, but they were to seize me if they came across me.

I was much affected when I did not find the ambassador in the boat. While I was waiting for him, I felt happy at having got away from the camp. Then the sentries reported to us how a *galliot* belonging to the Mahomedans was approaching. Putting my head to the window, I saw that it was Mīr Muḥammad, and thereby my courage at once evaporated.

He came aboard the envoy's boat, and earnestly entreated me to save his life; for the prince would never see him until I went back to the camp and spoke with His Highness, who was waiting for me. While we were still in talk, the sentry said that all the Mahomedan army had come from Vingorla. Thus I lost all hope of being able to flee, and, entering Mīr Muḥammad's *galliot*, we went off to find the prince, who had already gone four leagues farther off. The commander of the fleet notified my presence to the prince. But owing to the land route being closed by the enemy, who were plundering in all directions, thus causing great risk of the elephant's capture, which would be a disgrace, he ordered them to embark the horses and the troopers told off to escort me, while the elephant was put aboard some other vessel. Thus we all went to a port distant some two days from Vingorla, where the prince had gone to destroy a temple known as the White Pagoda, or of the Virgins. It was sent into the air by gunpowder.

The prince was pleased and happy at my return.

Remonstrating lovingly with me, he said he did not know what was to happen to me. For he saw that I had no love for him or for his family. Other Farangīs would adopt any and every method to find a prince who had for them a mere fraction of the interest he displayed in me. I replied that I admitted fully the love with which His Highness was pleased to favour me; but my expenses were heavy, nor did I deserve less pay than that given to the other physicians. Thus I could not continue to serve him. Besides this, his ministers and the officials made me wait a very long time for the little His Highness gave me. In this way, while in his service, I was expending my patrimony without benefit and with nothing but distress.

Before putting faith in this speech of mine, it is necessary for the reader to know my temperament, and he should, in addition, know the wonderful cures I had effected among the Mahomedans. Well might I talk thus, for I neither sought for, nor was I in need of, the prince's pay, and thoroughly content should I have been had he grown angry and said: "Be off with you." But he, instead of getting angry and expelling me, ordered, in my hearing, a guard of horse and foot to be put on me, as he did not want me to escape again. Seeing thus how determined he was, I said I could not follow him, not having the necessary equipment; all my baggage was in Goa. On this account I prayed leave to visit Goa to fetch my things, and bid farewell to my relations. I pledged my word to come back within the term of seven days.

He was reluctant to give me this leave, but in the end said he would grant it if I swore to come back again. I swore after the manner of Hindūstān—that is, by the feet of His Highness—I would come back again. But he refused this oath, and called upon me to swear by the name of the Messiah, and that then he would place faith in my words and permit me to quit the royal camp. Finding he required this of me, I swore by the terrible, venerable, and admirable name of Jesus that I would be faithful to my promise. Then he granted me the leave, and conferred on me another set of robes (*sarāpā*).

Though thus obliged to abandon Goa, which I had wished to serve to the utmost of my power, I resolved to seize the occasion for alleviating the great necessity from which it was then suffering. There was famine from want of supplies, especially of wheat, of which there was none in Goa—not even enough to prepare the Host. I asked the prince to let me have a cargo of wheat, his army being fully supplied. It was to be delivered at Goa on account of the merchants, for I wished to confer this benefit on my intimates by way of a parting gift. My petition was acceded to, and, embarking on the same vessel, I went to Goa, where the Portuguese were much pleased at the benefit I had gained for them from the prince, and the merchants acquired their profit. After two days I took leave of the viceroy and my friends, and returned to the royal camp, where the prince awaited me with great eagerness.

When I arrived I learnt that the prince was already prepared for the march, having completed the destruction of the White Pagoda and other edifices belonging to Sambhā Jī. We took the road for Bardes once more, halting on the bank of that river. Shāh 'Ālam had given orders that everyone caught entering or leaving the camp at night should be beheaded without fail. This was to frighten the spies, and hinder them from coming to pry about in the camp. It happened that they caught, among others, some Canarese, who had come from Goa to sell fruit, butter, *et cetera*, in the camp. Already they were on their way, early in the morning, to be beheaded, when my servants, hearing of this, informed me of the miserable plight of these Canarese. I therefore hurried to the prince, who was already on the march, and besought him for an order to release my people, who had carried me from Goa. He smiled, and directed the release of the men for whom I had petitioned. Thus some men were released whom I had recognised to be Christians.

After this we marched, and climbed a mountain called Ramgat (? Rāmghāṭ), a league and a half of ascent. Here Sambhā Jī might have killed the whole of us, for it was a place difficult to climb, with narrow paths passing through jungle and thorny scrub. But he did not choose to attempt it, and they said he was acting in collusion with Shāh 'Ālam.

But what Sambhā Jī did not do by attacking us, God carried out by the pestilence which raged in the army with such violence that in seven days of its prevalence everyone died who was attacked—that is, about one-third of the army. Of this disease there died every day five hundred men; nor was the mortality confined to men only—it extended to horses, elephants, and camels. This made the air pestilential, and, it being a confined route, supplies failed also; and this was like encountering another enemy. For although, as I said, wheat was abundant from this time, there were no animals to carry it. Thus the soldiers had more than enough to undergo. Many of those whose horses had died had no money to buy others, nor was there anyone in the camp ready to sell. They were thus forced to march on foot, and many died of the great heat and thirst they underwent. Having reached the top of this pass, we marched for the kingdom of Bījāpur. Several times we were watched on the march by the enemy, who, whenever occasion served, spared neither our baggage nor ourselves, plundering in all directions.

Finally we arrived at Aamadanaguer (Aḥmadnagar), where Chānd Bībī caused golden and silver balls to be fired from her cannon, with the inscription that the ball should belong to the finder. Here we met the army of Aurangzeb, who was waiting for the rainy season to pass before venturing farther into the kingdom of Bījāpur and Gulkandah. During these marches and halts it was observed that in the morning there were on the tents various scarlet imprints of hands. Every-one was in astonishment. We could never discover the signification of these imprints, unless it could be judged to be some witchcraft, for no one could climb so high as to make those hand-prints on the royal tents.

As I was already dissatisfied with all this marching, I continued to reflect on modes of retiring to Europe, there to enjoy the much or little that I had fairly earned by my labours. I therefore asked Shāh 'Ālam for leave to visit Sūrat on some business I had there. But as he knew by experience that my determination was to proceed still farther, he ordered his slaves to watch carefully that I did not take to flight. He refused to give any other answer.

Seeing him thus positive, I adopted another plan, which was to write to Muḥammad Ibrāhīm, begging him to assist me in my escape. He wrote that he would most willingly do so. To this end he sent daily four thousand horse to patrol as if they meant to make an attempt upon us, and this caused some anxiety to Shāh 'Ālam. This went on for several days, until the day fixed for my escape arrived. I sent my books out of the camp by the hands of my spies, who moved about in safety. Then, contenting myself by carrying off my hoard of gold coins and my case of instruments, I left my tent mounted on a horse followed by a palanquin, as if I were going to take the air. I halted at the tent of one of my friends, an Englishman named Thomas Gudlet, and there I drank a cup or two so as to mystify Shāh 'Ālam's spies. Then, on the pretext that at night I had to give a dinner to some friends, I sent the spies to procure dishes of food, some in one place, some in another. I also ordered my palanquin to be taken away, as I intended to ride home that evening.

When I found myself free of these spies, I sent out two faithful servants to wait for me in a village across the river, near which were posted the four thousand horsemen of Muḥammad Ibrāhīm. On arriving, they were to display a small white flag as a signal that the horsemen were there, and that I might come safely. As soon as I got this warning I rode out on my horse as if taking the air, but in truth I was on my way to escape. When I reached the river I moved most leisurely, as if I only meant to give my horse a drink.

When the sentries saw that I was crossing the river, they began to shout and warn the horsemen that I was clearing out. But they were too late to catch me, for giving my steed the rein I moved off in fine style. The horsemen of Shāh 'Ālam pursued me, describing a half-circle in the hope of surrounding me. But Muḥammad Ibrāhīm's troopers at once rode up, lance in rest, and put Shāh 'Ālam's horsemen to flight. Thus delivered I reached the village, and from the village the army, where I gave thanks to Muḥammad Ibrāhīm for the favour he had done me.

Nor must I omit to mention how some Christians in the service of the Gulkandah king, aware that I was seeking to escape from Shāh 'Ālam, came out to meet me and escort me, so as to take my side in case any of the Gulkandah troops attempted to interfere with me. Hardly had I reached the presence of Muhammad Ibrāhīm, when one of Shāh 'Ālam's spies turned up. He delivered letters to the general, and informed him in private that I was much valued by Shāh 'Ālam, who would take it very ill should he assist a person that the prince had sent after several times and put sentries over to prevent his escape.

The spy left, and also the other persons present, and I was alone with Muḥammad Ibrāhīm. He already regretted having helped me in my flight, and as he had been planning to desert to the prince's side, he feared being badly treated by His Highness. This was why, after having congratulated me on my escape, he prayed me to remain with him a few days; he said he felt unwell, and wanted to purge himself. I quite understood the design of Muḥammad Ibrāhīm; he meant to make me over once more to Shāh 'Ālam. Placing my hand on my dagger, I said to him that if he did not give me leave to go on to Gulkandah, I should without fail rip open my bowels in his presence, and would rather die than go back to the service of Shāh 'Ālam.

He became alarmed at finding me thus resolute, and, retiring inside, told me to wait a little. He wrote me a passport for Gulkandah, and coming out again handed it to me, telling me privately to make all the haste I could. As this was all I was waiting for, I jumped on my horse at once and travelled for three days, until I arrived at Gulkandah. There I repaired to the house of a friend, Monsieur Francisco Guety, and he conducted me to the mansion of Xarif Elmulq (Sharīf-ul-mulk), brother-in-law of the Gulkandah king. He had several conversations with me; and the king's sister suffering from palpitation of the heart, I was able to alleviate her complaint a great deal. In this way I began to be talked about in Gulkandah.

Thus the king heard of my arrival. As his European physician, a Frenchman named Monsieur Destremon, was dead, the king sent for me to his presence. There, after some conversation, he directed me to go and bleed a woman in his harem, much cherished by him, because she knew where the treasures of the King of Gulkandah Cotobxa (Quṭb Shāh) were concealed. She was a Georgian, and so extremely stout, and the fat covered the veins so much, that blood could not be drawn from her except from the capillary veins. Her arms were covered with lancet marks. I felt for the vein, and after fixing the bandage, I took a measure twice the size I used for others; and I reached the vein with such dexterity that the blood gushed out with great force. Everyone was in admiration at seeing a thing that had never happened before with this woman

The king himself, who was standing behind looking on, became desirous of being bled also. But though they made me wait for that day, in the end he would not have it done. It may be that someone had frightened him, that I might be an emissary from Shāh 'Ālam and Aurangzeb, sent to bleed him in such a way that he would never want to be bled again. In place of having himself bled, he made over to me for treatment one of his nephews who had an ulcerated leg, and for this purpose he presented to me seven hundred rupees for my expenses. [To evade capture by Shāh 'Ālam, Manucci again fled to Narsapur.]

While Shāh 'Ālam was halted in that province (Kohīr) waiting for the receipt of the treasure, elephants, jewels, and war materials, in accordance with the treaty, he requested the king to have a search made for me, and send me to him as he wanted me. Horsemen were sent by the king to fetch me, with orders to the governors that if I refused to come willingly, I was to be sent by force. The soldiers came upon me in Narsapur, and showed me the royal *farmān*, whereby the king recalled me to court, on the pretext of continuing the treatment of his nephew. He promised me that whenever I wanted my liberty it should be given without difficulty.

I could see quite well that there was no escape from going, for they would carry me off to the court whether I liked it or not. I therefore dissembled, and made display of goodwill, and a desire to be of service to His Majesty. I mounted my horse and went with them, in all pomp and magnificence, until we got to Gulkandah. When I appeared to make my obeisance to the king, he declared himself pleased at my coming. Urgently I begged him, as I had come under protection of his word, not to deliver me into the hands of Shāh 'Ālam. By this he was somewhat disconcerted, and fixed my pay at seven hundred rupees a month. But I declared that I would not accept pay, that I meant to serve him for nothing. Nevertheless, he sent seven hundred rupees to my abode, and while I was with him he ordered a set of robes to be conferred on me. He gave a private order to post a hundred horsemen in the street where I was staying, to prevent anyone interfering with me.

For the envoy of Shāh 'Ālam, called Momencan (Mūmin K͟hān), sought an opening for carrying me off to the prince. In addition to the guard of horsemen, Abu,l Ḥasan gave me over in charge to his *dīwān*, who was responsible for my personal safety. I began the treatment of his nephew once more, and remained two months in Gulkandah, by which time the patient had recovered. But I was obliged to seek safety in a secret flight. For the ambassador of Shāh 'Ālam, when he was taking leave, once more tried to induce the king to make me over into his hands. He (the king) replied that if at his departure he carried me away with him, no one would come forward to defend me. For this purpose he ordered the withdrawal of the hundred horsemen, placed as sentries to prevent interference with me.

This conversation was heard by one of the said ambassador's soldiers, who years before had come under an obligation to me for treating him in an illness, and he hurried to warn me of the ambassador's intentions. The information reached me when I was at cards, and, suppressing my tribulation, I went on for a time with the game. I then went out and betook myself to the house of the Dutch envoy, who was then Lourenço Pit, and begged his assistance in this delicate situation. After that I sent for the Father Vicar of Gulkandah, named Frey Francisco, of the Order of St. Augustin, and most earnestly entreated him to see Rustam Rāo and procure leave to remove to Machhlīpatanam a brother of his called Augustinho, who had fallen ill.

I furnished him with this name, so that if asked for his invalid brother's name he should be in no perplexity, and thereby avoid suspicion of there being some deceit. The arrangement succeeded perfectly, for the permit was obtained. I got into a palanquin, and feigned to be unwell; and praise be to God, the spies never discovered me. Thus did I make my journey without the envoy of Shāh 'Ālam being aware of my departure. I went on until I arrived at Madrasta (Madras) or Fort St. George, which belongs to the English, and there I was free of all danger. My escape from Gulkandah was the cause of some discomfort to the king, for Shāh 'Ālam made great complaint of his want of energy in arresting me, but he knew quite well that by that time I was no longer in Gulkandah. Still he made various searches, and in the end sent Rustam Rāo as a prisoner into the fortress, because he had issued the permit for my departure. The prisoner was forced to pay fifty thousand rupees, which were forwarded to Shāh 'Ālam as a present to procure pardon for the fault of the king's officer.

On my arrival in Madras, the Portuguese gentlemen, who knew the zeal with which I had served their nation in Goa, came to see me. They congratulated me on my arrival and offered their services in whatever way would be of use to me. Such help they would give most willingly. But I was all anxiety to see Senhor Francisco Martim (François Martin), Director-General of the Royal Company of France, who had come back to Pudichery (Pondicherry) from Sūrat. I got into a palanquin and went off to visit him, where I was well received, and well entertained for several days. He gave me the advice not to return to Europe, but to marry in India. He informed me of a lady born in India, but of good English Catholic parents. She lived in Madrastapataõ (Madras) and her name was Senhora Ilizabet Ihardili (? Elizabeth Hartley), legitimate daughter of (Mr.) Christovaõ Ihardili (? Christopher Hartley), president of Machhlīpatanam, and of Donna Aguida Pereyra, a Portuguese lady. At that time the lady Ilizabet Ihardili was the widow of Mr. Thomas Klark (Clarke), an English Catholic; he was a judge, and second at the station of Madras.

This is what I was told by Monsieur the General, confirmed by some Capuchin friars, and thus I began to relinquish the idea of going back to Europe. For, as they told me, having become accustomed to the climate and the food of India, and being already advanced in age, I should not last very long in Europe. Thus I quitted Pondicherry and returned to Madras, meaning to find out the intentions of the said lady. There I arrived at the end of June in one thousand six hundred and eighty-six, and I talked with the well-known Fathers Zenaõ (Zenon) and Ephrem (Ephraim), Capuchins, and apostolic missionaries in Madras, otherwise Fort St. George. They were aware of the virtues and sound doctrine of the said lady, and they gave me such a good report of her qualities and virtues that I decided to marry. By the favour of God I was married on St. Simon's and St. Jude's day of that same year (1686).

I had a son, but God chose rather to make him an angel in Paradise than leave him to suffer in this world. In this way I was fixed to a residence in the said Fort St. George, where came many that knew me, or heard speak of me, in order to be treated. Among those who came was Rajah Champat, son of Champat Bundelah, who, as stated in the first part of my history, was sacrificed by Aurangzeb as a foundation for his victories, in reward for having found him a route in his combat with Dārā.

Nor did Shāh 'Ālam fail to send in search of me in several directions, while the princess sent one who had formerly been my servant to seek me in Madras. She gave him as a present a dagger, which he sold to one of my friends for eight hundred *patacas* (Rs. 1600). This she did only through her desire to know where I was, so that she might send to fetch me.

All my acquaintances know that very few months passed without gifts coming from the Mogul grandees, who gave me many presents, and sent to me patients of title and many others. Experience was my great teacher, whereby I had acquired several secrets, in which it may be that I shall allow the world to participate, for I have no heir to whom to bequeath these treasures that preserve our bodily health. But among the others I may as well mention that I manufactured certain cordials regardless of expense, the same being wonderful in certain complaints, as many can testify. Yet it is only a short time ago that I began to distribute these cordials, for I have no wish to imitate those who, keener for others' gold than the health of their fellow men, make up mixtures of various things and sell them as cordials. I did not begin to sell mine until experience had taught me that the purchasers would not be cheated. My residence in Madras will offer no prejudice to the continuation of my history, for, besides the spies I employed, the nobles were pleased to forward me news of what took place in the camp.

I know quite well that some in reading this history will comment on my leaving the Mogul country so many times and then going back. Some will say to themselves that in those lands there must be some delectable fields which caused my return there. But in reality, granting that by God's favour I did have the luck to attain some good fortune, yet never had I any desire to settle there. For of a truth they have nothing that can delight or win people from Europe, or make them desire to live there. The country is not good for the body, much less for the soul; for the body it is requisite to live ever on the *qui vive* and keep your eyes open, since no one ever says a word that can be relied on. It is continuously requisite to think the worst, and believe the contrary of what is said; for it is the habit there absolutely to act according to the proverb of my country, "Pleasant words, sad actions." They deceive both the acute and the careless; thus, when they show themselves the greatest friends, you require to be doubly careful.

The country is not good for the soul, as much from the licence one has there, as from the absence of

Catholic observances. Thus, when I could leave it, I did so; nor should have I ever gone back there, had I not been forced by necessity. I offer up many thanks to God that at length He granted me means to deliver myself, and I assure the reader that few Europeans could live there with the advantages and honours I was able to achieve. Nor let him be led away by the hope that, resorting thither, he would be able to improve himself in any degree. For few indeed are they who return thence bettered, and many are those who have been made worse.

Among other occasions, there was one when the king's wife, the mother of Shāh 'Ālam, was graciously pleased to give me testimony of her goodwill towards me in recognition of my having accompanied the prince her son from Goa to court. This princess showed me great affection because I had attended her and bled her several times, in addition to which she had often to send for me, as she suffered much from gout. As it was I who prescribed for her, she often sent me some dainty, as is the fashion of these ladies to do to those whom they esteem. When I bled her she put her arm out from the curtain, but wrapped up, leaving only one little spot uncovered, about as wide as two fingers, close to the vein. For that attendance I got from her four hundred rupees and a *sarāpā* (set of robes) as a present, and I bled her regularly twice a year.

It should be understood that, before a European can acquire the office of physician among these princes, he must be put to the proof a long time, for they are extremely distrustful and nice in such matters. Every month the princesses and the ladies have themselves bled, which is done in the way I have above described. It is just the same when they want themselves bled in the foot, or have any wound or fistula dressed; nothing is ever shown but the part affected or the vein they wish opened. When I bled the wives and daughters of Shāh 'Ālam, each of them gave me two hundred rupees and a *sarāpā*, but when I bled that prince, who was my employer, and he was at court, I could not do it without the leave of the king. For this bleeding I got four hundred rupees, a *sarāpā*, and a horse.

When I had finished I had to report to the king the quantity of blood I had drawn, what was the prince's reigning humour, and reply according to circumstances to the inquiries made by the king on this subject. After this he would give me my dismissal, granting me a *sarāpā*. For each bleeding of one of the prince's sons I received two hundred rupees, a *sarāpā*, and a horse.

The distrust among these princes is so acute that the father does not trust the son, nor the son his father. Here is an instance: Sulṭān Mu'izz-ud-dīn, eldest son of Shāh 'Ālam, was graciously pleased to act as intermediary, and to intercede for me with his father to get me back into his service, as I have related more at length in my account of Goa. The father, without any other reason, commanded me not to go to the court of the said Sulṭān, giving him orders at the same time not to send for me. Let him, said Shāh 'Ālam, employ his own doctors, and not me. Upon this subject they had some words, and thereupon separated. Sometime afterwards Sulṭān Mu'izz-ud-dīn feigned the invalid, and no longer went to the court of his father. As soon as the latter heard of the illness he sent his Persian physicians, and these men reported that he was not in the least unwell. To give them the lie, and show that he required my treatment, he made one of his women servants suck a place in his neck, and thereby raised a blue mark. On learning that he was suffering from this blue mark, Shāh 'Ālam, without knowing the cause of it, had the idea that he required bleeding. So he ordered me to see him at his residence, and, with a view to satisfying his son, told me to go whenever he sent for me; and in this manner they made it up, and were at peace.

Perhaps it will be found not altogether devoid of utility if I impart to my readers several events that happened to me which are proof of the prince's kindness and of the friendship he bore me. Seeing that I was not married, he inquired from me, through the first princess in his *maḥal* (seraglio), why I did not take a wife. I replied that I found none of my standing that took my fancy. This lady and her husband were both desirous to get me married, so as to retain me and hinder my leaving Hindūstān and his court. She said to me that she would send for all the daughters of Christians, whether Europeans or Armenians, and I had only to choose the one I liked best. She would see that I obtained the girl, would give her away in marriage herself, and provide all the expenses necessary on such occasions, adding a number of other promises. I thanked her, and made her understand how grateful I was for all her favours, but being a man of family, it was not correct for me to accept a bride such as she proposed. To that she replied by a great many things; among others, that Mahomedans took anybody, without regard to their birth. Although Christians could never have pretensions to such an honour, yet, if I would agree, she would have all her maids-of-honour brought before me, and I had only to select the one I most liked, and she should be given to me as wife, nothing remaining but to carry her away to my dwelling.

Being weary of all this woman's talk, I gave an off-hand answer that I was incapacitated for marriage. But on she went, and, with a number of other remarks, refuted me by saying that my bearing and complexion showed the falsity of what I told her. Finally, after all this discourse, she ordered me to put my hand inside the curtains of the bed to feel her pulse; for this is the way one has to deal with these ladies, as I have said. I noted that the arm was thick, muscular, and hairy, and by these signs I knew at once it was a man's arm; and it turned out to be Shāh 'Ālam himself. Without delay I rose and said that the arm I had touched was a man's, and not a woman's, and it could be no other than that of the King of the World. At these words the prince burst out laughing, and told me that I knew how to distinguish the difference between a man and a woman.

Wishing to retain me and gain me entirely over to his interest, the prince thought that women would be a good vehicle to secure his object; for it is very common for men to be destroyed by this snare. Here is how he set to work. He asked me if I knew there was a European in his palace. I said I did not. Instantly, while we were speaking, there came out of a room a very pretty girl, dressed as a man in European style, with a gold-mounted sword at her side. As soon as she saw me she lifted her hat and saluted me. I was conscious at once that it was the prince who had put all this in play to amuse himself, and see if he could gain me over. But I feigned the ignoramus, as if I had not noticed anything, returned the bow, and proffered some compliments. Speaking French, I went up to her to kiss her, when at once she turned her back and fled. I ran after her, as if wishing to embrace her, but she ran faster than I did. However, I did my utmost to overtake her. Laughing, the prince cried out to me. At his voice I came back with slow steps close to him, much put out at not having succeeding in embracing the young person.

When I had come close, he asked me what I wanted to do. I replied that I wanted to embrace and kiss the would-be young man. He assumed to be astonished at such a piece of audacity, then took to smiling at it ever so long, as did all the princesses.

Afterwards he told me that the Farangī I had seen

was not a man, but a woman, and if I would have her he would give her to me, and she could serve to carry my medicines to the *maḥal.* I answered, with a serious air, that she was no use for that, as medicines administered by a woman's hand produced no effect. The prince joked for a long time with the princesses over what I had said. This is the greatest amusement he has. All other Mahomedans also pass the greater part of their time among their women. This is so much the case that through them important business at court is transacted. For my part I have done a great deal thus, principally through the first princess.

It is the custom in the royal household, when a physician is called within the *maḥal,* for the eunuch to cover his head with a cloth, which hangs down to his waist. Then they conduct him to the patient's room, and he is taken out in the same manner. The first time that I was led through the palace, I was fitted out in the above fashion, but, by premeditation, I walked as slowly as I could, in spite of the urging of my guides, the eunuchs. The prince, having seen this, ordered them to uncover me, and that in future I was to be allowed to come and go without being covered. He said that the minds of the Christians were not filthy like those of the Mahomedans.

This prince held me in such affection that he granted me permission to enter the *G͟husul-k͟hānah,* which is a secret place where the second audience is given and the council sits. Into it only the principal lords and officers of the court enter. If anyone fails to attend, whether by accident or otherwise, he cannot enter any more without fresh permission. To obtain this renewal he must make some present to the prince, at the very least one gold and nine silver coins; but with respect to me, I had liberty to enter and come out without anything of that sort. As the prince was in a fright that I would quit his service, he sought from time to time means of obliging me, and paid me all the honours such as I have reported. However, finding he could not capture me through women, he resolved to have a friendly talk with me on religion.

Having sent for me, he begged me not to take it amiss if he gave me a warning; his religion forced it upon him, and to discharge his conscience he was obliged to give it thrice. Following on this, he said it was his intention to elevate me to the rank of a noble at his court; but before this could be I must adopt his religion, which was assuredly the best, and through it I would gain salvation. The moment he had finished his discourse I made a very low bow, and said I knew very well what was contained in the Qurān, also what the Gospel imposed on me. There I had learnt that without baptism no one could enter the kingdom of heaven, and to gain it I was ready to spend and give up my life.

Seeing me so determined, he changed the subject, and he ordered me to send at once to procure him some crystal vessels for drinking water from. I sent off a man to Bombay to bring some. This order he executed—nay, those he brought were very handsome. These I presented to the prince. He seemed to be astonished to see so many crystals at once—more than he had ever seen in his life—for he imagined them to be of rock-crystal, which is extremely costly in the Mogul country. This is the reason of his asking me what the whole might be worth. Quite happy, I answered him that it was a present from me, and that Doctor Nicolas stated no prices to kings. He was so satisfied with this reply, that, coming to me, he patted me on the shoulders, and said that should God ever be gracious and make him king, he would remember my generosity. At the same time he ordered them to give me a very valuable set of robes and a very nice horse.

I must here make the remark that when these kings and princes give audience they display all imaginable gravity and majesty in order to inspire fear in everybody, but in their *maḥal* and in private they are as lowly as infants. This I have experienced several times, they going so far as to play with me with all possible familiarity. It is true that it may be said that all these pretty stories referring to me are of no great value to the public, but I thought a charitable reader would easily pardon this small satisfaction which I have ventured to give myself. Moreover, if anyone were about to travel in these far-off places, it may be that at some conjuncture these tales of my humble adventures will not be entirely useless to him.

As the entire thoughts of these princes are turned in the direction of the throne, they search out very carefully any means of conferring favours on the most powerful men, in the hope of having them on their side. Shāh 'Ālam had usually with him a Hindū prince called Bau Sing (Bhāo Singh), leader of twelve thousand horsemen, and a vassal of the king. He served under the orders of Shāh 'Ālam. Noticing that he had ceased to come to court, being unwell, the prince sent me to visit him on his behalf, and offer my services. This was merely to oblige him, and gain him to his side, should any occasion present itself.

The rajah was already old, and was suffering from his lungs. The prince, however, directed me to observe him and reckon how long he might yet live. Bhāo Singh received my visit, but refused my services, and told me if I gave him any medicines he would put them with the rest I saw there. He had a whole roomful. God might do with him according to His pleasure, but he would not take the medicines, beyond looking at them. All this care was because he was afraid of being poisoned. This fear was increased by the example he had in Rajah Jai Singh and several others to whom such a fate had happened. I must say the prince never had any designs of that sort, and all he did was intended to oblige. I may add that during all the time I had the honour to serve him, he never suggested employing me for such a purpose.

Still, he made a trial as to whether I was of a nature that would carry out such devices. This I discovered in the course of time. For example, he sent to me some unknown persons who offered me large sums to bring to their death other patients that I was treating. Others asked me to sell them poison, but no one ever got me to accede to such a demand. Another stratagem was also made use of to test me and attempt to find me out in a fault. This was the sending to my house of a young and very pretty girl, in charge of an old woman, on the pretext that the young beauty was ailing. She was barely eighteen, and I found out from her pulse that she was the very reverse of indisposed. I asked her if she suffered from any pain which could not be detected from the pulse. As I interrogated her, the old woman, making believe that she was a simpleton, left us and took a turn in the garden. The young girl seemed at once to grow very free with me, as well as by word as by deed. She told me she longed for my friendship, while hers would not be useless to me. She could secure me many advantages. As soon as I heard her talk I was disgusted, and, quitting her, I came out and shouted to the old dame to take her away. I then grew angry, and, calling my men, ordered them both to be ejected.

Two months afterwards there came another still more lovely; but she was alone, and in a palanquin. Under the same pretence of illness she told me she came from a great distance to procure a cure. She entered my house wrapped in a shroud, but on nearing me she uncovered, and throwing herself at my feet, implored me to keep her in my house; for, being a stranger, she knew not where to turn. Her prayer was repeated several times. I noticed that she had on her jewels of great value, and her clothes were those of a person of quality, so fine that her skin showed through. All this troubled me, and I fancied that it might be to betray me. Still more did I think so, for the same thing had happened to others; and as I had no intention of marrying, it did not suit my views to get entangled.

With the object, then, of getting her away, I expressed my sympathy, and by pleasant words sent her off. Some time afterwards I was warned that this was one of Shāh 'Ālam's tricks, only resorted to in the hope that she would take my fancy—that I should have an affair with her, and by this means he would obtain an opening for compelling my continuance in Hindūstān, with a change in my religion, or else the loss of my life, as has happened to many who have lost their souls for a woman's love. Only a few years ago two Capuchins, or rather Portuguese, in the town of Iṣfahān fell into this sad soul-destroying misfortune. One of them was prior of the convent, and both were forced to become Mahomedans through similar events. Afterwards, under pretext that they were of that religion, they robbed a merchant of their own nation. God forgive those who send out characters like these to be missionaries.

The kings and princes delight in showing themselves to be just, and when taking cognisance of important business, they endeavour to hold the balance even. Since I was in Shāh 'Ālam's service in the capacity of physician, I was an object of envy to other physicians, the Persians, who sought means to ruin me. It chanced that a brother-in-law of the prince, named Mirzā Sulaimān Beg, fell ill from a fullness of the blood. The prince directed his chief Persian physicians, named Aguins (Ḥakīms), Moquins (? Muqīm), and Mosencan (Muḥsin K͟hān), to prescribe for him. They failed in curing him, and instead of bleeding him and cooling him down, they gave him hot remedies. They treated him in such a way that in a few days he was in the throes of death. When he was in this state, one of his brothers, named Mirzā Mahomed Moquim (Muhammad Muqīm) took me to the patient's house, hoping I might help him. I saw at once that there was nothing more to be done. On the prince hearing the opinion I had expressed about his brother-in-law, he asked his physicians the reason he had fallen into this condition. They had the ill-will to say that I was the cause. To find out the truth Shāh 'Ālam sent the *nāẓir* Daulat, the chief eunuch of his palace. This man on his return reported that the patient complained that the said physicians killed him, whereas had the Doctor Nicolas only treated him, he would not have lost his life. While saying these words the poor man expired. But the testimony he had given me conferred much credit upon me at court, and gained me the esteem of everybody.

After a time it came to pass that Mirzā Muḥammad Muqīm, brother of the deceased, of whom I have just spoken, went out of his mind. In an access of madness he slew his father-in-law and some servants, and committed many other crimes. On hearing this, the prince made him over to his physicians. Their report was that such a man could never recover the senses that he had lost. To demonstrate the force of their opinion, they cited as proof a passage in the Qurān which says that for madness there is no cure.

Shāh 'Ālam heard this sad decision pronounced, and at once ordered the patient to be placed in my care, as he believed I should find a remedy. I know not whether this was actually because he thought me cleverer than the others, or because I was a Christian. For I had often noticed that many patients were made over to me when their health was in a desperate state, because they had taken it into their heads that the Saviour had invested me with some virtue or other. With the permission of God I cured this lord in a few days. To reward me for my trouble and for any expense I had incurred, he sent me a horse with very good paces, but made no other payment. The reason of such a meagre present was his miserliness. On my side I was much put out at getting so little for all the trouble I had taken. So, without any word of thanks, I sent the horse back, telling the groom who had brought him, when many men were present, that his master was in no state to send gifts before he had recovered his reason perfectly, and when he had recovered his health I would accept what he sent to me. He had hardly heard my message when he sent me the same horse with a thousand rupees and a very handsome set of robes. The truth is that he did not send me the present willingly, but felt constrained to do it for fear I might tell everyone he was still mad. By this means he would lose the office he held at court, and also lose everyone's confidence. Shāh 'Ālam, when he learnt what had passed, was very satisfied at the cure, and still more with the answer I had given about the present. On his part he gave me a horse and a set of robes, adding many praises from his own lips, a habit common enough to these princes with physicians who succeed in curing patients they have made over to their care.

Shāh 'Ālam had directed the physician Muqīm to treat the wife of one of his captains called Mabarescan (Mubāriz Khān), a man much beloved by that prince. This woman had been long in a decline, and was worn out by the quantity of blood she had lost. The doctor, finding that his remedies did her no good, lost all hope of her, and intimated to the prince that her life was in danger. On hearing this, Shāh 'Ālam ordered me to take over the case. I applied myself to her relief with all possible care and diligence, and in a short time I had pulled her through. The physician was vexed in his mind, but outwardly he displayed much goodwill to me, just the contrary of his real feeling. I was not taken in, for I had known that pilgrim for many a long day.

The physician Muḥsin Khān treated a uterine(?foster) brother of the prince, whose name was Muḥammad Riẓā. He had a severe fever, which made him delirious. The physician, not recognising the complaint, came to the conclusion that there was no remedy, and gave him up. After that I was ordered to treat the man, and in a short time I put him on his legs again. There were other patients who had been given up in the same way by these gentlemen, but subsequently recovered their health under my hands, to those physicians' disgrace and loss of reputation. This is the reason they were no friends of mine; still more so that, though their patients came to me, none of mine went to them.

I also cured a noble from Balkh called Fatḥ-ullah Khān, a title conferred on him by the king. He had afterwards married an extremely pretty woman, who had served up to him nothing but delicious *plâts* until he got ill, and lost his appetite. He grew so thin that he looked like a skeleton, and no physician was able to do him any good. In the end Shāh 'Ālam ordered me to take charge of him. I knew the constitution of these savages, so I gave him a comforting syrup, which could do him neither harm nor good. Then I ordered him to get his stews made of horseflesh, and by this means he was in a short time restored to his former rude strength.

From this I acquired such renown that many men of this race came to me for treatment. But I got very little out of them, for they are very avaricious and paid me highly in compliments only. Moreover, I had the reputation of being charitable and curing the poor for the love of God. Thus everybody flocked to my house. The Mahomedan and Hindū surgeons were very much provoked, for their interests were involved and they lost their practice. However, as they saw they could not injure me directly, they started the rumour that I drank the blood that I drew from Mahomedans, that it was by this means that I was made so brisk and energetic and had such a high colour. All this was simply to hinder people coming to me to be treated. Everybody supposed that what they had published was true, and great repugnance was shown to be bled by me. Aware of what it was that troubled them, I told them to bring with them a china vessel, and all they had to do was to carry the blood home, and there bury it, for fear any cat or dog might consume it; for if that happened, they would make noises exactly like those animals. By this measure I put an end to the false rumours, and they were no longer spoken of.

One day, as I was attending to the treatment of some patients with all possible care, there comes into my house a king's slave in a great rage and a great hurry, making much noise and throwing everything into confusion. This man I imagine had been sent by the other doctors, my enemies. I went up to him and begged him most civilly and even humbly to do me the favour of not upsetting the sick men. But he paid me no heed, and went on worse than before, and abused me. Seeing how insolent he was, I signed to my men to fall upon him without giving him time to draw, which they forthwith did. Our man, finding himself caught, flew into a fearful rage, and made more noise than ever. He said he would kill me and my men and other such outrageous speeches.

Thereupon I assumed an aspect of mingled severity and sadness, and said I had compassion for him, seeing he was suffering from blood to the head. His was a case for bloodletting. This remark made him more furious still and he struggled to get free. Without heat, I ordered them to undress him and then bind him; and sending for a lancet, I made ready to bleed him. The slave, still angry, insisted that I must not bleed him; if I did he would kill me. My answer was given in an amiable tone before everyone that it was absolutely necessary to bleed him, that the blood had gone to his head, and assuredly if not treated he would be the death of someone.

In the end, by force I opened two veins in his arm. The fellow was still angry and wanted me to close the veins; but ignoring what he said, I showed sorrow at beholding his blood, from time to time feeling his pulse, and saying that his blood was very vitiated. Then, raising my eyes, I looked in his face and asked if he did not already feel an alteration in his body. Finding that his menaces and loud talk were of no good to him, nobody listening to them, he adopted at last the mode of humble entreaty, and said in a feeble voice that God had brought him to my house to be cured of the ills he had suffered from through many years. He thanked me for my trouble. In spite of this I did not trust him without precautions, so, closing the veins with two fingers, I put several new questions. Having replied very properly and civilly to these, just as he ought, I closed the veins and had his clothes and weapons returned to him. After this he said a thousand flattering things about me, and never more passed in front of my door. When we met at the king's or elsewhere, he was very polite to me. I have always thought that he did this only from the fear he had that I might announce he was mad, or that I might drain all the blood from his body.

It is not the practice among these princes for nobles to have converse with the favourites and servants of other princes for fear they may spin some web of treason. If it is ever the case, it is always with the permission of their master. It happened that Diler Khān fell ill; he was Shāh 'Ālam's enemy, yet he sent for me to prescribe for him. He knew of the prohibitions on the subject; he sent word that if I went to his house, it would afford a good opening for him to become friends with the prince. He would always be ready to assist him with all the cavalry under his command on any and every occasion that might arise.

As I knew the custom of the court and the scurvy tricks of the Mahomedans, I informed the prince of this affair, and pointed out to him that Diler Khān had sent for me. Hardly were the words out of my mouth when his face began to flush and he asked me very hastily whether I wanted to go there. To that I replied with a smiling face that, if I was anxious to go there, it was only to see the state he was in— whether he would live or die, so that I might make my report to His Highness. These words appeased him, and he forbade me to go. Diler Khān died, and it was found to be poison administered by his son-in-law, Azil Can, and by one of the prince's commanders.

PART III

Governor Gyfford employs Manucci

In the year one thousand six hundred and eighty-six, seven days after my arrival at Madras, Governor William Guiford (Gyfford) sent for me and informed me that the governors and officials of the Mogul king in Bengal province had been ill-treating his (the English) factors. They hindered them from exercising the privileges conceded to them by the Mogul kings. For two years he had made efforts to bring his grievances before the king, and had spent much money, yet had been unable to impart to the king in person the damage they were doing him. On this account they had begun a war on the Governor of Hūglī.

He prayed me to find some means by which King Aurangzeb should take notice of the oppression inflicted on them by his officials. I wrote a letter to one of the king's eunuchs, a very familiar friend of mine, called Necruz (Nekroz)—that is, "Fortunate Day." In it I informed him with great politeness of the troubles suffered by the English nation within His Majesty's dominions, including many necessary particulars. I prayed him as a favour to deliver this letter to the king, and he, out of his great friendship for me, and aware also that His Majesty himself knew who I was, delivered the letter with confidence when the king was among his women. Having read it, the king put it in his pocket, then went out into the *'Am-Khāṣṣ* (the audience hall) and began to hold audience. After hearing several complaints brought before him by his officials, he drew the letter from his pocket and began to read it again, shaking his head meanwhile. Then he said aloud: "It is true that the English are in the right and the fault lies with my officials." The persons present were much agitated.

He turned his face in the direction of Mahābat Khān, and asked him if there was at the court any agent of the English. He answered that there was not. The king ordered him to write to the Governor of Madras, that he forgave the temerity displayed by the English in plundering the town of Hūglī, and on their side they must excuse the troubles caused to them by his officials. The governor should send to court persons properly empowered, and he might be assured of acquiring new favour. During this going to and fro, the war in Bengal went on.

By the time the answer arrived, Governor Gyfford was already out of office, and there governed in his place Alexandre Hayel. The latter, on seeing the goodwill shown by the king, was very pleased, but was unable to send off any representative at once, because he had to report to the general, who lived in the island of Bombajm (Bombay), at a great distance from Madras. The officials at the court finding that no agent appeared in time, and being aggrieved at what the king said in audience, so managed affairs that they forced the king into investing the fortress of Bombahim (Bombay). This place was so closely pressed that it very nearly fell into the hands of the Mogul. Finally the (English) general was obliged to send an envoy to the court. Great expenditure was incurred before he obtained entry in the manner that everybody obtains, and he received his leave to depart, when an order to raise the investment of Bombay had been issued. The English undertook to send orders to withdraw their fleet from

Bengal. If these efforts had only been made at the proper time, there would not have been much expense or damage, for from a single neglect flow many evils.

I will also recount what happened to me, and what I have seen and undergone. I have already told you in my book how, upon my arrival in these regions, the chief personages of San Thome did me the honour to receive me with civility, and offered to put themselves at my service. Among them were Manoel Texeyra Pinto, chief captain (*capitaõ, mor*), Joaõ da Costa de Sua, Cosmo Lourenço Madeyra, Antonio Palha de Lima, and Manoel da Silva de Menezes. I had treated them and their families gratis.

A year afterwards there came to me from Goa a sum of three thousand and seven hundred *patacas* (Rs. 7,400) which I had deposited with Father Salvador Gallo, prefect of the Theatines. The said Father handed the money to my attorney, Joaõ Lopes de Figueredo, a Portuguese born in India, to be delivered to me. When this man arrived at the port of San Thome the above named were at the time governing, and were also the magistrates. Thus, when the said Joaõ landed they seized him and confiscated everything he brought with him, taking possession also of his ship, under the false declaration that he was the debtor of certain Jews called Bertolameo Rodrigues, Domingos do Porto, and Alvaro da Fonçequa. These magistrates called upon him to pay a debt due from a man of his faction (Figueredo's), called Francisco de Lima, owed to the above Jews. These latter were much delighted at the benefit thus done them.

Finding this great wrong done, and that I should also lose my money, I had recourse to these same magistrates. I laid before them the receipt of Joaõ Lopes (de Figueredo) the letters of Father Salvador Gallo, and attestations by Dom Rodrigo da Costa,

Governor of India, who had also written a separate letter to the leading men of San Thome recommending me to their favour, because their Indian dominions were under great obligations to me. He certified that Joaõ Lopes conveyed this money to be delivered to me. Thus he had done his very best to carry through my business.

None of these efforts did me any good. Once more I presented fresh testimony received from Goa from Augustinho Ribeyro and Pascoal Gomes; also the Letters Patent with which the King of Portugal had honoured me. These men had been present when the said Father (Gallo) delivered the said money to Joaõ Lopes de Figueredo. He was under obligation to pay me in current coin, and to take seals (sealed receipts); Joaõ also demanded leave to pay me. He only owed money to me, and nothing to anyone else —as was the truth, for no statement was produced to show how he was a debtor. In the end the said Joaõ Lopes was ruined and destroyed. As for my claim, which they could not deny, after much worthless argumentation, they resolved to pay me two thousand *patacas* (Rs. 4,000). This they declared was a favour they were doing me; the balance they would not pay. One man so decided because I would not marry one of his relations; others said, if I settled among them in San Thome I should not lose my money; another said that there was no ground to complain, that the two thousand *patacas* sufficed, as I had a sufficient income to live upon all my life; the rest uttered similar irrelevant opinions, and I was sent about my business.

With regard to the wrong done to Joaõ Lopes, let the reader understand that there were two reasons for it. The first was envy at seeing him, a man born in India, with some fortune and the owner of a ship, a thing they did not possess. The second reason was because three of the said magistrates had asked the wife of Joaõ Lopes in marriage, she being a rich woman, and, as she had refused them all, this produced the hate and envy which impelled them to ruin the man.

When twelve years from this dispute had passed by, in the year one thousand seven hundred (1700), there came as Governor of San Thome, on behalf of King Aurangzeb, a friend of mine called Xefican (Shafī' Khān). He was told of the injustice and robbery done to me by the Portuguese of San Thome, and revived the suit. The men were summoned to his presence. He asked them about the debt to me, when they answered boldly that they knew of no such thing, nor did they owe me anything, and they offered to swear upon the Holy Evangelists.

As the governor did not know the European languages, he applied to Mr. Thomas Pitt, Governor of Madrasta (Madras), sending him my papers and affidavits, and asked him to decide according to right. The said governor sent the papers to be translated into English. There was a delay of two months in getting this done. At the end of this time he sent for the Portuguese, and asked them in a friendly way to give me satisfaction, because it seemed to him that Nicolas Manuchy (*sic*) was a most reasonable man, and they ought to come to an agreement with me. In a most haughty and contumacious manner they replied they owed me nought, nor would they pay me anything.

A few days afterwards he (Mr. Pitt) assembled the whole council, the magistrates, and the learned men of different nations. They all sat together and deliberated. The Portuguese were called in, and in their presence in a loud voice he (the governor) read my documents, when those present decided unanimously that I had been wronged. It was decreed that the debtors must pay me. They were thus unmasked before all the Europeans and Mahomedans, yet not for this would they reform and turn from their evil ways.

I will add another case which happened to me in the same San Thome with the aforesaid Manoel da Silva de Menezes in the year ninety (1690), in the month of March. I had advanced five hundred *patacas* to a Genoese merchant called Jorge Bianco for trading in Pegu. He sent the principal with the agreed profit to be paid to me in San Thome. The said Manoel da Silva de Menezes was then judge. He took possession of my money and wanted to pay with his usual arguments, and in spite of all my efforts I could not obtain payment of what was mine. In the end I made use of certain friars, who interceded for me with Thomas de Maya, the chief captain then holding office, and he did what he could out of friendship for me. He ordered me to be paid; but behold the way Manoel da Silva wanted to satisfy me! He had bought some *koṛis* (scores, or twenties) of cloth for thirty *patacas* the scores. He wanted to pay me in this cloth, entering every score in my account at eighty *patacas*. Since I declined to accept, I only received a little cash, losing part of my principal and all the profit.

It seems to me that readers will approve, also those intending to come to India, of having this information by which they can guide themselves, making use of my experience.

The reader will have seen in my Second Part the efforts I had made and the services I had rendered in Goa when the Portuguese found themselves in such great peril. Thome de Azevedo, the chief physician, a priest of Jewish birth, ordered the bailiffs to seize me and thrust me into prison. The bailiff had compassion on me and sent me secret word of these orders, and advised me to get out of the way. At that moment I was entering the house of the Secretary of State, called Luis Gonsalves Cota, to translate the reply to a letter from Sambhā Jī, which the viceroy was about to send. After the letter was translated I mentioned to the secretary the orders that had been given by the physician. The secretary answered very frigidly that the physician could act thus, as he had the leave of His Excellency. If he had me arrested, he had cause, for I had no permission to treat the poor. He reprehended me, and said I was acting ill; he had also heard it stated that I had some little pills with which I made an easy cure of wounds and buboes. I answered that I treated none but mendicants and the indigent, and that without fee. It was my habit wherever I travelled to help the necessitous, and for such good deeds I was esteemed throughout the Mahomedan country, where I was held in much respect. Thus I would seek some other place, so as not to give annoyance, and preserve my liberty. The secretary was very stiff, and gave me not a word of reply, instead of paying some attention to or remedying my grievance.

I concealed my feelings, though disappointed in him, and lost no time in placing myself (in sanctuary) within the church of the Theatines. Thence I sent information to Dom Rodrigo da Costa, who at the time was in command of the fleet, and on hearing from me he went to see the viceroy, Count Francisco de Tavora. The latter was annoyed with the chief physician for wishing in that dangerous time to interfere with me. The physician was sent for, and also the chief surgeon, Francisco da Silva, and they were told by the viceroy in an angry voice that, if they touched me, he would have satisfaction from them. I was let alone, and in freedom.

I believe the reader will not be astonished at my writing with so much liberty, for I profess to declare the truth, which, as it seems to me, is the only thing likely to be of use as a warning to any curious person undertaking any long voyage, or in especial one coming to these parts of India. Many is the time I have wished to do good to and help necessitous persons; but afterwards, instead of being thanked,

I issued from the matter under sentence of crime as a misdoer and a rogue. Thus was it with what happened to me in the year one thousand six hundred and eighty-two.

Taking with me the ambassador from Goa, Joaõ Antunio Portugal, I set out for the army of Shāh 'Ālam, then lying near Goa territory. In our company were twenty men of rank, one Jesuit called Antonio de Barro, a Theatine called Dom Joseph Tedesqui, and a priest known by the name of Gonsallo Lopes. The whole party was put up by me in a large tent which the prince had assigned as my quarters, and there I entertained them as befitted them.

The next day I brought them to the court of Shāh 'Ālam, and there with the greatest difficulty I obtained leave for the entry of three persons only; but out of respect for me they were relieved of the heavy expenditure which has to be incurred by custom at all such courts. The Prince Shāh 'Ālam desired me to remain with him, and in order to compel or induce me, sent his confidant, Mirzā Muḥammad Riẓā, officer of his table and a great friend of mine, to make over to me two thousand rupees, which I was to accept, giving as a reason that I had spent considerable sums on His Highness's service. He had express orders that he must make me accept the money. I brought forward some objections to receiving it, but he embraced me, and, encouraging me, earnestly besought me to accept. The supplicant, finding that I did not want to accept, left the money and beat a hasty retreat, and I gave orders to lock up the cash.

The ambassador and some others were present. They began to talk softly to each other, and then angrily asked me in a loud tone who the rupees were meant for. I replied that the prince had sent them to me for my expenses. In their anger they answered me with misplaced words, and such-like talk, so that I held it better not to answer ignorant men who did not speak to me in a proper manner. It was reported among them that the prince had sent the two thousand rupees to the ambassador and that I had usurped them.

This matter was not such a secret that it did not come to the prince's ears, and he was annoyed, saying he could not have supposed that such people could have been so ignorant, and the higher he had thought of them, the more aggrieved he felt. To restore my honour, he ordered one of the principal officials of his court, Mīr Muḥammad Ṣādiq, to send for the ambassador to his tent with all his retinue, and apply a remedy for the above false statement. With me standing near him and the others round him, he asked if I had received the above-mentioned money. I replied in the affirmative. Then in a loud voice, with his hand raised, he said it had been heard that there was someone rash enough to assert that Manuchy had stolen the said money. If he could only find out who were these slanderers, he would unfailingly cram their mouths full (be it said with all respect) of dirt. Most of them hung their heads and said not a word; they had imagined they were sent for to receive some present.

When I had finished the negotiations in favour of the viceroy, Shāh 'Ālam ordered that in his presence the three persons should receive each a *sarāpā* (set of robes). At that moment appeared two men with two thousand rupees in two bags, and from behind the ambassadors shouted in a loud voice these words: "Here are the two thousand rupees that Your Majesty confers on the Portuguese ambassadors." They recited these words three times. Joaõ Antunes Portugal was alarmed at such shouting, as he did not know the language, and asked me the reason. I told him it was about the two thousand rupees that the prince had ordered to be given, and that it was in this manner that the gift was made, instead of sending the money to his tent. He cast down his eyes, recognising the reason why the prince acted thus. It was solely that no doubt might be thrown on my good faith. Joaõ Antunes Portugal was incensed at this affair, and, in place of being sorry, sought means to take mý life. If he did not succeed, it was because I did not remain in Goa, but returned to the Mogul prince's service.

I will insert a small affair that happened to me on the same occasion. In Goa there was a well-born man called Lourenço da Cunha, who pretended to be my friend. On my taking leave of the viceroy, at the time when I was about to start for the Mogul army to undertake negotiations for the State, this man carried me to his house, where I stopped all night. He asked me to convey in my boat a box containing various Chinese curiosities, which might be worth fifty rupees, hoping to sell them in the army. I excused myself for two reasons. The first was that the goods were not suitable for Mahomedans, being images of tigers, cats, cocks, *et cetera*. The second was because the things could not be carried safely, owing to the difficult marches we were to make. On hearing these objections he said nothing; but at midnight, when I was asleep, he made over the box to the boatman, with an order to inform me after I had reached the army. When I arrived at the army the boatman told me about the box, but at the time I passed the matter over in silence. The next day my friend Lourenço da Cunha turned up, and demanded from me four hundred and fifty rupees for the goods he had put into my boat. My arguments were of no avail, he talking preposterously. Finding all this trouble, and being careless about money, I ordered the payment of the amount claimed, and before his face caused all the contents of the box to be distributed to common people. He declared he was doing me a favour in letting me have the things so cheap.

These fellows glory in cheating foreigners without scruple.

This incident brings to mind that in seventy-six (1676) I left the Mogul territory, and stopped a few days at Damaõ (Damān). At that time a Portuguese fleet arrived as convoy to the ships going to Sūrat and Kambāya. The principal men in this fleet begged me to open my boxes, as they wanted to see some of my curiosities. I could not refuse, and, holding them to be gentlemen of position, I allowed them an inspection; but it was not long before some of the articles had disappeared. I suppressed any remark, for if I had taken any action they would have assassinated me without fail, as is customary among them.

In the year ninety-two there came a Hindū officer from the army in the Karnātik, a commander over five thousand horse, recommended to me by the Nababo (Nawāb) Julfacarcan (Ẕu,lfiqār Ḵẖān), Mirzā Mahdī, the captain of cavalry, and other friends. He wanted to be treated, and promised me four thousand rupees. The Portuguese of San Thome now interfered, including the head of the bishopric, a priest, then in charge also of the civic government, who was under obligation to me for having cured him of an obstruction. All these men, hearing of the above Hindū, took him to a physician, who offered to effect a speedy cure at a less price. They arranged matters so that the said officer believed them, and sent me a message that I need not trouble, and if he wanted me he would let me know.

After the lapse of a few days he sent a message to me, because he had not recovered his health as he desired, but I declined to attend him. I replied to those who had written to me that the said captain had declined to listen to my advice; and he went back as he had come lamenting his evil fate, for thus do the people of India talk when things do not succeed with them as they would wish. This captain was a rajah, his name was Dalpat Rāo, son of Champat Bundelah, he whom Aurangzeb sacrificed after crossing the river Dholpur (*i.e.* the Chambal) to give battle to Dārā, as described in my First Part.

Once in Goa, being in my house, there suddenly appeared a gentleman of birth who, with much assurance, took a seat without uttering any words of politeness. At his back stood four Kaffirs with staves in their hands. He said he was a gentleman of high rank, and occupied an important position in His Majesty's service, but fortune had not been kind to him. He had been wealthy, the lord of many plantations, but to pass the time he had gambled and lost all. Then raising his eyes, he looked at me and said: "I have heard that your honour is a merchant, a person of position, and the reputation you enjoy has induced me to visit you." But he could not stay long, because the viceroy was waiting for his presence to begin his dinner; and since he was in want of pocket money, he would borrow a sum from me. I replied that I was a poor soldier, and not a merchant; he had been misinformed. Raising his voice he said: "These arguments will not do for me. Either lend me or give me what I need." At these words the Kaffirs raised their staves. On seeing this I fell into a quandary, and began to reflect on what might be the result. I tried to retire into my room, when he said to me roughly, raising his voice, that I was not to stir from my place. Then dissimulating as to the pressure put upon me, I told my boy to bring my writing-desk. I opened it in front of him and showed what it contained—namely, thirty *ashrafis* (gold coins). I handed him this amount with the greatest politeness, saying that, had there been more, I should most willingly have offered it to him. He felt so honoured that he took twenty-five coins, saying that would suffice for his wants during that day. He put his good services at my disposal, instructing his Kaffirs that when I needed them for giving anyone a beating with bamboos, or stabbing anyone, they must carry out my orders. He then departed. Conceiving that I had got rid of him very cheaply, I gave thanks to God, and at once changed my quarters, going to live close to the Convent of the Carmelites, and there I lived with my doors barred, for I had seen many houses robbed by bodies of masked men entering them.

The first time I was in the city of Goa I lived in the street called Santo Aleixo, opposite some large houses. In one of these lived a widow called Dona Christiana; she was rich and led a quiet life. She wanted to marry me, a thing I never dreamt of. Seeing that I made no approaches, and made no effort, she resorted to a trick. This consisted in sending for the prior of the Carmes, Friar Pheliciano de Santa Teresa, a native of Milan and a great friend of mine. To him she complained that I had been pursuing her, sending her offers of marriage, to which she replied that she had no thought of such a thing. The Father believed her words, being unaware of Indian women's trickish ways; and coming to pay me a visit, as he constantly did, he prayed me with the greatest gentleness not to persecute Dona Christiana with such proposals as I had sent her, saying that I wanted to marry her. When I heard the padre talk like this, I was plunged in thought, trying to remember if on any day I had given the widow occasion for such a complaint about me. Examining my mind thoroughly, I found I had not the least remembrance of her, and said so to the Father. He smiled and said he hoped there would be no more complaints about me. As a satisfaction to him I left the neighbourhood and lived elsewhere.

Eight days afterwards the same priest came straight from the widow's house to find me, and directly he saw me began once more to complain harshly, saying that I should be the cause of that woman losing her reputation. He begged me for the love of God to abandon such thoughts. Feeling myself quite innocent in the matter, I replied to the padre that never had I dreamt either of stopping or of marrying in Goa. As it seemed to me, it was *she* who wanted to marry me, and had thus called in the padre as intermediary and made use of this artifice. I laid before him many similar affairs that had happened in India. But the priest was not a practical man, and had not been long in India, so he believed what the woman had said, and made me out the culprit. He told me I was not speaking the truth; and finding my arguments did not prevail, I gave my word to the priest that in a short time I would quit Goa, if he would only give me the time to prepare, and this he did.

Apropos of this case I may mention that, on arriving in the town of Bassaim (Bassein) in one thousand six hundred and sixty-six (1666) I was sent for by the commissary of the Inquisition. He was the prior of the Franciscan Convent, and three times over he examined me to find out about me and my life. Discovering nothing suspicious by his interrogatory, he made me swear upon a holy crucifix. Then, finding there was nothing wrong in my replies, he embraced me, and, treating me as an educated man with a clear conscience, he sent me away, saying that now I was free, and he would not send for me any more. I came to discover in the course of time that my accuser was the Father Damaõ Vieira, a man expelled from the Jesuit order. This is the man who came as an envoy to Rajah Jai Singh, and promised to reduce the city of Bījāpur by miracle.

Owing to the hatred in which he held me, he denounced me, and I was sent for by the commissary as I have said. I was innocent, and could not make out why I had been sent for. As the friar found he could not harm me in this way he came to Goa while

I was living there, and urged a well-born man called Antonio de Couza Coutinho, who had once been governor of India, to put an affront on me. But, like a wise man, he would not consent; he invited me to his house, and in his conversation told me to live very cautiously, for the friar in question was not fond of me. Thus I was far from secure, and for this and other reasons I quitted Goa.

After some time there arrived at the town (San Thome) the most illustrious Lord Dom Gaspar Alfonço, Bishop of Meliapur (Mailāpur) and other places. This prelate held in his hands both civic and ecclesiastical jurisdiction. Yet he did not meddle much in the former branch. However, as I noticed that he did me the honour to like and esteem me, I begged him to see me righted to the injustice that had been done me (see pp. 217, 218). After I had told him my story a few days elapsed. He then gave me his reply, telling me that I was in the wrong, that the judges owed me no redress, that it was the chief captain who had done the wrong, and it was he who ought to do me amends. "But," he added, "he is no longer in this world, and has left nothing. That is a misfortune for you, but you must bear it, as one must the other ills of this life."

I resented acutely the inequity of this answer; however, I did not show this for several years. All the time I was reflecting how I could bring him to feel the injustice of his finding. Finally I determined to take as my model what the prophet Nathan said to David to bring home to him his sin. Full of this thought, off I went to visit the said bishop, putting on a vexed and melancholy air. When we had exchanged compliments, I told him I had come to ask him for advice on a thing that had happened to me. To this he replied that with all his heart he would render me such service in all matters as was within his power.

"Monsignor," said I, "when I lived with my fellow-countryman, Hortense Bromsoune (Ortenzio Bronzoni), we were both very well known, had good credit, and everybody esteemed us. This induced Juan Dias d'Almeda and Diogo Mendez Botelho to confide to us a chest which contained a quantity of money. My comrade, driven by I know not what necessity, or perhaps by envy, had a false key made, and withdrew one thousand rupees from the chest. This he did in the face of all I could say to prevent him. Some months afterwards the two Portuguese came and removed their chest. It was not long before they noticed that one thousand rupees were deficient from the total sum. They complained, but as we were well supported we rejected their demand in sharp terms, and ejected them from our house, protesting that they were forgers and rogues.

"Some time afterwards my comrade died, and left me as his testamentary executor. However, as a long time had passed, the affair was no longer spoken of. Now they wish to revive it, and a few days ago I received a letter from the aforesaid Portuguese in which they set forth the distress they are in, that they have a daughter to be married, that I should reflect whether in conscience I do not owe them for that deficiency of one thousand rupees which occurred within my house."

I added some words praying the bishop to tell me as a matter of conscience whether I was under an obligation to pay that money, with the interest accrued since that time. It was to be remembered that I had not consented to the theft. He answered that I was under an obligation to pay. I took my leave and went to see the Jesuit and other regulars and priests, men learned in the law. I told them the same story and all replied to me in the same terms, but had no idea of the inference I intended to deduce from their answer. It was my object to make them admit out of their own mouth that what they had decided in my case was unjust, for my case was absolutely identical, changing only the persons. I had been robbed, the inhabitants of San Thome were consenting parties to the theft, and Manoel Texeira was the Ortenzio Bronzoni who had taken my property.

Some of those religious persons read the riddle after I had left, and they told me afterwards I was very clever. But all that was no more than compliments, for that did not hinder the greater number of them giving certificates in the very teeth of the equity of my demand, clear and evident as that was. Although this business has no interest for the public, I have thought it might serve as a warning to those who travel in these distant parts. It will teach them not to allow their property to be taken from them, for once it has gone the best arguments in the world will be useless in procuring them redress.

But now let us come back to the persecutions at Tanjor, of which I have already spoken at some length. It is my duty, dear reader, to tell you what has since taken place. At the beginning of December (? 1701) the Reverend Father Martin, Jesuit, appeared at my house. After a good deal of ceremony and compliments, he produced a letter from Monsieur Martin, Governor of Pondicherry, in which he begged me as a Christian to be so good as to interest myself in the protection of these oppressed believers, and procure for them some respite, they and their imprisoned pastors. He represented to me that their misfortunes arose from nothing but certain acts and importunities of this, that, and the other person in the king's entourage, whereby from being their friend he had been turned into their enemy.

The Reverend Father (Martin) had brought with him a large present made up of European curiosities, a mirror of crystal, and a poignard mounted with jewels in the style of this country. He expected by means of these presents to procure some letters of recommendation from the Governor-General Daoutan (Dā,ūd Khān), who had taken the place of Jufacarcan (Zu,lfiqār Khān).

He had been sent into this kingdom of the Karnātik by orders of Aurangzeb, whose domination extends over all the petty Hindū kings and governors of these countries, all of them being tributary to him, as I have (I think) already explained.

I took into consideration in a Christian spirit the misfortunes to which this new Christian community was exposed. I was also of opinion that all these presents would be useless and in vain; for this reason I did not think it advisable to present them, because these Mahomedans are very touchy, and I feared that the general might conceive some idea quite opposed to the facts. Neither did I desire the Father to go to him, though this was his intention; and he meant to take me with him, he meeting the necessary expenses of the journey. I made up my mind to avoid all this labour and expenditure by writing a letter on the subject to this nobleman. In it I besought him as a friend, and by reason of the obligation that he had always professed to be under to me, to look with a favourable eye upon the Christians of Tanjor. They had been cruelly persecuted by their king, who had unjustly imprisoned two Jesuit Fathers, my near relations. Would he have the goodness to interpose with his authority to protect the said Christians, and get those Fathers out of prison, where they were so unjustly and narrowly detained, and also procure the restitution to the former (the Christians) of the goods so unjustly forfeited? I wrote other letters on the same subject to the first minister of the Karnātik province (? the *dīwān*), who is always in attendance on the above general; also to other officers of the army with whom I was acquainted and who were great friends of mine. I sent all this correspondence to the camp by one of my servants.

After these dispatches had started, Père Martin proposed to leave for his college at Pondicherry, which is part of the same mission, and by his hands I sent a letter in reply to that of Governor Martin, detailing what I had done for the relief of the Christians at his solicitation, and as a response to the friendship with which he honoured me.

As soon as my man arrived at the army he presented my letters to the general commanding, Dā,ūd Khān, along with some presents that I sent him on my own behalf. He also delivered the other letters to the first minister and the other officers to whom I had the honour of writing. These men, having read them and learnt that the captive Fathers were my near relations, were extremely incensed against the King of Tanjor. The commanding general, in particular, and the first minister displayed much resentment on the subject; and on the spot they sent for the envoy of that prince, who is always present in the army of the general, to secure the interests of the king, his master. They blamed the king loudly for his hardihood in imprisoning the poor European Brahmans from Rome (that is the name they give the priests). To this they added some harsh and severe language, and told him they were amazed still more at the acts of the king, his master, when he knew that these Fathers were near relations of the Doctor Nicolas Manuchy, physician to the Mogul Emperor, his suzerain. To this Dā,ūd Khān added the words: "He is also my physician and my father." These last words were said by the general because from his early youth, when I still lived in the Mogul country, he had called me "father." Falling into a great rage, he ordered the agent to put such pressure on his master that the captive Fathers, the Roman Brahmans, should be set at liberty, and the Christians allowed to live according to their religion. He added: "If you do not obey my commands, I will have you put to death, and wage continual war against your master. Do not fail thus to write to him. I also require him to restore all the property that has been confiscated from the Christians."

The envoy, upon receiving these orders, wrote in the above sense to his prince, and described the manner in which he had been treated by Dā,ūd Khān. The cause of this harshness was the persecution he had commenced against the Christians, and the confiscation of their goods. He prayed, therefore, first of all for the release of the Jesuit Fathers, known as the Roman Brahmans, the cessation of all persecution of his Christian subjects, and the rebuilding of the ruined churches. As a consequence of these acts he stood in danger of his life, and His Majesty ran the risk of a war if these demands were not conceded.

While this correspondence was in progress, Dā,ūd Khān, the first minister, and all the other officers, gave indications of taking the matter very much to heart, and swore with most terrible strength at the malignity of those deeds at Tanjor. The crime was so much the greater at being perpetrated upon poor people living peaceably, who had never given their king any cause for complaint.

Thus, no sooner had he received the letter of his envoy than the king sent forth edicts, whereby he permitted his fugitive Christian subjects to return unmolested to their houses, and there enjoy their possessions as heretofore. He ordered the release of those who were in prison, and all Christians were free to follow their religion. The two European Fathers, the Roman Brahmans, were taken out of prison; but as the remedy came somewhat late, through the fault of the Jesuit Fathers of Pondicherry, it appeared that one of them, attacked by fever and dysentery, had succumbed. He was a Portuguese, and his name was Simon Carvalho; but the other, a French Father, was released, as well as the other Christians.

I also received in connection with this affair a letter from Dā,ūd Khān, addressed to the King of Tanjor. It was full both of menaces and compliments; its purport was the securing to these poor persecuted men the liberty they had lost. I caused it to be conveyed to its destination, and by way of reply he (the king) announced that on the receipt of his envoy's letter he had complied with everything: the Christians were at rest, the Roman Brahmans at liberty—though it was known that they were not Brahmans, as they asserted, but of the same profession as those that dwelt at Pondicherry.

In spite of this, the prince was terribly enraged against the Christians, even going so far as to write to all the kings, his neighbours, asking them to destroy everyone of that faith found within their states. But the letters and menaces of Dā,ūd Khān put an end to all these disorders, and not a single prince was found willing to follow the king's suggestion.

Upon the departure of the Reverend Father Martin for Pondicherry, I determined to visit that place myself, and send some of my most trusted servants to Tanjor. The latter were to make inquiries as precise as possible into the truth of the reports about the persecution. My object was to satisfy myself if what was said about the reverend French Jesuit Fathers in regard to the Hindū ceremonies they practised was true or false. On this head I assure you that the whole is quite true, following the report of my servants and the statements of certain merchants I know. In addition, there is also what I learnt about it from several French clerics and secular priests, who had seen the reports and found them to be quite consistent and in accordance with the truth.

From what I have said, and from what I said earlier, about the persecution it will be clearly seen what were its causes, its commencement, its results, its termination. In dealing with this matter, I took my part so far as my duty and my insufficient zeal impelled me.

I have already spoken of the General Dā,ūd Khān on several occasions. Here I must remark that he came to this province of the Karnātik in the month of January 1701, and on his arrival he camped below the great fortress of Arcat (Arkāt), an ancient strong place of the Hindū kings, at a distance inland from Madras of about thirty-four leagues. Thence he did me the honour of addressing me a very civil letter, inviting me to pay him a visit. To do this I had not the slightest intention.

But the governor of this locality (Madras) and his council having heard what was passing, made use of the occasion to send him a present and congratulate him on his auspicious arrival. With this object they prayed me to render this service to their company, and they associated with me in the task a Brahman clerk long in the service of the Company, whose name was Rāmāpā. At that time he was not in their service.

I started and carried with me a fine present, consisting of two cannon, several lengths of broadcloth in scarlet and other colours, other pieces of gold cloth of Europe and China, and several rarities, such as mirrors of all sizes, different kinds of crystal vases, and some weapons such as fusils, pistols, and sabres; also different kinds of wine; added to all of which was a sum of five thousand rupees. As soon as Dā,ūd Khān heard that I was coming, he desired to honour me so far as to send a captain with thirty horsemen and fifty musketeers to receive me at a distance of five leagues from his camp.

On the following day I gave myself the honour of going to visit him, when he displayed much tenderness and friendliness. Next I conveyed to him compliments on behalf of our governor, but he let me understand that he felt much resentment, and complained that they had not already paid him a visit. They had not taken the same trouble as the Portuguese to pay him the usual compliments. My answer was that when other governors had come to occupy the position he held, it was the custom to visit them at this very place where he now was. I could not run the risk of going any farther, on account of the great forests there were, filled with robbers, where I might possibly receive some injury and lose much of what I was bringing. The Portuguese could run a greater risk, for they brought nothing with them, and came only to demand favours.

He seemed satisfied with these reasons, and others that I gave him, on the subject, and after much discourse on divers matters I laid before him a letter and said to him that I had a present to offer on behalf of the governor and of the company; and I prayed most humbly that he would deign to accept it. His reply was that I need then only retire for repose to a tent which he had had erected for me close to his mansion. He would send word to me of the hour at which I could appear, as is the custom among the Mahomedans. Thereupon I took my leave of the general and retired to the tent, and it was impossible for me to get away from it to pay my respects to the first minister, Mahamad Sayd (Muḥammad Sa'īd, the *dīwān*), and all the other officers. For I expected from one moment to another to be called, nor did I wish to allow any opening for the complaint that I was not found in my lodgings.

With this thought in my mind I wanted to send the above-mentioned Brahman to visit the chief minister, but he objected that it was late, and he wanted to bathe his body according to their custom, which is to bathe every day. Although he deceived me, I believed him all the same. However, not to neglect entirely my duty, according to the customs of the court, I sent a very honest youth, that I had brought with me from

Madras, to make my compliments to the chief minister, and intimate to him my arrival in the army. I sent him word that it was late and I was unable to acquit myself of what was due from me to him, but that in the morning I would do so without fail.

About half-past seven o'clock Dā,ūd Khān sent me word that I might bring the present before him. This I did to a great extent, only keeping back in my custody the money and some of the trifling things. The reason for my so acting was that I could not then give him the money secretly, by reason of his being accompanied by many officers and other persons of consideration. Moreover, they look on it as a distinction and an honour to receive presents in public, but as regards money they never take it but in secret. I was thus obliged to beg him in a low voice to give me instructions to whom it should be delivered. He replied in the same way that I must keep it, that afterwards he would dispose of it as he judged most fitting. The Brahman Rāmāpā did not fail to notice the good reception given me, and all the honours showered upon me, as also the friendliness displayed more and more by Dā,ūd Khān. Besides, the Nawāb had fed me splendidly that evening, and had directed his major-domo to supply my table all the time I was with him just as if it were his own. For these reasons he (Rāmāpā), like a fool, proceeded to imagine that this would suffice, that the present had done all that was required, and thus it was of no use to give him (Dā,ūd Khān) anything more. It was advisable, Rāmāpā thought, to keep the money, and on this he imparted to me his idea.

He suggested that we should all the same enter it without fail in our account, and tell the governor that we had paid it over. To speak the truth, I was surprised at such a proposal, and to start with fell into such a violent rage with this Brahman that, in opposition to my nature, I spoke several sharp and harsh words to him, and went so far as to style him a thief and a traitor. For he knew very well that with the

Mahomedans no present was better or more esteemed than money.

The following day Dā,ūd Khān sent one of his servants to spy out the land, and discover from the Brahman how much money he had with him, and bring back a faithful report. He (Rāmāpā) quite forgot that the day before he had reported to another servant of this same Dā,ūd Khān that in addition to the presents we had brought some money, and this he had let out without first speaking to me.

He told the second messenger that we had brought no money at all. At this information the general was so irritated that he sent back the present he had already accepted, and displayed extraordinary indignation against the Company. Yet with regard to me, he showed me still the same esteem, and did me always the same honour as before, in my quality as his sincere friend. As for the Brahman, he declined to see him again, and ordered the door of the house to be shut against him.

However, as soon as I saw the present come back, I went off to see Dā,ūd Khān, to whom in the sweetest and most flattering language I pointed out the injury that might be inflicted on me. I prayed him most humbly, even if he had no concern for the Company, at least to call to mind our ancient friendship. I was rather esteemed and liked by the English and the gentlemen of the Company. As they had heard of the friendship and respect that he (Dā,ūd Khān) had for me, that fact had induced them to send me to him to carry through their business with him. Furthermore, they knew my honesty and loyalty.

His reply was, that as for me he would do anything I wanted, but that the English settled in the country of the king, his master, possessed a strong place most useful and highly suitable for all sorts of merchandise and traffic. They had always been left undisturbed, and yet, without regard to the past, they now treated him in the most cavalier spirit, and gave him next to nothing. They failed to reflect that they had enriched themselves in his country to a most extraordinary degree. He believed that they must have forgotten that he was general over the province of the Karnātik, and that since the fall of the Gulkandah kingdom they had rendered no account of their administration, good or bad, commencing with 1686. Nor had they accounted for the revenues from tobacco, betel, wine, *et cetera*, which reached a considerable sum every year. In his capacity of governor-general of the province he was forced to work for the progress and benefit of the king's interests. The English were very much mistaken if they thought by two thousand four hundred *patacas* (Rs. 4,800) to discharge the whole of their debt and enjoy freely all the revenues appertaining to the crown of his prince.

All this he said with the greatest imaginable fury and passion, which were increased by his hatred of the English for having killed his brother-in-law, who was slain in the fight at Cuddalore, as I have stated, while serving in the army of Sulaimān Khān, the general's brother. After his rage had cooled a little, he made me sit down beside him, and caused Rāmāpā to be sent for. To him he said in harsh words that he did not mean to accept the present, he might carry it back to the governor; for his part he did not accept presents of that sort. He would come himself with all promptitude possible to take what he anticipated would suit him better. As regards Manouchy, he would not allow of his return to Madras; he meant to retain him for himself, and still more so because he happened to want him for the treatment of some ailments.

At these words the Brahman withdrew and repaired to the tent and waited for me, so that we might concert what ought to be done at this conjuncture. But at the same moment the general called a captain known to me, named Mirmoin (? Mīr Mu'in), an Uzbak by race, and ordered him to take two hundred horse and two thousand infantry, and proceed to Madras with all the haste he could. He was to invest that place, and prevent anything going into or coming out of it. He meant to follow in person very shortly. But the coming of night hindered the execution of these orders with all the haste he desired, for they are very slow at making a start.

Thus after supper I had the time to hold a conversation with Dā,ūd Khān at great length, and still more easy was it to do so that he was in high spirits, having drunk copiously of the European wines that I had brought for him. I began this talk by remarking to him that if he was so kind as to hold me in such high esteem, I must humbly supplicate him not to send either the captain or the soldiers. The matter was of the utmost importance for my reputation, which I placed entirely in his hands. If these soldiers proceeded to Madras, all the European nations as well as the English would attribute the fault to me; I should pass among them for a man void of either faith or fealty in any business confided to me.

I also prayed him to hinder the Brahman's departure, telling him the reasons I had for this course. In no shape or form was it advisable for him to leave except in my company; to do otherwise would be to put the fat in the fire. As concerned the revenues, I pointed out to him that at the time when the English came and occupied Madras it was nothing but one vast plain full of sand, uninhabited, and without any name or fame in India. On the other hand, it should be remembered that it was now highly populous, full of active merchants and other residents. It was the money of the English and their good government that had created all that prosperity, coupled with the justice they administered to everybody without fear or favour. If he intended to act with so much harshness and injustice, all the nations of Europe would abandon India. He must recollect the income and benefits which Aurangzeb had acquired; for from what entered and left Madras alone he collected more than one hundred thousand *patacas.*

In addition, there were many merchants, weavers, cloth-printers and others, for all of whom the English provided a livelihood. Many subjects of the king of this realm and others knew very well that every year there were earned in Madras five *lakhs* of gold *pagodas* (equal to about one million *patacas* more or less), and over ten *lakhs* of silver rupees (which amounts to five hundred thousand *patacas*). The whole of this money remained in the country, and in exchange for all this the English carried off to Europe no more than some cotton-cloth. Let him reflect that if he objected to the residence of the English in Madras, and if he bothered his head about their gaining such considerable sums, it was requisite for Aurangzeb and his subjects to give them time to withdraw to Europe. They (the English) set little store by the place; yet if they were forced to abandon it, they would also give up the other towns and factories they held in the Indies. In that case they would cease to be friends and become enemies. Upon their departure they would without fail seize every ship they came across, and thereby spread ruin and desolation throughout the Mogul empire.

I pointed out to him these things, not solely in respect of the English, but also as generally applicable to the other nations of Europe who were to be found in that empire. Dā,ūd Khān was favourably impressed by all these arguments, and gave me reasonable and satisfactory answers. In brief, he issued orders to stop the departure of the troops and the Brahman.

The next day I paid a visit to the chief minister and to all my other friends, and to them I related what had happened to me, although they knew it already. However, they felt my troubles acutely, and generously endeavoured to protect me. In this way, after a few days, I was given my dismissal, carrying a confirmation of all the *farmāns* and favours accorded to the English just in the manner that they desired.

Dā,ūd K͟hān now took the present again ; and as he knew that I had the money, it being only the Brahman who denied the fact, because he wished to embezzle it like the thief and the traitor he was, he (Dā,ūd K͟hān) accepted the present favourably and thought highly of it. He told me to retain the money until he sent someone to receive it. Upon this I took my leave of him.

Next day I sent on the present that I had for the chief minister, who took it with much politeness and many thanks. This lord is one of the most polished men to be found among the Mahomedans. He invited me to his table and entertained me magnificently, one of the greatest honours that these people can confer. However, the Brahman was jealous beyond measure of all the honours received by me from Dā,ūd K͟hān, from the chief minister, and all the other officers of the army, a feeling intensified by seeing himself despised and hated.

For this reason he designed covertly to make me lose the esteem and reputation that I had among the Mahomedans, and the property I held within the English jurisdiction. To this end he tried to make use of the spies who were on the spot, men of his tribe, and wished to force them into writing to the Governor of Madras and his council that I was the sole cause of failure and the producer of all the disputes between the Mahomedans and the English. But the most intimate friends of the man knew that all he said was false, and all his inventions diabolic. They refused, but instead gave me warning of what was going on. They advised me not to put much trust in Rāmāpā. He, on the other hand, became more and more eager for my ruin and destruction, and had recourse to other methods. In pursuance of this idea he sought the advice of another Brahman he knew, and then returned to our quarters. I asked him where he had been, and he told me he had come from the general's. The latter had given him an order to place the money in the hands of the servant of a Brahman called Longcarne (? Langkaran). Directly this servant came to us, we must obey the order forthwith and without objection. He added to this several words to persuade me that such was Dā,ūd Khān's wish.

When he had finished these words he went off on other business, and instantly those servants appeared and claimed the money. They told me they came on behalf of Dā,ūd Khān. There were several of them, and as soon as one had entered, another put in an appearance. They solicited and importuned me to such an extent about this money, for which they said Dā,ūd Khān was waiting, that I remembered what the other Brahmans had said about not trusting Rāmāpā.

Then I recollected that Dā,ūd Khān had said he would inform me of the name of the person to whom he desired that I should count out this money. For these reasons, then, I would not deliver it to these servants; but to escape from their importunities I said that they had only to wait a little while I went to fetch the money. However, instead of doing this, I made all the haste I could to get out and find Dā,ūd Khān. I discovered him in the midst of many officers conducting a review of his cavalry. In spite of this, I went close to him, and twice over whispered in his ear, asking him to be gracious enough to send someone to receive the money.

To these words he replied by telling me to wait a little. When he had finished his inspection I renewed my prayer that he would be good enough to relieve me of that burden, since he knew very well that I could not guard it securely. At last, to satisfy me, he sent for his treasurer, and, after having had a good look first one way and then another, to see that no one was watching, he said to him privately, and to me also, that he must go to receive that money.

I returned to my quarters highly pleased, and there I found no trace of the lackeys I spoke of above, nor have I ever seen them since. In a little time the treasurer arrived, and I delivered the money to him in the presence of several of my friends and some servants of the Company. He, too, was very joyful at receiving it, for there is no greater pleasure to these men than when they behold the store of their master on the increase.

Some little time afterwards the Brahman Rāmāpā returned, and, although he knew all that had happened, he made no sign; on the contrary, he asserted he knew nothing whatever. But I told him I had paid over the money to the general's treasurer, and not to the men of the Brahman Langkaran. Upon this, in the humblest tone and his eyes swimming with tears, he began to make excuse, just as is their habit; for it may be truly said that these people are very much like crocodiles (*cocordilles*), whose skin changes at their will and pleasure.[1]

These difficulties occasioned me much trouble, and were all due to the Brahman; so great were they, that I was not far from losing my life. The whole affair caused me the more vexation because this Brahman had many friends at Madras, and many relations among the merchants who were influential with the governor, *et cetera*. In spite of this, by Heaven's help I was delivered entirely, upholding my own honour and that of the Company. Upon quitting the army I had the delight of hearing, mingled with other compliments, that all which had been gained was on account of me; I found myself also regaled by a very rich *sarāpā* (set of robes), which I showed to the Brahman, who also received one for himself.

About fifteen days afterwards I returned to Madras, and rendered an account to the governor of all that

[1] Does he not mean to say "chameleons."

I had done in regard to the interests of the Company and to the matters he had committed to me. This generous man, having obtained full confirmation of my story, was very satisfied, and gave me many marks of his gratitude. I did not tell him all that the Brahman had done to me, for he had besought me with tears in his eyes not to say anything. His tears compelled me to have compassion, and, instead of telling, I made over to him two lengths of cloth, thereby rewarding his ingratitude and infamous conduct by a largesse. I let him see that a generous and Christian heart (be it said without boasting) never resents the wrongs or injustice done to it.

[Some months later Manucci had further dealings with Dā,ūd Khān, who arrived at San Thome with his army, on his return from collecting tribute in Tanjor and elsewhere.]

Lastly he reached Madras with all his army. At this spot the Governor of Madras sent out to salute him Mr. Ellis, the second in council, accompanied by two other officials. They carried with them a present similar to the one I had given him when I applied for confirmation of the *farmāns* to the Company. Their orders were also to pay many compliments to the chief minister. Of all these duties the Englishmen acquitted themselves.

By chance I happened to be present when these gentlemen arrived at the camp, because I had gone there also to pay my respects to the general and the chief minister. The visitors were badly enough received; for Dā,ūd Khān declined to receive this "ordinary present" as he styled it. He told them plainly that these articles were not such as could be presented to a man of his rank. He felt astonished that the governor should send presents of such small importance; he should remember that he was the first man in the province, and lieutenant-general for the Great Mogul. He also said to them that he was greatly amazed at the governor sending a Brahman to Arkāṭ in the company of Dr. Manouchy, to take part in the discussion of their business. The matter was fully important enough to demand a man of another stamp than this Brahman, a nobody and of no standing. His amazement was all the greater, since the man had tried to do harm to Dr. Manouchy, who had been brought up in the courts of Asia, more especially that of the Great Mogul. He added some further words in my praise and to my honour, such as is not meet for me to repeat.

In the end the Englishmen were given leave to depart, and they received some very fine cloth-of-gold and silver, of which he made them a present. He added many soft and sugared words, for he declared to them that he was a firm friend of their nation; they ought to repose entire confidence in him, for he would at all times be ready to do them a service in all matters. But along with these speeches he did not omit to tell them that presents sent to a minister of his standing ought to be large and proportionate to his rank and authority.

Those gentlemen wished to make excuses, but he declined to listen. Whatever efforts they made to persuade him that they were treating him exactly like all the other *nawābs*, his predecessors, and above all, Z̲u,lfiqār K̲h̲ān, who is generalissimo at the court of the Mogul, he remained deaf to all their arguments. The English were much put out by this treatment, which was founded on nothing but cupidity. Therefore, foreseeing the inconveniences likely to be produced by his displeasure, they decided to employ some friends to plead their cause. They applied to the chief minister and others, who adjusted the quarrel. The conditions were that the same present should be sent again, adding five thousand rupees and some very rare European curiosities. After this they became friends.

Dā,ūd K̲h̲ān subsequently (July 11) sent a message

to the governor that he was desirous of visiting him, as he (Pitt) could not come to San Thome. The governor requested me to go to that place (San Thome) to receive him (Dā,ūd Khān) (July 12), and escort him to this fortress (Fort St. George). This I did. We left San Thome with fifty horsemen, as previously agreed on. On our way we met the councillors from Madras, accompanied by a part of the garrison. After reciprocal compliments between the two parties, we resumed our journey.

Upon reaching the gate of the town, we perceived all the soldiers—European and Indian—under arms, and drawn up in single rank on both sides from that spot up to the fort gate, while a number of armed men were on the town wall and the fort wall. These were arranged in excellent order, much to the astonishment of Dā,ūd Khān, who could not repress signs of admiration. Still greater was his amazement when, as they drew near the fort gateway the soldiers and officers, on catching sight of the governor, drew themselves up in line and went through divers movements which were quite unknown to him. They were only done in his honour and that of the governor. But being unaccustomed to all this military ceremonial, he was thrown into a state of confusion and apprehension. He believed himself to be already a prisoner. For this reason he spoke to me in a loud voice, requesting that all these men might be withdrawn. I reassured him, saying it was nothing but the usual ceremonial and method among these troops; he should not be in the least afraid, or suspect anything. At the same time I took care to cry out to the soldiers that they must retire.

While I was speaking the governor arrived, accompanied by a large number of officials and servants. I told him (Pitt) he must embrace Dā,ūd Khān, who by this time had dismounted with all his retinue. This embrace was given, and then the chief minister and the *bakhshī* were received in the same fashion.

Then we entered the fort, where the governor paid him innumerable tokens of respect and friendship and conducted him to his rooms. These were magnificently furnished. The bed in his room was covered with a quilt of (blank). He admired it in a way to show that he had never seen one like it before, and he begged me to ask the governor if he could give him a pattern of that coverlet, and this I did in a low voice.

The latter (Pitt), readier even to give than the other to ask, made him a present of two others. He even offered to give him the whole bed. Dā,ūd K͟hān would not accept this, contenting himself with the two bed covers, these being of a wonderful, extraordinary, and strange workmanship. Upon entering the room the governor presented to him a ball of ambergris mounted in gold, with a rich chain of the same metal. After this was done they sat down, and the conversation turned on various subjects with offers of service. When the talk was finished, the governor sent for wine, and drank to the health of King Aurangzeb to a salute of thirty-one guns.

Dā,ūd K͟hān responded to this by drinking the health of the King of England to the sound of as many cannon as before. Then they drank the health of the chief minister (*wazīr*), Asad K͟hān, who is nowadays Mirolo Morao (*Amīr-ul-umarā*)—that is "Noble of Nobles." This title was borne by Aurangzeb's uncle and father-in-law (*i.e.* Shāistah K͟hān, died 1695). A salute of twenty-one guns was fired. This was followed by a toast to Zul,lfiqār K͟hān, and one to Dā,ūd K͟hān himself, each with the same number of cannon. To end with, they drank to the *Dīwān*, the chief minister of this general, and to his *bak͟hshī*, each time to the sound of fifteen cannon.

He was astonished at the rapidity and dexterity with which everything was carried out, and was highly gratified by it all. While these ceremonies were taking place, they made him a present of several cases of liqueurs, spirits, and wines of Europe of different sorts. All these he greatly prized. Next he was led into a large hall adorned with all kinds of arms. There he found a magnificent dinner prepared in European and Indian fashion. He admired the variety of the arms, for which, however, he had no envy, unless for the spears. Having asked the governor for one, two were given to him.

He then went to seek repose for an hour, and after that took his leave. The governor accompanied him as far as the fort gateway, the general protesting against his coming any farther. There they reiterated their compliments and polite speeches, and Mr. Pitt wished him a pleasant journey. On his side the general put forward many offers of service, and assured him of a perpetual peace, wishing him every success in his enterprises and trading; and said he would ever remain his friend and protector so long as he ruled the province.

The governor did not withdraw until Dā,ūd Khān had mounted his horse—nay, wanted to hold the stirrup for him, but this Dā,ūd Khān would not allow. But to me he said in a low voice that he would like to be saluted with some salvoes of artillery as he was leaving the town. This desire was carried out, the musketeers also accompanying him to the boundary of San Thome. I went with him half-way there, when he said that as it was already late I might go back to Madras. All this he said with many compliments and a thousand expressions of civility, ending by saying that he hoped to pass still two or three days in my house at the Big Mount, and rest himself there. I consented with the greatest pleasure, as may be imagined. I went there to see him before he started for Arkāt, when he gave me a valuable set of robes, and repeated his offer of serving me just as he was used to do on previous occasions.

The above is the mode in which things happened and an arrangement was arrived at, the Mahomedans making profuse protestations to the English of service and friendship. We shall see next how these perfidious men acquitted themselves of such promises. At the end of December 1701 I was at Pondicherry on business connected with the Tanjor persecutions, of which I have already spoken. At the end of January in the next year (1702) I had trustworthy information that Dā,ūd Khān and the *dīwān* and the whole army were about to leave Arkāṭ again for Madras. This fact I learned from different sources through various friends and officials known to me, some of whom sent a warning to me that during this march some harm was intended to Madras.

He had received peremptory orders from the court to deal rigorously with the English.

This news forced me to forsake the pleasant company of the French, in order to return with all possible haste to Madras. I arrived there on February 2 of the same year (1702). On my taking leave of them the governor, François Martin, and the other officials of the Royal Company, strongly enjoined me to let them know what happened between the English and Mahomedans, sending off immediately express messengers (*pions*). This requisition I executed without fail.

A few days afterwards I warned Governor Pitt of Dā,ūd Khān's approach. In fact he arrived at San Thome two days afterwards. On my advice they sent him a Mahomedan servant of and trader under the Company, named Coja Ammad (Khwājah Aḥmad), as also another merchant of the town named Narāpā. But the second man fell ill and only the first named went; I went also.

There I found the general, the *dīwān*, the *bakhshī*, and all the officers assembled. They received me most cordially, showing many signs of joy and embracing me. They sent without delay for Khwājah Aḥmad, who appeared at once. They directed him to inform the Governor of Madras that they desired his presence at San Thome. They had important matters to communicate to him. If he could not come himself, would he send the second and the third in council (February 4 or 15)? Then Dā,ūd Khān and the *dīwān* turned towards me, and said I must confirm to these gentlemen (the English) whatever Khwājah Ahmad had been ordered to report to them. Then taking me aside privately, they told me to be sure to tell the said governor to come himself without fail; or send the two others of his council. Then they said we must both return to San Thome, showing thereby that they had no confidence in Khwājah Ahmad, and had no belief in his truthfulness.

When we arrived at Madras we went together to see the governor, and told him what the Mahomedans had charged us to say to him. To this he replied that he neither meant to go himself nor send any of his council. He declined to do so on several grounds, principally because neither the second nor the third nor anyone else could speak " Maure " (the language spoken by the Mahomedans). But he urged me earnestly to return to the general (Dā,ūd Khān) along with Khwājah Aḥmad, and explain the reasons which hindered him from complying with his request. If he had any negotiations to make with him and his council, he could conduct them safely through Khwājah Aḥmad as their qualified procurator.

The real reason why the governor declined to send anyone is that he feared the Mahomedans might oblige them by force to execute some writing by which they undertook to be responsible for all piracies throughout the seas, and on all the coasts of India. This is what they (the Mahomedans) had done at Sūrat to the other directors of the companies of France, Holland, and England. Or he feared they might be seized and constrained to pay considerable sums to recover their liberty. This was a customary enough act among the Mahomedans, and yet it would greatly injure their company.

However, Khwājah Aḥmad and I returned to San Thome. I repeated to Dā,ūd Khān and the *dīwān* all that the governor had said to me. As I was about to leave I perceived that things were approaching a rupture, whereupon I humbly besought them not to employ me in such thorny affairs. The intention of the two Mahomedans was to make use of me as mediator between the two parties. They had great faith in me because I spoke the language fairly well, and they imagined that without harming much the one or the other, I should deal with things to their advantage and that in some degree I should adopt their side rather than the other.

Thus they laid before my eyes the great danger the English stood in of losing Madras. In so doing they somehow forgot that I, too, had been suckled in Europe as much as the English; that, for the honour of my country and of all the other European nations, I was under greater obligation to them (the English) than I could possibly be to the Mahomedans. Under these circumstances I parted from them as civilly as I could, and on sufficiently good terms, in order to be able to advise the governor of what I thought best for his reputation and the defence of the town.

[The English made preparations to resist any attack, protesting at the same time against the high-handed methods of Dā,ūd Khān, who confiscated thirty loads of fine cloth and also took possession of three villages. Their protests were of no avail.]

However, Dā,ūd Khān and the *dīwān*, having come to the conclusion that the English were quite resolved on resistance, that the town was fairly strong and very well provided with artillery, and had a garrison of eight hundred seasoned soldiers, decided to send a message asking the governor to send me to San Thome. They were ready to discuss matters with me and settle the dispute to the advantage of the company. In spite of some time having elapsed without my having seen the one or the other of the parties, the governor lost no time in sending me.

After an exchange of the usual compliments, Dā,ud

Khān began his reproaches about the English, whom he designated as over-proud and defiers of his king's orders. In reply, I laid before him several arguments, which I will not set forth, to avoid wearying my readers. All I will mention is that I showed to him the great harm being done to the king's interests by the way he was acting. For these nations, worn out by such continuous ill-treatment, must inevitably in the end leave the country and close their trade; but as soon as ever they got out to sea they would capture every merchant vessel they came across. They would make descents upon the ports upon the sea-shore, would carry off all they could find, would give quarter neither to rich nor poor, and wherever they landed would spread fire and desolation.

To all this I added that, if they declined to listen to these arguments, so important in the interest of their king, I would, being his (the king's) servant, go to the court myself and prove to him the innocence of the English and the injustice being done to all Europeans. No consideration was being paid to the fact that these merchants were neither the defenders nor the protectors of these pirates, from whom they also suffered, and it was this very cause that made it impossible for any of the European nations to suppress them, or give the king the undertaking that he demanded.

In spite of this, Dā,ūd Khān wrote to the French at Pondicherry, the Dutch at Negapatam, and the Danes at Tranquebar, calling on them to send men and ships to help him against the English at Madras. These people, all of them, made excuses. While this was in progress attempts were made to appease the Mahomedans by pleasant words, and making them limited promises. They were not thereby deterred from continuing their investment (of Madras), although carrying it out less rigorously than at first; in fact, four Englishmen who had been made prisoners at San Thome by Dā,ūd Khān's orders, when on their way from Cuddalore, were now released and sent here (Madras), each being presented with a *chaal* (shawl).

I communicated to Monsieur Martin, Governor of Pondicherry, all that happened between the Mahomedans and the English. I told him it would be a good thing to send some men to Dā,ūd Khān and the *dīwān*, so as to turn their minds from doing at Pondicherry what they were then doing at Madras. Thus that governor (Martin), who is extremely prudent and well versed in the Mahomedan way of governing, decided to send one person with some presents for Dā,ūd Khān, the *dīwān*, and some other officials. Consequently, on the 15th of the month of March of this year (1702), Monsieur Desprez, a merchant of the Royal Company, arrived at San Thome, and at once informed me of his presence, sending me a letter from the governor. In it Monsieur Martin recommended me to this gentleman, and prayed me to aid and assist him in his negotiations with Dā,ūd Khān and the other officials.

As soon as I heard this news I threw up all the business I had at Madras, and transferred myself in all haste to San Thome, wishing to be of use to the French to the utmost of my powers. This desire was increased by the fact that I have always esteemed, and shall continue to esteem, them by reason of their fine qualities and the honourable attentions with which they have overwhelmed me.

After I had arrived at San Thome I had a conversation with the said Monsieur Desprez. I found him very much troubled; for never before, all his life long, had he been concerned in a similar business, and had never paid a visit to a Mahomedan of this rank. I gave him encouragement, and told him I would do all that was necessary to carry through the affairs of the Royal Company. I would accompany him on his visit to Dā,ūd Khān, the *dīwān*, the *bakhshī*, each one separately. This I did, and he was well received by these lords, who gave him many testimonies of the regard in which they held the French, and betrayed to him their pleasure at the French having sent to compliment them so very politely.

Monsieur Desprez had brought a present for Dā,ūd Khān, and one for the *dīwān*, and never dreamt that the *bakhshī* would also require to be remembered. But I adjusted all that; I observed that there was enough in what he had brought to bear division into three parts; this I did. In this way they were highly contented, and he obtained his leave to depart after a very short delay. It took him only eight days to get through the business. When he said good-bye, the *nawāb* and all the other officials requested him to assure his governor of their friendship. He might live unconcerned, nor need he have the slightest doubt about the respect they had for his personality; and in all that lay in their power they would be always ready to help the French of the Royal Company. It sufficed that Monsieur Manouchy was the governor's friend to ensure their giving all the help that lay in their power, for was not he (Manucci) loved and respected by all the ministers of Aurangzeb?

Dā,ūd Khān sent to Monsieur Martin a very fine horse, valued at one thousand rupees, along with a costly set of robes; another set was given to the said Monsieur Desprez. The *dīwān* and *bakhshī* also gave him a very good set each, and sent him off in a satisfactory manner. He bore with him a complimentary letter to the governor, and the latter was highly satisfied, being hardly able to contain himself for joy at being thus delivered from such rascals.

In the year 1703 I received a letter from Dā,ūd Khān and another from the *dīwān* Chaadetulcan (Sā'ādatullah Khān), and several others from other lords. By these letters they entreated me to visit them, especially as they had much need of me. I began my journey on

February 27 of the same year (1703), and found the said general at the town of Carpa (Cudapah, Kaṛapa), distant one hundred and twenty leagues from Madras. I was very well received by these gentlemen according to their customs. They asked me to be so good as to treat a captain named Mohamed Jafar (Muḥammad Ja'far), a Persian by race. I would not undertake the case, for he was already moribund—in fact, he died a few days afterwards. During the short time I was with their army I got no time to rest, for everybody pestered me, as their way is, for medicines—even those who had no need of them. They would say as a reason: "I have no appetite; give me some medicine to make me eat like an elephant, or like a camel, or, at any rate, like a horse." And all these brute-like demands simply to have strength to slake their sensuality, for their minds are filled with, and they have no other diversion than, the desire to steal all they can, for no other object than the accomplishment of their carnal desires.

At the end of fifteen days they gave me leave to go in an honourable manner, conferring on me a *sarāpā* (set of robes) and enough money to pay the cost of my journey. These gentlemen gave me a letter for the governor of this place (Madras), conveying many thanks for having sent me, and they told him other details of my journey. Verbally they directed me to say to the said governor that he must give back three villages, those that Ẕu,lfiqār Ḵhān had presented to the Honourable Company of England in the days of his being governor; since then fresh orders had been received to take possession of them again.

I arrived at Madras, and carried out the orders that had been given to me. But the governor, Thomas Pitt, paid no heed to the message; for having much experience he knows perfectly the manners and customs of this kind of people. They seek continually fresh methods of capturing some money. His reply to them was, that he was the owner of the villages, and that he meant to keep them, so much so that to this day he remains in possession.

On this reply there came certain menaces, but in the end the thing blew over without further disturbance.

The said *dīwān* gave me another letter for the Governor of Pondicherry, Francois Martin, which contained but some compliments and friendly expressions. But the said *dīwān* or governor directed me verbally to say to the said Sieur Martin that he had received orders from the King Aurangzeb to obtain the lands controlled by Pondicherry. The answer given (by the French) was that they had been bought from the hands of Roma Raja (Rām Rāja), son of Shivā Jī, that afterwards they had received them back at the hands of the Dutch; that the lands were in their possession, and they meant to keep them to all eternity. After this reply they sent him a few presents, and since then nothing more has been said about the matter. It is the fashion of these Moguls to make a display of power (in this way) and proclaim themselves all-powerful and masters of everything. Subsequently, when they discover that they cannot overcome either by force or artifice, they dissemble, but if at a future time an occasion presents itself, they keep neither their word nor the friendship that they had promised.

Country between Madras and Cuddapah

I noticed in this little journey that the country is full of hills, and that the roads are very narrow. Thus, had the inhabitants displayed any courage or valour it would never have been possible for the Moguls, with all the forces at their command, to make themselves masters of it. I also beheld several ancient fortresses built by the Hindū princes of the Karnātik; for those who are nowadays in command on behalf of the Mogul had been warned of my approach, and invited me to visit them. Each one made me a present, such as some pieces of silk, some shawls, *et cetera*, and treated me most splendidly according to their fashion. It is true that they did not present these things to me for nothing, for in return I gave them such medicines as they wanted.

I noticed that these fortresses had not been designed by good architects or engineers. The works are (? weak) in spite of their walls being built of great hewn stones fixed in cement, and their being provided with hollows or ditches right round them. In some ditches there is a water supply, in others none. The forts have also some pieces of artillery twenty to twenty-five feet long, of which the calibre is so extremely large that a big fat man can easily get inside. The greater number of these guns lie on the ground outside the fort gates. There are, in addition, a few inside in different positions. I also noticed some small pieces on the walls and bastions, carrying a ball of from one half-pound to three pounds weight. They were mounted on heavy blocks of wood, without carriages or wheels, and their muzzles pointed into the air.

Their only use is to make a noise and smoke on the days when a new moon appears, or when it is intended to frighten someone, for to go through any drill with them, or to teach how to aim them in one direction or another, that is an impossible thing. Nevertheless, the Mogul never omits to sanction the money necessary for efficiently providing all these fortresses, and sees that there are faithful officers in charge, such as Darroges (*dāro͟ghah*) Ammy (*amīn*), and Morseg (*mushrif*)—that is to say (blank in the original). In addition there is a commandant at each fortified place. But the whole lot are thieves, and the places are kept like cowsheds.

During this journey I also received an invitation from Gulla Maly Can (G͟hulam 'Alī K͟hān), governor of the fortress of Velours (Velūr, Vellore), my ancient friend who gave himself up to Dā,ūd K͟hān, as I have related. This lord received me with great joy, the more so that at the moment they were in the midst of feasts and banquets in honour of some grandson of his. This event he had looked forward to for several years past, and now attributed to the virtues of my medicine the appearance in the world of this new heir to his wealth. For this reason he gave me several things and uttered many expressions of gratitude; in addition he sent with me as an escort twenty-five horsemen and five matchlock men.

The fortress of Vellore is large and well built. It has lateral supporting walls and the ditch is large, about fifty cubits in width, and filled by springs rising in it. The water is full of crocodiles, and if by misfortune anyone falls into it he is at once torn to pieces and eaten up by them. Out of curiosity I went quite close to the ditch; these animals, seeing on the water the shadow of human beings, at once opened their jaws. I threw them a goat, which they tore to pieces at once and ate, snatching the pieces out of each other's jaws. I observed that at the noise these made other crocodiles rushed from different parts of the ditch. They were in such great numbers, and there was such confusion, that they could not be counted. They kept their heads out of the water and their jaws wide open. As a pastime I threw them several goats in pieces; they fell upon the pieces, and without any chewing swallowed them at one mouthful. At another place I made the men throw in some heads of goats with large horns. But no sooner had they been thrown in than the crocodiles with a toss of the head had at once swallowed them, for these animals are monstrous. It can also be said that they render the fortress stronger, and defend it from any assault that might be delivered. But what protection are they against the high hills surrounding the place, from the summit of which the walls could be knocked down by pieces of artillery?

According to the custom of the country there come at times strange men who, as a sacrifice for their sins, throw themselves into this ditch. The Mahomedans often sacrifice buffaloes, cows, goats, *et cetera*, and all this forms the food of the crocodiles. Dā,ūd Khān, when he mastered the fortress, had all the thieves caught in the army thrown to these crocodiles. This he did by way of a thanksgiving sacrifice for the reduction of a place of such fame. This is what they ordinarily do to secure good success in their designs.

PART IV

Dā,ūd Khān visits San Thome

After Dā,ūd Khān had taken the fortress of Pilconda (Penūkonda), as already stated, he came to San Thome in the month of November (1706). Before entering the town he rested for one day and one night in my house, situated at the foot of Monte Grande (the Great Mount, of which I have already spoken). I was unable to go out myself to meet him by reason of the heavy rain then falling.

The following day he came on to San Thome, and went straight to see the Lord Bishop, prostrating himself at his feet, as is their custom in the case of religious mendicants. The bishop received him in the church with music and instruments. On his leaving he presented three hundred and fifty rupees to the household of the said Most Illustrious, and then retired to his tents.

As I was anxious to pay him a visit, the Governor of Madras, Thomas Pitt, asked me to go in company of the envoys he must that day send. I acceded to the governor's wishes.

The envoys were the following: Mester Rabart (Raworth) and Mester Fedorik (Frederick), both of the Council; the third Mester Devenport (Davenport), secretary, the fourth Mester Canosbin (Coningsby), both well-born, well-instructed young men of good carriage. Joined with them was the doctor of the Honourable Company, called Doctor Botler (Bulkley).

The four above-mentioned gentlemen were mounted on handsome Arabian and Persian horses, while the doctor and I were in palanquins. During the march there went in front one hundred halberdiers, men of the country; behind them were carried two flags, and after these marched sixty-two European soldiers, commanded by a sergeant. We went on and found Dā,ūd Khān in a large tent erected on the sea-shore, and fitted with carpets. He was seated on a small bedstead and clothed in simple raiment. On our entering the tent he rose and embraced us all, then made us sit near him. He displayed much urbanity, and was most courteous. After exchanging compliments, we passed an hour and a half in conversation with him. He professed himself a warm friend of the governor, praising his good administration.

Upon giving us our leave he presented us each with an emerald ring worth two hundred rupees, and placed in the hands of Mester Rabart (Raworth) a jewel to be presented to the governor; it was worth five hundred rupees. He remarked that he was sending it in sign of remembrance, and he would be glad to meet him and drink a glass or two to his health in his company.

The next day the governor sent him a messenger, a person of standing, with many compliments, to say that he would expect him during his march. Dā,ūd Khān started, but half-way reflected that the English would never permit his entry with a number of retainers and that some dispute might arise between the soldiers on both sides. Thus, stipulating with me to get his salute of guns from the city, he halted. He proposed going to a garden belonging to an English resident of that city, and sent word to the governor that from certain reasons he had changed his mind as to his visit. At once there started to greet him the same Englishmen as specified above, and with them a young man, a private merchant named Mester Lester (Lister), son-in-law of Daniel Chardin, also a famous merchant, and much esteemed by him (Dā,ūd Khān). I, too, was of the company.

The banquet which had been prepared was carried to the garden along with several cases of good wine. When the meal was finished they made him a present of eight pieces of broad-cloth of various colours, different pieces of silver plate, such as candlesticks, *pān*-boxes, basins, inkstands, boxes, scent-sprinklers, *et cetera*, two large mirrors in gilt frames, several chests of liqueurs, Persian wine, and rose-water, a large quantity of dried fruit, almonds, walnuts, filberts, pistachios, apricots, *et cetera*, the whole amounting in cost to seven thousand rupees. The Nawāb, pleased and satisfied, resumed his journey, and passed six days in San Thome. I felt it my duty to pay him a visit every day in return for the obligations I was under, and also because he asked me.

As Dā,ūd Khān was suffering from sciatic pains, he sent a man to beg the governor of this place (Madras) to do him the favour of lending him the services of his medical man to treat him. In reply the governor sent his doctor with all the articles requisite.

At this time (when Dā,ūd Khān was laid up) the Lord Bishop went to pay him a visit, and gave him a present of some torches and candles of white wax. He explained that he was a poor "darvesh" and had no wealth with which to find presents. He was received most courteously. On the next day Dā,ūd Khān went to see him, and said good-bye. He was received in the way I have already described, and once more he gave the bishop three hundred and fifty rupees. He drank a considerable quantity of wine, and the principal Portuguese inhabitants, to the number of four, were present.

One day before his departure I went to take my leave. We then had a long conversation, and he expressed his approval of the liqueurs and cordials that on several occasions I had forwarded. I now presented some more. He gave me a present of a costly set of robes, and of three hundred and fifty rupees. He added that it was only a small sum, and must be made over to the little children in my house; and he would not ask me to accompany him, so as to spare me the fatigue of the march, I being a man already getting on in years. He begged me to continue my friendship as before, and he would never forget me.

During the conversation a dispatch-rider arrived from the court with a number of letters. Among them was one from Ẕu,lfiqār Khān, of whom I have already spoken. By it he entrusted him with some business, and also in it directed him to make over to me seven hundred rupees as a present. Dā,ūd Khān executed this second commission on the spot. That noble (Ẕu,lfiqār Khān) had been condescending enough to write to me several times to ask for some lotions and medicines, by means of which his wife, who suffered from her eyes, had been cured.

Dā,ūd Khān started, and took with him the doctor. Before they left he gave him one hundred and fifty gold pagodas, which comes to five hundred and twenty rupees in silver, and a valuable set of robes.

Marriage of F. Martin's Granddaughter

Two days after the departure of these French captains the marriage took place of the Lord Governor Martin's granddaughter to Monsieur Ardancour (Hardancourt), commissary and second councillor. A grand banquet was given, followed by music and dancing, at which were also present the son of Governor Ruberto (Gabriel Roberts) of the fortress of Tevanapatam, and a councillor called Mester Barlu (Mr. Berleu). When the festivities were ended, they returned to Tevanapatam, and I in their company, wishing to pay a visit to Governor Ruberto (Roberts), my old friend. This gentleman received me with great politeness, and after several healths were drunk we had music and dancing.

In the midst of this joyous intercourse there reached me, almost at midnight, a mounted orderly bearing a letter, which recalled me with all urgency to Pondicherry. I was wanted at once to treat the Lord Governor Martin, who was seriously ill. Upon hearing this sad news I and the rest of the company were much pained, not merely at having to break up our feast, but equally at learning of the grave indisposition of an old and affectionate friend. At once I was given my leave to depart, on condition of paying another visit to Tevanapatam, which I promised to do.

I began my journey at once, and at break of day arrived in Pondicherry. I found the good old man, then seventy-three years of age, in a high fever, with pains in the head, absence of sleep, and other symptoms. I started on the treatment forthwith, and held a consultation with the doctors of the Royal Company, one of whom was named Monsieur Maquari, and the other Monsieur Albert. By our efforts and the drugs we administered he was placed out of danger, and by dieting and care was restored to perfect health.

Not to break my word, and in compliance with the messages sent me, I went back to Tevanapatam, to the contentment of all my friends; thence back to Pondicherry, and finally back to my own house in Madras. Here I received news that a Monsieur Delavale, a married man and resident of Junçalam (Ujung Salang), a land belonging to the King of Siam, had turned pirate. It is three years ago that he came to Madras in the guise of a merchant. I gave him money to trade with, as did many other persons of this settlement. Having acquired enough money and a supply of goods in this country, he left it. To disabuse his creditors of any hope they entertained of being repaid—at any rate, the capital amount—he captured an English boat loaded with cloth from Bengal, and took its captain a prisoner.

The governor of the place (Ujung Salang), on the facts being reported, sent orders to seize Delavale; but he fled, followed by all his companions, taking with him the prisoner, but abandoning his house and wife. The governor of the country took possession of his wife and of all the merchandise. Monsieur Delavale sought refuge in another province of the same kingdom, ruled over by a man who was an enemy to the other governor. The followers of this pirate Delavale are two in number, one called Monsieur Masson, the other Monsieur de Roubal. These events have caused such consternation among the merchants, that not one of them will venture on a voyage to that port.

Family Troubles of a French Doctor. Manucci Concerned

[A certain French doctor being on bad terms with his wife, she left him, and, taking her youngest son with her, fled to her relations at Lāhor.]

The afflicted surgeon made great efforts to recover his little son, but never succeeded. The child's detainers were too strongly protected. Maria de Ataides taught him in the Mahomedan way, and he learned to read the Qurān. The Maria de Ataides in question had an ancient eunuch in her service who directed her household. He was a very avaricious man, and advised his mistress to kill her niece and take possession of her property. The lady, without further consideration, accepted the proposal, and gave her niece poison.

While the niece was in the throes of death, an old woman-servant of hers came secretly to call me in. I started in all haste, but did not arrive in time to be of any use to her, the whole of her body having already become black. Therefore, when I had enjoined her to ask God's forgiveness, she called upon the name of Jesus as well as she could, and shortly afterwards expired. When the surgeon heard of his wife's death he was quite happy, and over and over again asked the king for leave to return to his own country, but all in vain. Once more he wrote a letter to Maria de Ataides, in which he said she ought to send back his son at once. If she did not, he had decided to make the boy over to Begum Ṣāḥib, who would send men to seize him.

Maria de Ataides was annoyed at this threat, and was, in addition, afraid of some censure against her being issued by the court. Thus she had the boy circumcised at once, and continued his training in Mahomedan tenets. Whenever I had the opportunity I never omitted to console the boy, to teach him, and to hold out hopes that his father would still be of some benefit to him. Seeing that the youth received consolation from, and believed in, my words, and being also anxious to deliver him from Mahomedanism, I took the liberty of saying to him that if he wanted to leave that house and go to his father, I would help him, and provide the necessary expenses. I knew that his father was waiting for him, and meant to marry him to the daughter of the officer in command of the fortress of Damān, who was providing her with a dowry of twenty thousand rupees. To these overtures the youth replied that he would carry out all my orders. At once, and in secret, I found four guardians who could represent the youth before the courts if, upon obtaining his liberty, he should endeavour to recover part of what belonged to his mother. The youth left the house secretly and joined these guardians, who were waiting. They took him without delay to the *qāẓī's* court, a man who was my friend, and to whom I had in addition recommended this client's interests in the shape of some presents I had given him.

The guardians' action was such that the boy Ignatio was restored to liberty, and recovered something, though nothing of consequence, out of what had belonged to his mother. This small effort cost me two thousand rupees, which equals one thousand *patacas*. I reported to his father, then at the court in Dihlī, what had been managed, at the same time advising him that as soon as his son arrived he should send him into Portuguese territory, so as to be protected from Mahomedan outrage.

When Ignatio reached the paternal dwelling he was very pleased, but, finding that his father was not sending him away from Mahomedan territory, as I had suggested, he said to him: "My father, why do you keep me in the house and do not at once send me into Portuguese territory? Do you not see that one of these days the Mahomedans will come to steal me?" The ignorant father answered that he kept him in his house to revenge himself on Maria de Ataides, and to be able to recover the plunder that his wife had robbed him of. What an impossibility!

Thus my counsels were of no use to him, nor did in aught avail the words and repeated insistence of his son. We shall see what things came to pass. After twelve days the men of Maria de Ataides went to Dihlī, and, asserting that the youth was in his father's house, they went before the king, and recounted to him the above circumstances. Forthwith the king ordered soldiers to be sent to seize the youth and bring him to the presence. As soon as the king saw him he appointed him one of his pages, with charge of carrying his sword during audience, being a well-formed and graceful youth. Then after some years he was appointed captain of artillery, and at the present time is married and has sons and daughters.

The old surgeon stayed on at court without obtaining leave to depart. Then he decided on flight from Aurangābād for Damān. This he managed to do, but the end was not favourable. At the time I arrived at Sūrat orders had been received to catch the surgeon, who had fled from the court. He was very easy to recognise, for he bore a knife scar across his face from one ear to the other, due to a wound inflicted by one of his compatriots. I was then in Dihlī newly from Persia. The governor, in his attempts to find the surgeon, learnt that a surgeon (that being I) had arrived from court.

At once he sent off a messenger to my house, who informed me, on behalf of the governor, that I must at once appear in his presence. At that time I had fever, and the insolent fellow (they are all like that) would not take my excuses, or accept the complimentary message I sent to the governor, whose name was Cartalapan (Kār-ṭalab-Khān). The man spoke with great rudeness, and made as if he meant to take me away by force. At this movement I lost patience, and, getting to my feet, gave him several shoe strokes, and threw him downstairs. Thus, beaten as he was, he returned to the presence of the governor with outcries, making out a little more than he had suffered. As the governor was a cautious man, he sent a person of standing, making over to him a letter from the court, in which was entered the mark on the face as a means of recognising the surgeon.

On his reaching my house, as soon as I saw him I recognised that we were old friends. He reported the facts to the governor, and he sent word to me that as soon as I was well again he would come to see me. Three days having elapsed, the fever left me, and I repaired to the governor's. I was well received by him, as he required medicines from me. Whilst we were in conversation they brought in the surgeon. He was taken away that night to another house, and next morning was sent back to court. These events took place in 1680, in the month of September. In 1686 the king consented to his leaving, looking on him as a man already old and no longer of any use.

This same doctor in 1672 had another mishap. Being then, as I have said, desirous of leaving for Europe, he expended seven thousand rupees on diamonds. He showed his purchase to a young man who in his wanderings had arrived at his house. Being a fellow-countryman, he placed great faith in him, and never dreamt of his plotting treachery against him.

One day when the doctor had gone to make his appearance at court, the ungrateful youth opened the casket with a key that he had got made, and took the diamonds and as much money as seemed to him necessary for expenses. He then fled. He might have carried off a great deal more than he actually took, but this he refrained from doing, not wishing to carry such a weight as would hinder the celerity of his movements. When the surgeon returned from the audience hall to his house, he perceived the loss he had suffered. By much exertion he sent off different persons in many directions to search for the thief. He also wrote to the (European) factors living at the seaports. But all his efforts produced no results, for never more was that young man heard of. It may well be that he was robbed by other thieves and his life taken, as on many occasions I have seen happen.

I pray the prudent reader not to grow angry at such advice, but if I write it so often, I do it solely to warn any inquiring traveller who may wish to wander through the world, and teach him at others' cost how to look after himself. In voyaging prudence is required, and, above all, patience, for in most instances it is only through the rashness of youth that such difficulties arise ; and men are generally the originators of their own ruin, and may even risk the loss of life. The following story may serve as an example :

When I was a youth, at the beginning of Aurangzeb's reign, it was my custom to go out on Thursdays. On that day there is a great concourse of men and ladies of the city (Dihlī) who come out to visit sepulchres and obtain recreation in the gardens of K͟hwājah Quṭb-ud-dīn, outside the city of Dihlī—as I have said before—some to pray and some to enjoy themselves. I, too, went to take the air in those gardens. I was also curious to see certain festivals that it is usual to hold several times in the year in the fields and gardens, and on the banks of streams, reservoirs, *et cetera.*

While returning one day from the garden of K͟hwājah Quṭb-ud-dīn on the way to my house, I saw a carriage coming a long way off. It withdrew out of the direct road, and went down into the open fields. Seeing this manœuvre, I assumed that it had moved out of the highway for fear that I might do it some harm. I knew that in the carriage was a public dancing girl; it was surrounded by fifteen pages, and followed by a horseman. Without taking time to reflect, I turned my steps with all possible speed towards the carriage, shouting to it to stop. It paid no attention, however, to my voice, but went on its way peacefully.

Seeing that I was not obeyed, I decided to make a display of courage, so I seized a stick, and, going up to the carriage, gave the pages several blows. Seeing that the game was not a joke, these men followed the example of the horseman, abandoned the carriage and took to their heels. At that point I raised the cloth that covered the carriage, and saw the dancer. I gave her some abusive language, not forgetting, however, to keep my eyes open to see if succour was on its way.

This precaution of mine was not uncalled for, since at this moment I saw afar off a troop of cavalry coming in my direction. I left the carriage at once and directed my steps slowly towards the horsemen in question, while I adjusted my turban firmly on my head, and handled my sword to see that it would come easily out of the scabbard, just as if I was making ready for a fight, should I be opposed. During this interval I had drawn near the horsemen, making these preparations meanwhile. They now drew rein; one of them, however, who was in advance, came on towards me. In spite of having his face half concealed, I could see he was a man of some age. When he was near me he spoke to me politely and modestly. However, I gave no answer to his words, and went on my way with my eye fixed steadily on the other horsemen, who were standing still. I believed they meant to bar my way. I was greatly mistaken, however, for on my passing quite close not a man of them said a thing to me.

The following day I made the same excursion, taking my lance with me this time. While I was in a plain of some size and fairly level, I saw the carriage of the previous day a little off the road guarded by some horsemen. I knew at once that these were the same men as before. Nevertheless, not to show that I had any fear of them, I would not retrace my steps, but continued my journey, flourishing my lance about a bit, until I was quite close to them. Then the elderly horseman, with the greatest politeness and a smiling face, asked the favour of speaking a word with me. Directly I heard the voice I stood still, and turning towards him the point of my lance, I asked what it was he wanted.

He answered modestly that he was the brother of Allahwirdī Khān, that he had fallen in love with this dancer, on which account the king had reduced his high pay. Out of love for her he endured all this hardship, and gave up everything. Therefore he asked me the favour of permitting him to go and come freely. Without changing my position I answered that I granted what he asked, on condition, however, of his throwing over the carriage a scarlet covering, so that I might identify it. He answered that he would do so, and went away after saying good-bye.

The man's name was Mirzā Arjanj, brother of that Allahwirdī Khān who betrayed Prince Shāh Shujā' when he delivered battle against Aurangzeb, as will have been seen already in my First Part. This Mirzā Arjanj, being resolute in not giving up the said dancer, was content that the king should take away two hundred horses from his command, and leave him only ten, with twelve thousand rupees of yearly pay. He endeavoured to become friendly with me, but I declined to waste my time on him or put any trust in him.

One day, while I was out on one of the above excursions, I amused myself in those gardens for longer than usual, and night came on before I had half completed my journey. By the light of the moon, which was now very bright, I observed coming towards me some strings of camels and oxen laden with goods, guarded by mounted soldiers. To afford myself a bit of a game, I drew my sword and charged them, with shouts of "Mora, mora!" (*Māro, Māro!* ("Strike, strike!") On hearing my cries, all the men fled and abandoned the animals. When I had arrived quite close, and found there was no one there, I rode my horse in all directions, crying out that I was only joking. Moreover, I was no thief, therefore let them return and look after their animals. My voice was given to the winds, since no one appeared. I resumed my journey and made for my house. Afterwards I learnt that it was the baggage of a viceroy, who was proceeding to his government of the province of Ajmer; but no one over found out that it was I who had caused the stampede.

It is the custom in the Mogul country for the royal elephants, whether those meant for war or those which fight before the king, to be kept outside the city near the gardens. They stand in a field below some trees, they are bound with heavy chains, and their keepers live with them. I once went at night to tease these animals with fireworks. They broke their chains and rushed wildly over the fields, doing a great deal of damage. Next I received word that some cavalry soldiers had been posted on guard to seize the insolent intruder; thus I forbore to molest the elephants any more. Just let the judicious reader imagine what would have been my punishment had I been taken, and into what disgrace I should have fallen. To-day, although now in old age, when I remember this and other similar escapades I committed, I never fail to sigh over them and grieve at my misdeeds.

I must not forget to tell what happened to me on the day of the Virgin's Feast—that is, on December 18, 1705. It was at Monte Grande (Big Mount) at three o'clock in the afternoon. I was in the middle of entertaining several guests, who on that day never fail to appear, for a great crowd assembles there for this solemnity.

While I was in the middle of conversation with my friends, men of different nations, I noticed that a serious dispute was going on at my gate. My servants were hindering the entrance of certain audacious persons who wanted to come in by force. I, too, proceeded to the spot. Although I saw they did not mean to listen to argument, all the same I attempted to prevent any violence, but quite in vain. The insolent fellows persisted in their attack, but were finally put to flight.

There remained in our hands the captain of the men; he was a Brahman officer, who ruled over some villages not far from Big Mount. He was drunk. I ordered the man to be tied to a tree over against my gate, and he received a good thrashing. He was then taken before the Mahomedan governor (*faujdār*) Mullā Murād, in San Thome. He is the present governor of the territory, and is a nominee of the great *dīwān* and minister of the Karnātik.

When the captive reached the *faujdār's*, the principal officers and some of his relations presented themselves. They tried hard to throw the whole blame of the misdeed upon me, and they accused me as the culprit. Some of the Mahomedan officials supported their contentions. The judicious governor was not taken in by these fabrications, but on dismissing my servants he sent me a letter full of ceremonious expressions. He paid no heed to the contrary suggestions of the Brahmans, my enemies.

Perhaps he had doubts that if he had acted otherwise he would be either reproved from court or dismissed from his office. He knew very well that the chief ministers were my friends. The man who has no friends in these lands is nowadays despised, and it is of no use for him to be in the right.

As it seems to me, I have not explained in detail the way in which I was treated when in the service of the Prince Shāh 'Ālam. Now, to demonstrate once more their policy, their style of government, and the mode in which their business is done, also how much the ladies at this court can accomplish, I will resume the subject. By this means the reader will learn what is the value of friends upon occasion.

There was at the court of the Prince Shāh 'Ālam a European blood-letter who, when he entered the service, was granted two rupees a day. This was done by the influence of the chief physician, Muḥammad Muqīm, of whom I failed not to speak on other occasions. The blood-letter, finding the prince had a good opinion of him, and having by this time acquired a little money, made a most unreasonable demand from the prince to the detriment of the said physician. He said to the prince that Muḥammad Muqīm had an annual salary of over one hundred thousand rupees, besides the other great profits that he received. But Muqīm was not any wiser than he, the European, was, and therefore he, too, was worth quite as much pay. The prince, upon hearing this preposterous claim, was much put out, but concealed the fact, and gave not a word of reply. The physician Muḥammad Muqīm heard of the affair by means of his friends. He was much annoyed, but made no sign, and did not betray his feelings in the least.

I had already been known in the empire for many years when I reached the court after the heavy loss of money in Portuguese territory of which I have already spoken. I was then much in need of money for my support. As soon as my arrival was heard of, I was at once invited by the prince and several of his princesses to accept service with him. The message was conveyed to me through a eunuch of some standing named Meccaian (? Miskīn). To this proposal I replied that I would be really glad to accept the honour done to me by His Highness, but I must decline to accept his service unless the physician, Muhammad Muqīm, conducted the negotiations with me. Thereupon it was at once ordered that he should present me to the prince, as is the custom.

At this time Shāh 'Ālam was making his preparations for starting to take charge of the Dakhin. The physician Muḥammad Muqīm, remembering what the European blood-letter had done to him, feared the same conduct from me also. He further reflected that I had cured several persons of quality whom he had given up as beyond hope, whence he was afraid he might lose his reputation and be ejected from the service. Thus, in spite of his promises, he took no steps to push my interests.

The leading princess, as a sign of her affection for me, sent me food daily, and made me presents of different kinds of fruit. Seeing that the date of departure was close at hand, she asked my permission to deal herself with the prince on my behalf, since the physician had done nothing. Before this, I had requested her not to speak on the subject. My reply to her now was, that I begged as a favour she would not speak to the prince on the subject, as I had left it to the discretion of the physician. This I said in spite of my being in great straits from the want of money, and my sufferings from the persecutions of my adversaries, the aforesaid (European) blood-letter (of the prince) and the (European) surgeon of the king, of whom I have spoken above. I stood strong and firm in my decision in order to prove to the physician, Muḥammad Muqīm, and those others, the vast difference there was between one person and another, and that he might see my upright modes of action.

I held my tongue for several days, looking out for some movement on the physician's part. Finally, seeing that he was not forwarding my interests, in spite of his making a great show of wishing me well, I left the court, gave up my house, and took refuge in the house of a friend named Luis Gonzalves, intending subsequently to remove to the city of Lāhor, where I had lived for a number of years. On the day that I disappeared the princess as usual sent me some gifts of food. When it was reported to her that I had gone, and it was not known where (the news reached her rather late) she was much grieved. She shut herself up in her room, and would not go to the garden to join the prince as was her custom. He passed his time there listening to music and other pastimes.

The prince noticed the absence of the princess. Not aware of the cause, he sent to invite her, letting her know that he was waiting in the garden most impatiently, for without her there could be no joy. The princess, aware of the great love the prince bore to her, sent back to say that she had been kept awake and troubled by a slight ailment; would he, therefore, excuse her for that day? Hardly had the news reached the prince's ear, than he quitted the entertainment, and with all possible haste made for her apartments. He saw she had nothing the matter beyond being in low spirits, so he pressed her to tell him the cause of her melancholy.

But the princess in a graceful way made excuses, just exactly as ladies do when they are intent on having their own way. Finally, being forced into consenting to explain her ill-humour, she said it all sprang from the thought that His Highness did not love her to the extent that he asserted; because, if his love were really such, he would not have neglected to entertain at court, and taken into his service, the physician Manuchi, a man who knew her constitution, a man who had nursed her as a little child in his arms.

Taking her by the hand, to these words the prince replied that when morning came he would send in search of me, and pledged his word of honour that he would do so. Women can do much, and demand a good deal as soon as they perceive that they are held in estimation. On this occasion, that was how the princess acted; therefore she replied to the prince that that very moment he must write an order to the principal eunuch, Nāẓir Daulat, directing him to send off a troop of soldiers, who at the time were on guard, to trace me out. Prince Shāh 'Ālam gave way to the wishes of the princess, and the soldiers, rushing about all night, made a fruitless search for me.

However, they came in the end to know that if I were in any place in the suburbs of the city, I should not be found anywhere else than at the king's artillery park, in the house of my great friend, Luis Gonzalves. In fact, when it was already full daylight, being seated in the garden, I observed one of the prince's guard thrusting his head in at the door, but as soon as he saw me he withdrew it at once. Having seen this man, I was a little reassured, guessing what it might be for, when in a moment or two there entered twelve troopers in the highest glee. They treated me most ceremoniously, and in a few words conveyed to me that the prince was waiting for me, and I must start quickly.

At these words I pretended to turn a little uneasy, as if they had need of me for some case of illness. They assured me that everybody was in good health, and I was sent for solely with a view to do me honour.

The men urged me to start, and, to tell the truth, I was extremely eager myself, yet concealed it, and gave signs of the exact contrary of what I desired. I told them to let me go to sleep, during which time they, too, could sit down and rest. To sum up, we began our journey about nine o'clock in the morning.

Meanwhile, let us look at what was going on about me at the court. By this time the princess had given up hoping for my return, and carried her lamentations to the prince. Shāh 'Ālam went forth to hold audience, and asked his chief minister and counsellor, Casmir (Qāẓī Mīr), where Manucci had gone to. The Qāẓī, knowing nothing about my disappearance, replied that I was in the city. Shāh 'Ālam then ordered him to include me among the servants of His Highness. Upon receipt of this order, Qāẓī Mīr suggested that Manucci had heavy expenses; it was therefore necessary to give him an honourable rate of pay. The prince thought over this for a little, and then instructed him that he should give me seven rupees a day, the sum that his blood-letter had received. My friend Qāẓī Mīr put on a dejected air, and made this suggestion: "Your Highness ought to know that the father of your blood-letter was barber to the father of Manucci; thus he would never accept that rate of pay."

At these words, another friend of mine who was present, named Mirecautaula, came forward three paces, and, making obeisance, said, "If Your Highness permits me to speak, I will inform him of what I know about Manucci." The prince turned his eyes in his direction, and with a smiling face said he might speak. Mirecautaula then started: "Does Your Highness know that Nawāb Mahābat Khān offered him through me three hundred rupees a month, with a palanquin, robes, and food, yet Manucci would not enter his service?" Having said this much, he bowed and returned to his place. The prince asked him whether, if he were to offer me three hundred rupees a month, create me *manṣabdār* (noble) of the court, would I accept? Mirecautaula replied: "Maybe he will agree, this being a royal establishment." The prince ordered Qāẓī Mīr to settle with me, and obtain my consent. This is the way they are accustomed to act in this court when they want to give a helping hand to anyone.

While this was in progress, I arrived at the house of my friend, Qāẓī Mīr, not far from the court. He was not long in making his appearance. As he was coming in at the door, I went to meet him with the usual compliments, but with a very long face, in spite of my knowing all that had taken place. The moment he saw me he put his hands to his sides, halted, and showed all the signs of being quite worn out, telling me: "To-day I laboured in a cause which very seldom is carried to success in the Mogul court; you are already made a servant of the Prince Shāh 'Ālam, and have as pay three hundred rupees a month, and in addition you are a noble of the court."

With a humble countenance, making an obeisance, I rendered him sincere asseverations of my gratitude. But Qāzī Mīr, observing that I had not changed my expression one little bit, nor shown any sign of gladness, came to the conclusion that I was dissatisfied. Therefore, coming closer to me, he suggested that for the time being I ought to accept the pay that had been fixed. He could assure me it would very soon be increased, and this he repeated at least twice.

Discovering by these remarks that he had not perceived that I was more than content, in order to let him see the truth, I drew back one pace, and lifting my head and my voice, I said: "I accept with all goodwill the honour that, through your mediation, His Highness has done me, and I live in the hope of receiving through your protection still greater." Thus did I reassure Qāẓī Mīr, and inform him that I was satisfied. Embracing me, he took me by the hand and led me into the house. We had dinner together, then he presented me with a horse (which I was much in want of) and a valuable set of robes, thereupon I returned to my own house.

As soon as I reached my house, the princess sent me her usual gift of food, together with a thousand rupees, giving me to understand that this money should serve as a help for the expenses I might have to incur in connection with the ensuing march, which was to begin a few days afterwards.

The eunuch Nāẕir Daulat sent a man to call me, whereupon I paid him a visit and sat down in his presence. On seeing me he shook his head and said: "You are the man who had the royal gates opened at unsanctioned hours, a thing never allowed in the royal palace." I replied that to have the royal gateway opened at that hour was due to the generosity of His Highness, who desired to favour a foreigner.

This man (Daulat) was a great friend of mine, as I experienced on many necessary occasions, as will have been seen. In opposition to the habits of his class, he was of a good disposition, and very liberal. He had sixty horses in his stalls, and sixty camels loaded with pieces of cloth and other valuables. His tent was like a general's, and in his suite were noble horsemen. He was much esteemed at the court because he behaved prudently; his income was very large, owing to the offices he held, and his words were listened to by the prince.

I likewise give an account of the manner in which it is usual to bleed the princes, at what seasons it is done, and what happened to me on such occasions.

Ordinarily the princes and princesses have themselves bled twice in the month of March, and the interval between the two bleedings does not exceed twenty-four hours. The operation is begun half an hour before the setting of the sun. Three days afterwards they take a purge; but if necessity demands a shorter interval they do not wait the three days, but are governed by the requirements of the case. In the month of September the same procedure is repeated.

The first time that Shāh 'Ālam had blood let by me I was summoned to the *Maal* (*maḥal*), which means the palace, and went into the *saral* (*ṣarāe*)—that is, seraglio. He showed me his arm, inquiring if his veins were visible, and asked if I should give him any pain when I drew the blood. When I heard this question, I took hold of his arm, and looking at it, said without a pause that the vein could be opened without the least difficulty, and he would be quite satisfied. I quickly tied his arm with a bandage of fine broad cloth without stretching the skin very much. As I took up my lancet to make the incision, he stopped me, and said I ought to stretch and rub the arm well, as other blood-letters did. I answered that His Highness need not be alarmed, that I knew what I was doing.

I took hold of the arm again and at once made the incision, opening the vein without going so deep as other practitioners do, by which practice some days must be passed without being able to move the arm. What I noticed on this occasion was that the prince betrayed signs of fear, turning away his face until the blood had been taken. It is customary to keep ready for these occasions a set of silver scales and weights; the basin for receiving the blood is also of silver.

On the ground is spread a large sheet, in order not to dirty the carpets and floor-cloths; over the body of the prince is cast another sheet, somewhat smaller. All the princes are present at the operation, as also the principal eunuch, and some under-eunuchs who act as attendants. It is the business of one of these to throw a little charcoal into the blood that is collected from the vein, also a little bit of iron, some small coin, and a few grains of raisins for the preservation of the blood. After all these ceremonies they bury the blood in the garden, also performing other customary superstitious observances. When the incision is made all those who are present make profound bows, adding the words: "May the blood-letting be to your benefit." The same ceremonial is followed in the case of a princess.

As soon as the surgeon has left the room alms are distributed. When I had finished the blood-letting the prince ordered them to give me four hundred rupees. At the time of my reaching the gate a eunuch handed me the said money on a salver, telling me it was proper for me to make a bow with my face turned towards the palace. I did so, according to the custom of this court.

When I gave an order to my servant to take charge of the said rupees, the insolent eunuch said to me, "It seems to me you could never have had as much money in all your life." At once I took the salver and emptied out on the ground all the money in it in the presence of the gate-keepers, telling them I made them a present of it. Then I turned to the eunuch: "Do you not know that I am the son of the chief physician of the King of Spain, who is lord over half the world and owns the mines of silver? My father, being tired and in a hurry, on one occasion missed the vein; but, seeing that the king required to be bled, he made another stroke, and hit the right place. In spite of this my father was so sorrowful for the error he had committed that the consolation offered by the king had no effect on him. Therefore, out of the love he bore him, and in the hope of restoring him to happiness, the king gave him a town as large as the town of Sihrind, together with a galleon laden with silver, which had just reached the port of Cadiz. Out of these revenues and moneys my father sends me twenty-four thousand rupees for my expenses, since the pay I receive from this court barely suffices for the expenditure in my kitchen."

All this I did and said solely to the end that it should not be thought that I was needy, and also to let them know my lofty way of looking at things. My prince, when he knew what had happened, said that he felt I must have been brought up in the midst of riches. He sent me the money over again, recovering it from the porters, and added to it a valuable set of robes and a fine horse. He said he must maintain the customs of his court, but without my being subordinate to anyone, and that I should have entire liberty.

Another mysterious thing happened to me when first I drew blood from the wife of the prince, called Nurnixam (Nūr-un-nissā) Begam. The lady thrust her arm out from the curtain, as is the custom, and, holding my lancet, I moved forward to open the basilic vein. I was still at a distance of six inches from the arm, when suddenly the princess turned round and threw up her arm violently towards the lancet—I know not whether through fear, or simply in changing the position of her body. The instrument went into the basilic vein, and blood flowed.

The prince, who was present, patted me with his hands on the shoulders (a sign of pleasure), and applauded my ability in having opened so skilfully so difficult a vein as the basilic. At this unrehearsed success I cannot tell you how I felt. Pallor spread over my countenance at the thought that all that portion of the lancet which projected from my finger-ends had entered the basilic vein, and might cut the artery. Having this in my mind, I stood watching the blood flow with no little apprehension. However, when four ounces had been lost, I noticed that I had not in any way touched the artery; on the contrary, I had struck exactly on the basilic, and thus I was reassured without having betrayed my concern.

The princes who were in attendance, although they had observed the difference of method in this extraction of blood, nevertheless did not attribute it to accident, but to the dexterity of my hand, and as such they spread it abroad, talking me up as a great master of surgery, although it was really an accident. In this way I left the court, after obtaining great honour and valuable gifts, in addition to being praised by everybody.

I have already spoken of the Persian physicians, and of their inability to believe or admit that European doctors are acquainted with medicine, but I will insert, nevertheless, an instance that occurred in 1679.

While I was at the court of Shāh 'Ālam in Aurangābād, there arrived a Venetian physician named Angelo Legrenzi. He came from Aleppo, having quitted the service of the Most Serene Republic, and at the age of thirty-five had set out in search of fresh fortunes. He had thought out various ideas, and collected in his head many thoughts.

He came to see me, and delivered to me a letter of recommendation from the Reverend Father Fra Ivo, Capuchin, of Sūrat. I received him with every civility, making an offer to him of a share in my house, including a companion of his called Signor Protazio, a German gentleman. I was highly delighted at his arrival, in the hope of ridding myself of several patients, who all day long came in search of me personally. Forthwith I gave him out to be my relation, in order to obtain him more respect. I took him to the presence of the chief physician, Mamed Muquin (Muḥammad Muqīm), of whom I have already spoken, with the object of getting him, too, entry to the court, with handsome pay from the prince, and thereby prevent any hindrance to his practising. The chief physician promised me the new-comer should have a place, but patience was required.

The worthy patrician, seeing how well I was treated, was full of joy, but would not comply with my advice. He showed he was in too great a hurry to enter the prince's service and draw his pay. As a proof of his ability, and that he was not a surgeon, but a physician, he prepared a pamphlet, in which he discoursed on the four principal fevers, of their causes, and the remedies for driving them away. Seeing that he had little confidence in my word, and none at all in that of other friends, I took him with me to the said chief physician; Legrenzi presented the pamphlet, and its contents were explained.

Muḥammad Muqîm, while listening to this talk, seemed pleased and contented, and by his face indicated that he approved of such good arguments. On his side Legrenzi was equally satisfied, in the belief that he had done rather well by presenting his work, which would cause him to be valued at the court. Knowing the contrary, I said to him how much I should rejoice if he met with success. At the time of saying good-bye the chief physician said to him that he could repeat his visit to the court.

I continued to aid him with a horse and servants, who every day attended to him, for the chief physician lived over half a league from my house. This going and coming lasted for over half a year without the chief physician making over to him any patient, or speaking any more to him. Our patrician did not perceive what it meant. Finally, one day, to undeceive him, Muḥammad Muqîm ordered one of his servants, an Armenian, called Joseph, who acted as interpreter, to sit down near him.

Our patrician was offended at this act, and on his return home he reported it to me. I did not know what else to say to him than that we must have patience. The following day he went back to the court, and wasted his time seated there for over three hours. Finally the chief physician accosted him by asking him whether he knew what thing God was. At such a demand Legrenzi was stupefied, and made no sort of answer. By this request he understood that he had received his dismissal, and his joy was turned into sadness. Thus he went back the way he came with lamentations over his strange fate. He was well received, and appointed again to the place that he had quitted. Mr. Protazio remained with me, having no money to pay for his journey. After a year, however, he started, and I helped him so far as I could, and I heard no more of him.

I now state what happened to me. On December 15, in the year 1706, it was the pleasure of the Divine Power to remove from this world my wife, with whom I had lived more than twenty years. The grief I underwent at that melancholy moment I neither know how to, nor ought I to, recount. All I will say is that it was the more profound for never having been experienced before. But, just as it appears to be the way of the world that sad events always come in company, and are never solitary, on the 29th of the same month Monsieur Martin died; he was the Governor of Pondicherry, nowadays called Fort St. Louis. By this second death I was plunged into nearly the same grief. He had been very much my friend, my true and ancient friend, and I had received from him great—very great—kindness, civility, and honour.

Still, in spite of all these misfortunes, I was well able to console myself by placing reliance on the Divine Will.[1]

[1] There are no further personal details in the original MS., which closes with a lengthy and detailed account of disputes between the Jesuits and Capuchins at Pondicherry. We have no further trace of Manucci at Madras or Pondicherry, and only slight evidence of his death in India in 1717 (see Introduction).

INDEX

'Abbās II, Shāh of Persia, 9, 10, 11, 12, 14, 16, 20; gives banquets in honour of Lord Bellomont, 11, 14, 15, 20; parades his cavalry in honour of Lord Bellomont, 16; and the Island of Ormuz, 27; and the eunuch Daulat, 159

Abu,l Ḥasan, King of Gulkandah, and Manucci, 193, 194, 195; and Shāh 'Ālam, 194, 196

Āgrah, Aurangzeb and Murād Bakhsh arrive in, 73

Āgrah, Bellomont at, 36; Bellomont's remains removed to, 37

Āgrah, Dārā and his army leave, 53, 54, 55; directed to retreat to, 58; takes flight to, 69

Āgrah, English factory at, 36, 38

Agrah, Manucci at, v., 36, 124, 141, 163, 164; takes flight to, 71; tries to leave, 72; has to remain in, 73; leaves in disguise, 74; starts for, 110

Āgrah, Shāistah Khān, appointed governor of, 74

Āgrah, references, 33, 87

Āguada, fort at Goa, 179

Aḥmad, Khwājah, sent as envoy to Dā,ūd Khān, Pannī, 251, 252

Aḥmadābād, Dārā takes possession, of, 86

Aḥmadnagar, Manucci accompanies Shāh 'Ālam to, vi; Shāh 'Ālam and his force arrive at, 190

Akbar, King, ordered fortress to be built at Allahābād, 112

Akbar, Prince, son of Aurangzeb, asks permission to build a ship on the river of Goa, 166, 167; builds the ship and has it removed to Vingorla, 168; a watch set to prevent his leaving Vingorla, 169; writes for Sambhā Jī to the Viceroy of Goa, 171; at Vingorla, 175

Albert, Mons., doctor at Pondicherry, 267

Aleppo, 287

Alexander the Great, 25

Algarves (a province of Portugal), 184

'Ali Mardan Khān, who made over Qandahār to Shāhjahān, 159

'Alī, tomb of, at Iṣfahān, 23

Allahābād, account of fortress and rivers at, 112, 113; Manucci at, 112, 113, 114, 124

Allahwirdī Khān, at the battle of Khajwah, 104; 274

Almeda, Juan Dias d', 230

Alreu, Joaõ Rodrigues de, prevents Manucci's marriage with the Pathan widow, 158, 159

Alvor, Count of. *See* Tavora, Francisco de

Amānat Khān, at Lāhor, 150, 151

Andrada, Andre da, Portuguese renegade at Masqaṭ, visits Goa, 137

Apollo, the god, 36

Arabia, 28, 184

Ararat, the mountain called, 6, 7

Aras, the stream called, 6

Arfaxad, King of the Medes, 7

Aristotle, 160

Arkāt, Dā,ūd Khān, Pannī, at, 236; leaves for Madras, 251

Arkāt, references, 247, 250

Armenians: at Smyrna, 2; merchants with Lord Bellomont's caravan, 3, 7; at Erzerūm, 5; at Erivan, 6; merchants at

Tabrīz, 8; Lord Bellomont in debt to, 15; at Iṣfahān, 22; at Shīrāz, 24; merchants at Burhānpur, 32; musical instruments employed by, 107
Asad Khān, 249
Asia Minor; Bellomont and Manucci travel through, v.
Assam, Mīr Jumlah in, 117, 118
Ataides, Maria de, and the French doctor's son, 268, 269, 270
Audience-hall of Shāhjahān, 42, 43
Augustinians, Portuguese, their church at Iṣfahān, 23; valiant resistance against Sambhā Jī, 170
Aurangābād, Aurangzeb at, 32; Manucci at, 140, 141, 287; with Jai Singh at, 129
Aurangābād, 270
Aurangzeb: at Aurangābād, 32; prepares to seize the throne, 51; stratagems and intrigues, 55, 56; his army, 56, 57, 58; signal to traitors in Dārā's camp, 58, 62; advances with his army against Dārā, 60; in danger of being taken, 65; arrives in Āgrah, 73; communications with Shāhjahān, 73; succeeds in making a prisoner of Shāhjahān, 73, 74; starts in pursuit of Dārā, 74; appoints Shāistah Khān Governor of Āgrah, 74; makes Murād Bakhsh a prisoner, 74; leaves Lāhor, 82; arrives at Multān, 83; tempts Dā,ūd Khān with high pay, 84; leaves Multān, 85; and the Rajah of Srīnagar, 87; how he rewarded Jīwan Khān, 97; offers to take Manucci into his service, 98; details of march to Kashmīr, 102; the royal kitchen, 103; an early start, 104; order of the march, 104; how the route is measured, 105; the royal standards, 106; Roshan Ārā Begam and her retinue, 107, 108; plan of camp, 108; special royal tents, 109; Manucci's aversion to, 111; orders destruction of an idol at Benares, 114; in Kashmir, 124, 125; sends Mahābat Khān to Gujarāt, 125; orders Mahābat Khān to be poisoned, 149; Manucci translates his letter for the viceroy of Goa, 166; orders Shāh 'Ālam to march towards Goa, 176; at Aḥmadnagar, 190; M. negotiates with, on behalf of Governor Gyfford, 215; and the English, 216; sends Dā,ūd Khān, Pannī, to the Karnātik, 232; and the English in Madras, 242; references, 36, 54, 59, 67, 72, 81, 88, 112, 119, 130, 141, 167, 169, 181, 183, 197, 226, 249, 258, 274
Avicenna, 160
A'zam, Mīr, second envoy sent by Shāh 'Ālam to the Viceroy of Goa, 177, 178, 179
A'zam, Sulṭān, on the march to Kashmīr, 106
'Azamat-ud-daulah, chief minister of Shāh 'Abbās, 9, 11, 12, 14, 20; interviews with Lord Bellomont, 13, 15, 16, 17, 18, 19
Azevedo, Antonio de, brings news of Dārā's defeat to Āgrah, 71
Azevedo, Thome de, physician at Goa, jealous of Manucci, 220, 221
Azil Can, poisons Diler Khān, 213

Bahādur Khān (Mīr Bāba), advances with Aurangzeb's army, 60; sent to patrol roads west of Āgrah, 72; commands troops sent in pursuit of Dārā, 84; and the surrender of Bhakkar, 90, 91; governor of Allahābād, 114; story of his vain-glorious behaviour, 126
Balasor, the harbour of, 118
Balkh, the envoy from, Manucci doctors a relation of, 99, 100, 101; manners and customs of Uzbak nobles from, 100, 101, 102; the King of, 101; the holy man of, story of his madness, 150, 151, 152
Bandar 'Abbās, 25; Manucci and Bellomont at, 26, 27; English factory at, 27; bad effects of water at, 27, 28
Bandar 'Abbāsi. *See* Bandar 'Abbās
Bandar Congo, 138
Bandora, on Salsette Island, Manucci settles at, vi; resolves

to retire to, 162; arrives at, 163; leaves, with A. Machado, 164
Banquets, given by Shāh 'Abbās in honour of Lord Bellomont, 11, 14, 15, 20
Bardes, taken possession of by Sambhā Jī, 170, 174; the town of, plundered by order of Shāh 'Ālam, 182; the river of, 178, 181, 182; reference, 189
Barqandāz Khān, Manucci's commander, pleased at his rejoining, 77; leaves Multān with Dārā, 83; Manucci hires house belonging to, 142
Barro, Antonio de, Jesuit, 222
Basant, Khwājah, in command of boats sent to Bhakkar, 82; put in command at Bhakkar, 84; at Bhakkar, 86; defends Bhakkar against Khalīlullah Khān, 87; enraged by letters from Khalīlullah Khān, 88; his reply to the letters of Khalīlullah Khān, 88, 89; receives orders from Dārā to surrender Bhakkar, 90; and Lashkar Khān, governor of Multān, 91; and Manucci, at Lāhor, 91, 92; receives messages from Khalīlullah Khān 92; in danger, 93; is killed, 94; reference, 97
Bassain, Manucci at, v, 134, 135; warns I. Sermento of, 133; and the commissary of the Inquisition at, 228
Bautista, Frey Iraõ, Father Prior of St. Augustin's at Huglī, Manucci visits, 118, 119, 122; reference, 121
Begam Ṣāhib, revenues of Sūrat given to, 31; farewell to Dārā, 53, 54; message from Dārā to, 69, 70; answer to Dārā's message, 70; reference, 269
Begum Ṣāhib. *See* Begam Ṣāhib.
Beiçaõ, Luis, assists Manucci to demonstrate European mode of fighting, 128, 129
Bellomont, Lord, takes Manucci into his service, v, 1, 2; travels through Asia Minor, v; Persia, v; in India, v; death of, at Hoḍal, 1656, v, 37; at Raguza, 2; at Smyrna, 2; arrives Brūsa, 2; departs, 3; at Tokat, 3; Erzerūm, 5; at Erivan, 6, 7; at Tabrīz, 7, 8; at Qazwīn, 9, 10, 11, 12; at Iṣfahan, 12, 13, 14, 15, 16, 17, 18, 19, 20; interviews with 'Aẓamat-ud-daulah, 13, 15, 16, 17, 18, 19; haughty behaviour at audience with Shāh 'Abbās, 20; ill at Shīrāz, 24; leaves Shīrāz, 25; at Lār, 25, 26; at Bandar 'Abbas, 26, 27; at Sindī, 28; at Sūrat, 29, 31; supplied with money by Henry Young, 31; at Burhānpur, 31, 32, 33; at Sironj, 33, 34; at Narwar, 35; at Gwāliyār, 35, 36; at Dholpur, 36; at Āgrah, 36; remains removed to Āgrah, 37
Bellomont, Viscount. *See* Bellomont, Lord
Benares, rivers at, 113; Manucci at, 114
Bengal, Manucci's journey by boat to, 116, 117, 118; reference, 268
Berleu, Mr., 266
Berlin, Königliche, Bibliothek at, purchases MS. of Manucci's "Storia," 1887, viii
Bernier, François, Manucci comments on his inaccuracy, 110
Betel leaf. *See Pān*
Bezoar stones, 24; Manucci makes use of, in treatment, 144
Bhakkar, fortress of, Dārā's army leaves for, 82; Dārā and his followers arrive at, 84; besieged, 86; the evacuation of, 91; references, 50, 98, 110, 111
Bhāo Singh, Manucci attends, 205
Bhīmā, the river, 138, 140
Bhiwandī, 134
Biāh, the river, Manucci meets Dā,ūd Khān at, 76
Bianco, Jorge, a Genoese merchant, 220
Bibliothèque Nationale, Paris, volume of portraits now in, ix
Big Mount, Dā,ūd Khān stays at M.'s house at, 263; attack on M.'s house at, 276; M.'s house at, reference, 250
Bījāpur, city of, 134, 136, 228; Manucci at, 134; the King of, 133; Kingdom of, M. in, 138; references, 176, 190, 191

Biyās, the river. *See* Biāh, the river
Blood-letting, mode of, with royal patients, 199, 200, 283, 284, 285
Bombay, fortress of, invested by the Moguls, 216
Botelho, Diogo Mendez, 230
Boureau-Deslandes. *See* Deslandes
Bridges at Iṣfahān, description of, 21, 22
Bronzoni, Ortenzio, friend of Manucci, 230, 231
Brūsa, Bellomont and M. arrive at, 2; depart from, 3; Anthoine Cheleby, Governor of, 2, 3
Bulkley, Dr., English envoy sent to Dā,ūd Khān, 263, 264
Burhānpur, Manucci and Bellomont at, 31, 32, 33; Armenian merchants at, 32; description of, 32; Manucci at, 141

Cadiz, 285
Capuchins, Manucci's account of their disputes with Jesuits, vii; their church at Iṣfahān, 23
Carmelites, bare-footed, their church at Iṣfahān, 23
Carvalho, Simon, 234
Castro, Antonio de Mello de, Viceroy of Goa, 136
Catrou, Père, and Manucci, viii, ix; publishes book in 1705, founded on Manucci's "Storia," viii
Cavalry, Persian, parade of, 16
Chaghatāe Khān, 90
Chambal, the river, 36; Dārā and his army reach, 55
Champat Bundelah, 33; helps Aurangzeb, 56; fate of, 58; references, 197, 226
Champat, Rajah, son of Champat Bundelah, treated by M., 197
Chānd Bībī, her defence of Aḥmadnagar, 190
Chardin, Daniel, 264
Charles I, King of England, 13
Charles II, King of England, 2, 7, 12, 13
Chaul, the town of, 112
Chāwal, the Hindūs of, complain to Jai Singh, 132, 133
Cheleby, Anthoine, Governor of Brūsa, 2, 3
Chhatarsāl Rāe, advances with Dārā's army, 61; reinforces Dārā, 64; killed, 65
Chināb, the river, 146, 157
Chiūtia, the Rajah of, Manucci sent as envoy to, 129, 131
Christian religion, the, Manucci and, 126, 127
Christiana, Dona, a widow, and M., 227, 228
Clarke, Elizabeth, *née* Hartley, Manucci marries, 197; her death, 289
Congo, Port of, 25
Coningsby, Mr., English envoy sent to Dā,ūd Khān, 263, 264
Costa, Dom Roderigo da, commander of Portuguese fleet, 174, 178, 217, 218; M. applies for protection to, 221
Cota, Luis Gonsalves, secretary at Goa, 185, 186, 220, 221
Couza Coutinho, Antonio de, friendly to M., 229
Crocodiles, at the fortress of Vellore, 260, 261
Cromwell, 2
Cudapah, Kaṛapa, M. visits Dā,ūd Khān at, 257; country between Madras and, 258
Cuddalore, 240, 255
Cunha, Joaõ Nunes da, Viceroy of Goa, organises expedition to Masqaṭ, 137, 138; Cunha, Lourenço da, of Goa, tricks M., 224, 225

Dakhin, the, M. follows Shāh 'Ālam to, vi; 33
Dalmatia, 2
Dalpat Rāo, M. refuses to attend, 225, 226
Damān, the Portuguese of, 131; Portuguese territory extending to, 133; M. at, 163, 166, 225; references, 269
Damaõ. *See* Damān
Danes, the, Dā,ūd Khān asks, to help him against the English, 254
Dangim, the fortress of, Viceroy of Goa receives Sambhā Jī's envoy at, 173
Dārā, M. enters service of, v; to, petition of Thomas Roach, 40; expresses a desire to see Manucci, 47; interviews Ma-

nucci, 48; takes Manucci into his service, 49; and Shāhjahān, 51, 52; farewell to his father and Begam Ṣāḥib, 53, 54; leaves Āgrah with his army, 53, 54, 55; his army encamps at Dholpur, 55, 56; receives letter from Shāhjahān, 58; leaves camp, 59; advances with his army, 61; adopts counsels of Khalīlullah Khān, 63; shows great valour, 63, 64; receives bad news, 65, 66; routs Sulṭan Muḥammad and Najābat Khān, 66; listens to traitorous advice, 67, 68; takes flight to Āgrah, 69; sends message to Shāhjahān, 69, 70; advised to proceed to Dihlī, 70; starts for Dihlī, 71; hostile reception at Dihlī, 71; starts for Lāhor, 71; raising a new army in Lāhor, 74; pleased at Manucci's fidelity in rejoining him, 77; starts for Multān, 78; at Multān, 81; leaves Multān, 82; discharges Dā,ūd Khān from his service, 83; arrives with his army at Bhakkar, 84; makes Manucci captain of the Europeans left at Bhakkar, 85; leaves Bhakkar for Sindī, 85; reaches Gujarāt, 86; takes possession of Aḥmadābād, 86; raising a new army in Gujarāt, 87; a prisoner, 90; orders Primavera to surrender Bhakkar, 90; his dismissal of Dā,ūd Khān, 116; references, 36, 42, 97, 98, 111, 197, 226

Dārā, Prince. *See* Dārā

Dārā Shukoh. *See* Dārā

Darius, King of Persia, 24

Dā,ūd Khān gives Manucci a passport, 76; marches with Dārā to Multān, 81; fidelity to Dārā, 83; takes service with Aurangzeb, 84; Governor of Paṭnah, Manucci visits, 116; reference, 117

Dā,ūd Khān, Pannī, in Madras, vii; deputy governor in the Karnātik, Manucci writes to, 232, 233; causes cessation of persecutions at Tanjor, 234, 235; letter to the King of Tanjor, 235; at Arkāt, 236; Manucci sent by the English on deputation to, 236, 237; course of negotiations, 238, 239, 240, 241, 242, 243, 244, 245; his opinion of the English, 239, 240; at S. Thome, 246; an English deputation to, 246, 247; visits Governor Pitt, 248, 249, 250; returns to S. Thome, 250; hostile return to Madras, 251; Manucci goes to interview at S. Thome, 251, 252, 253, 254; writes to the French, Dutch, and Danes to help him against English, 254; Mons. Desprez sent as envoy to, 255, 256; sends a horse to Fr. Martin, 256; Manucci visits, 257; stays at Manucci's house at Big Mount, 263; visits S. Thome 1706, 263; receives the English envoys, 264; banquet given for, 265; at S. Thome, 265; visit from the Lord Bishop, 265; gives presents to Manucci at leave-taking, 266; references, 259, 261

Daulat, the eunuch, and Manucci, 159, 160

Daulat, Nāẓir, eunuch in service of Shāh 'Ālam, 208, 280, 283

Davenport, Mr., English envoy sent to Dā,ūd Khān, 263, 264

Delavale, Mons., a French pirate, 267, 268

Deslandes, brings home MS. of Manucci's "Storia," viii; suggests to Manucci that he should write his memoirs, 110

Desprez, Monsieur, sent by F. Martin as envoy to Dā,ūd Khān, 255, 256

Destremon, Monsieur, French physician to King of Gulkandah, 193

Ḍhākah, the river Jamnah at, 114; the city of, metropolis of Bengal, 117, 118; English and Dutch factories at, 118

Dholpur, Manucci and Bellomont at, 36; Dārā's army encamps at, 55, 56; the river (Chambal), 226

Dias, Agostinho warns Manucci of danger, 91

Dihlī, Manucci at, v, 38, 39, 74, 97, 99, 110, 141, 165, 271; enters

service of Jai Singh at, 125; Shāhjahān at, 37; Bellomont's property removed to, 38, 39; Dārā advised to go to, 70; Dārā badly received at, 71; references, 72, 91, 123, 270
Dilāwar, a servant of Manucci, warns him of danger, 92
Diler Khān sends for Manucci, 212; dies of poison administered by Azil Can, 213
Dindar Khān, of Qasūr, Manucci thinks of marrying daughter of, 157
Dulhā, Mahomedan friend with whom Manucci seeks refuge, 95, 96
Dumans, Frey Raphael, Capuchin, 10
Durgā Dās, sent by Akbar as his representative during negotiations with Sambhā Jī, 171
Dutch, at Smyrna, 2; factories at Iṣfahan, 23; at Patnah, 115; at Ḍhākah, 118; at Qāsim Bāzār, 123; Dā,ūd Khān asks them to help him against the English, 254

Ecbatana, 7
Ellis, Mr., sent on deputation to Dā,ūd Khān, 246
England, the King of, 10
English, at Smyrna, 2; factory at Iṣfahān, 21; factory at Bandar 'Abbās, 27; factory at Āgrah, 36, 38; factory at Paṭnah, 115; in India, Manucci speaks in defence of, 241, 242; in Madras, prepare to resist attack of Dā,ūd Khān, 253
Ephraim, Father, Capuchin, missionary at Fort St. George, 197
Erivan, Bellomont and Manucci, at, 6, 7
Erzerūm, Armenians at, 5; Bellomont and Manucci at, 5; the men of, 6
Ethiopia, 184
Europe, the Kings of, 16, 132
Europeans, artillerymen in service of Dārā, 49, 51, 52; permitted to distil spirits, 50; persecute Manucci, 155, 156
Eusebius, of Bourges, brings home MS. of Manucci's "Storia," ix

Factories, Dutch, at Iṣfahān, 23; at Paṭnah, 115; at Dhākah, 118; at Qāsim Bāzār, 123; English, at Isfahān, 21, 23; at Bandar 'Abbās, 27; at Āgrah, 36, 38; at Paṭnah, 115; at Ḍhakah, 118; French, at Qāsim Bazar, 123
Fahīm, the eunuch, sent to Dārā, 70
Fahīm, eunuch, servant of Aurangzeb, employed to carry messages to Shāhjahān, 73
Fatḥ-ullah Khān, Manucci cures, 210
Fidā,e Khān, on the way to Lāhor, 147; Manucci appeals to troopers of, for protection, 147, 148; and Manucci, 149; permits Manucci to have fat removed from two condemned rebels, 153; leaves Lāhor, 154; Manucci appeals for protection to, 156, 157; references, 150, 152
Figueredo, Joaõ Lopes de, Manucci's attorney, 217, 218
Fonçequa, Alvaro da, of S. Thome, 217
Fort of the Kings at Goa, 179, 181
Fort St. George (Madras), Manucci takes refuge at, vii; Manucci arrives at, 196; Manucci married at, 197; Dā,ūd Khān, Pannī, visits Governor Pitt at, 248
Foscarini, Doge Marco Nicolò, only authority for death of Manucci in 1717, viii
Francisco, Frey, Father Vicar of Gulkandah, Manucci appeals for help to, 195
Frederick, Mr., English envoy sent to Dā,ūd Khān, 263, 264
French, at Smyrna, 2; factory at Qāsim Bāzār, 123; Dā,ūd Khān, Pannī, asks them for help against the English, 254

Galen, 160
Gallo, Father Salvador, prefect of Theatines at Goa, 217, 218
Ganges, the river of Allahābād, 113; course of, 113, 114; Hindūs bathe in, 113
Gaspar Alfonço, Bishop, at S. Thome, 229, 230, 231

Ghulam 'Alī Khān, Governor of Vellore, invites Manucci to visit him, 259, 260
Ghusul-Khanah, private audience chamber, Manucci allowed to enter the, 203
Gitar, provisional governor of Lāhor, 146
Goa, Manucci at, v, vi, 135, 136, 137; Manucci decides to return to, 166; under government of archbishop Dom Manoel de Souza de Menezes, 168; Sambhā Jī's designs on, 172, 173; Shāh 'Ālam approaches, 175; the river of, 178, 181; Aguada fort, and Fort of the Kings, at, 179; Manucci obtains leave to visit, 188; takes wheat to the Portuguese, 189; jealousy of doctors in, 220, 221; Lourenço da Cunha, of, and Manucci, 224, 225; Manucci's stories of life in, 226, 227, 228; references, 186, 217, 229
Gombroon. *See* Bandar 'Abbāsi
Gomens, Ignacio, searches for Manucci's body, after his reported death, 96
Gomes, Pascoal, of Goa, 218
Gonzalves, Luis, a friend of Manucci, 279, 280
Great Mount, the. *See* Big Mount
Gudlet, Thomas, an Englishman, friend of Manucci, 191
Guety, Francisco, friend of Manucci at Gulkandah, 193
Guilherme (William), an Englishman, assists Manucci to demonstrate European mode of fighting, 128, 129
Gujarāt, Dārā reaches, 86; raises a new army in, 87; Mahābat Khān at, 126; Little, 146
Gulkandah, Manucci in, vi; Manucci reaches 193; flies from, and is brought back, 194; Abu,l Hasan, King of, and Manucci, 193, 194, 195; references, 24, 191
Gūl Mirza, Governor of Hūglī, grants Jesuits permission to build a church at Manucci's request, 119
Gwāliyār, the fortress of, described, 35, 36; Bellomont and Manucci at, 35, 36
Gyfford, Governor, employs Manucci, vii, 215

Hāndiyah, the town of, 33
Hardancourt, Monsieur, marries granddaughter of Fr. Martin, 266
Harem, the Royal, Manucci visits, in his capacity as physician, 203
Hartley, Christopher, president of Machhlīpatanam, 196
Ḥasan, tomb of, at Iṣfahān, 23
Ḥasan 'Alī Khān on the march to Kashmīr, 104
Ḥasanqala'h, 6
Hayel, Alexandre (Elihu Yale), Governor of Madras, 216
Hindū princes, of the Karnātik, 258, 259
Hindūs, at Lār, 25; the strong places of, 35; bathing in the Ganges, 113; the ancient idol of, at Benares, 114; the way of fastening their gown, 126; the, of Chāwal, complain to Jai Singh, 132, 133
Hindūstan, 33
Hixin, 28
Hoḍal, death of Bellomont at, 1656, v, 37; Manucci buries Bellomont at, 37; references, 40, 44
Hormuz. *See* Ormuz
Ḥūglī, the Ganges at, 114; Manucci at, 118, 119; a marriage proposed by the Jesuits, 120, 121; interference of two friars, 121, 122; Manucci leaves, 123
Ḥusain, tomb of, at Iṣfahān, 23

Iago Sant. *See* St. Iago
Ibrahīm Khān, one of Dārā's generals, 57
Ignatio, a French doctor's son, and Manucci, 269, 270
India, 2; Manucci with Bellomont in, v.
Iṣfahān, Manucci and Bellomont at, 12, 13, 14, 15, 16, 17, 18, 19, 20; description of, 21, 22, 23; Mr. Young, head of English factory at, 21, 23; Christian churches in, 23; tombs of 'Alī, Ḥusain, and Ḥasan at, 23; references, 10, 11, 12, 25, 207
Italians, at Smyrna, 2

I'tibār Khān, offers Manucci employment, 110, 111; harsh treatment of Shāhjahān in prison, 111, 112

Ivo, Father, Capuchin of Sūrat, 287

Jacob, a Dutch surgeon, assists Manucci with a case, 124

Jai Singh, Rajah, Manucci enters service of, v, 125; and the Rajah of Srīnagar, 87; on the march to Kashmīr, 107; Manucci describes European modes of fighting to, 127, 128; a demonstration, 128, 129; presents Manucci to Shivā Jī, 132; Hindūs of Chāwal make a complaint to, 132, 133; Manucci grieved at death of, 141; references, 205, 228

Jamnah, the river, at Allahābād, 113; course of, 113, 114

Jānī Begam, goes to Dihlī with Dārā, 71

Jesuit Fathers. *See* Jesuits, the

Jesuits, the, Manucci's account of their disputes with the Capuchins, vii; their church at Isfahān, 23; Manucci meets, at Āgrah, 110; ask Manucci to take two friars with him to Bengal, 112; at Hūglī ask Manucci to use his influence on their behalf, 119; at Hūglī try to arrange a marriage for Manucci, 120, 121; at Hūglī, and the Father Prior of the Augustinians, 122; at Āgrah, Manucci visits, 141; at Bandora, 162; and Antonio Machado, 164, 165; references, 132, 234

Jew's stones, from Mecca, 28

Jhon, Mestre. *See* Young, Henry

Jīwan Khān, and the reward of treachery, 97

Jonh, Mestre. *See* Young, Henry

Judith, the Book of, 8

Kābul, Kīrat Singh ordered to, vi, 141; Muhammad Amīn Khān, ordered to, 145

Kaliyānī, 134

Kambāya, 225

Kāmbe, village called, 134

Karapa, Cudapah, Manucci visits Dā,ūd Khān at, 257

Karnātik, the, Dā,ūd Khān, Pannī, in, 236; Hindū princes of the, 258; reference, 225

Kār-talab Khān, Governor of Dihlī, 271

Kashmīr, Aurangzeb's march to, 102; Aurangzeb in, 124, 125

Khajwah, battle of, references, 104, 117, 119

Khalīlullah Khān, the traitor, 53; gives traitorous advice to Dārā, 57, 62, 63, 67, 68; advances with Dārā's army, 61, 66; goes off to join Aurangzeb, 68, 69; Manucci spreads false report of his death, 71; sends force against Bhakkar, 87; letters to Primavera (Khwājah Basant), 88; leaves Lāhor, 88; returns discomfited, 89; sends messages to Primavera, 92; Basant's head laid before, 96; orders Manucci and his companions to proceed to court, 97; his excuses for the murder of Khwājah Basant, 97, 98

Khwājah Bahā-ud-dīn, tomb of, at Multān, 81, 82

Khwājah Khidr, island of, 86

Kīrat Singh, Manucci takes service with, vi; generous treatment of Manucci at Dihlī, 141; ordered to Kābul, 141; reference, 125

Kohīr, province of, Shāh 'Ālam in, 194

Kolīs, petty rajahs of, 129

Lāhor, Manucci goes to, vi; Dārā starts for, 71; Dārā in, raising a new army, 74; Manucci rejoins Dārā at, 77; Dārā leaves, 78; Aurangzeb leaves, 82; Khalīlullah Khān leaves, 88; returns to, 89; governor of, 91; Khwājah Basant and Manucci at, 91, 92; Manucci goes to, 141; sets up as a physician, 142; his first patient, 142–44; gains a reputation for skill, 144, 145; Manucci at, affair of the holy man of Balkh, 150, 151, 152; affair of Thīkā, Arāin, 153, 154, 155; Manucci at, story of eunuch Daulat, 159,

160 ; Manucci at, practises as an exorcist, 160, 161, 162 ; Manucci leaves, 162, 163 ; references, 86, 268 ; the river of, 146
Langkaran, Brahman, 244, 245
Lār, Hindūs at, 25 ; Manucci and Bellomont at, 25, 26
Lashkar Khān, Governor of Multān, and Khwājah Basant, 91
Legrenzi, Angelo, and Manucci, 287, 288
Lima, Antonio Palha de, of S. Thome, 217
Lima, Francisco de, 217
Lister, Mr., English envoy sent to Da,ūd Khān, 264
Lopes, Gonsallo, priest, 222

Machado, Antonio, leaves Bandora with Manucci, 164 ; causes trouble for the Jesuits, 164, 165
Machhlīpatanam, Christopher Hartley, president of, 196
Madeyra, Cosmo Lourenço, of San Thome, 217
Madras, Manucci in, vii ; Dā,ūd Khān in, vii ; Manucci's house and garden at, vii ; (Fort St. George), Manucci arrives at, 196 ; Thomas Clarke, second at the station of, 196 ; (Fort St. George), Manucci marries at, 197 ; English in, 241, 242 ; Manucci returns to, 245 ; renders account of his deputation to the Governor, 246 ; the Governor sends deputation to Dā,ūd Khān, Pannī, 246, 247 ; (Fort St. George), Dā,ūd Khān, Pannī, visits Governor Pitt at, 248 ; Manucci's return to warn English in, 251 ; English in, prepare to resist attack of Dā,ūd Khān, 253 ; Manucci leaves for S. Thome, 255 ; Manucci returns to, with a message for Governor Pitt, 257 ; country between Cuddapah and, 258 ; Manucci returns to, from Tevanapatam, 267 ; town of, references, 236
Magic and spells, stories of, 131, 132
Mahābat Khān, ordered to return to Gujarāt, 125 ; suspects Manucci of poisoning him, 149 ; his death, 150 ; ordered to write to Governor Gyfford, 216 ; references, 145, 146, 281
Maḥal. See Harem, Royal
Mahdī, Mirzā, captain of cavalry, 225
Mahomed, the prophet, 5
Mahomedans, way of fastening the gown, 126
Mailāpur, Gaspar Alfonço, Bishop of, 229
Mālabārīs, 162
Malier, Clodio, visits Manucci, 39, 40 ; befriends Manucci, 46, 47 ; presents Manucci at Court of Prince Dārā, 48 ; Manucci lives in his house, 50
Mālkher, Manucci escapes from, vi
Manucci : and Abu,l Ḥasan, King of Gulkandah, 193, 194, 195 ; at Āgrah, v, 36 ; leaves with Dārā and his army, 53 ; retreats to, 71 ; tries to leave, 72 ; is obliged to remain, 73 ; leaves in disguise, 74 ; at, offered employment by I'tibār Khān, 110, 111 ; he leaves, taking two friars with him, 112 ; treats the governor, 124 ; visits Jesuits, 141 ; at Āgrah, 163, 164 ; at Aḥmadnagar, accompanies Shāh 'Ālam to, vi ; at Allahābād, 112, 113, 114 ; at Allahābād, 124 ; and Monsieur Albert, doctor at Pondicherry, 267 ; Joaõ de Alreu prevents his marriage with the Paṭhan widow, 158, 159 ; and Amānat Khān, 150, 151 ; at Arkāt, sent with a deputation to Dā,ūd Khān, Pannī, 236 ; travels through Asia Minor with Bellomont, v ; at Aurangābād, 140, 141, 287; with Jai Singh, 129 ; and Aurangzeb, refuses offer of employment, 98 ; his aversion to, 111 ; and Aurangzeb, translates his letter to the Viceroy of Goa, 166 ; and Aurangzeb, negotiates with on behalf of Governor Gyfford, 215 ; and Mīr Azam, envoy sent by Shāh 'Ālam to Viceroy of Goa, 177, 178, 179 ; and 'Azamat-ud-daulah, present during his interviews with Lord

Bellomont, 13, 15, 16, 17, 18, 19; and Thome de Azevedo, physician at Goa, 220, 221; treats a relation of the envoy from Balkh, 99, 100, 101; story of the holy man of Balkh, 150, 151, 152; describes manners and customs of nobles from Balkh, 100–2; at Bandar 'Abbās, 26, 27; at Bandora, vi; resolves to retire to, 162; arrives, 163; leaves with A. Machado, 164; and Barqandāz Khān, 77, 142; and Khwājah Basant (Primavera), recommended to his care by Dārā, 85; and Khwājah Basant, under his command at Bhakkar, 85, 86, 87, 88, 89, 90; and Kh. Basant, leaves Bhakkar with him, 91; at Lāhor, 91, 92; stands by him, 93; at Bassain, v, 134, 135; questioned by the commissary of the Inquisition at, 228; and Frey Iraõ Bautista, 118, 119, 122; and Luis Beiçaõ, they demonstrate European mode of fighting, 128, 129; and Bellomont, is taken into his service, v, 1, 2; travels with him through Asia Minor and Persia, v, 2–27; and Lord Bellomont, present at his interview with 'Azamat-ud-daulah, 13, 15, 16, 17, 18, 19; with Bellomont in India, 28–37; buries Bellomont at Hoḍal, 37; at Benares, 114; journey to Bengal by boat, 116, 117, 118; comments on Bernier's inaccuracy, 110; makes use of *bezoar* stone in treatment, 114; at Bhakkar, arrives with army of Dārā, 84; at Bhakkar, made captain of the Europeans left in the fortress, 85; at Bhakkar, the fortress besieged, 86, 87; at Bhakkar, wounded by an arrow, 88; at Bhakkar, in command of the artillery, 88, 89, 90; at Bhakkar, leaves with Khwājah Basant (Primavera), 91; attends Bhāo Singh, 205; at the river Biāh, meets Dā,ūd Khān, 76; his house at Big Mount, Dā,ūd Khān stays there, 263; his house at Big Mount attacked, 276; his house at Big Mount, reference, 250; at city of Bījāpur, 134; in the Kingdom of Bījāpur, 138; blood-letting, describes his mode of treating royal patients, 199, 200, 283, 284, 285; his friend Ortenzio Bronzoni, 230, 231; at Brūsa, arrival, 2; departure, 3; at Burhānpur, 31, 32, 33, 141; and Capuchins, account of their disputes with the Jesuits, vii, Père Catrou, viii, ix; treats Rajah Champat, son of Champat Bundelah, 197; sent as envoy to the Rajah of Chiūtia, 129, 131; and the Christian religion, 126, 127; and the widow Dona Christiana, of Goa, 227, 228; marries E. Clarke, *née* Hartley, at Fort St. George, vii, 197; her death, 289; and Dom R. da Costa, commander of Portuguese fleet, 174, 178, 217, 218, 221; and Luis Gonsalves Cota, secretary at Goa, 220, 221; and Ant. de Couza Coutinho, 229; at Cudapah (Karapa), visits to Dā,ūd Khān, 257; tricked by Lourenço da Cunha, of Goa, 224, 225; follows Shāh 'Ālam to the Dakhin 1678, vi; refuses to attend Dalpat Rāo, 225, 226; at Damān, 163, 166, 225; and Dārā, the prince expresses a wish to see Manucci, 47; he interviews Manucci, 48; Manucci enters his service, v, 49; with the army, 53–59; the battle-array, 60, 61; describes course of battle and defeat of Dārā, 62–70; Manucci rejoins the prince at Lāhor, 77; follows Dārā from Lāhor, 80; the army leaves Multān, 82, 83; arrival at Bhakkar, 84; Manucci begs for leave to go with Dārā, 84; the prince makes Manucci captain of Europeans left at Bhakkar, 85; date of death, vii, viii, 289 *n.*; Dā,ūd Khān gives Manucci a passport, 76; Dā,ūd Khān, Manucci visits him at Paṭnah, 116; Dā,ūd Khān, Panni, a letter to, 232, 233; and Dā,ūd Khān,

Pannī, sent with a deputation to greet him by the English, 236, 237; and Dā,ūd Khān, Pannī, course of the negotiations, 238–45; and Dā,ūd Khān, Pannī, 246, 247; and Dā,ūd Khān, Pannī, sent to meet him at S. Thome and escorts him to Fort St. George, 248; and Dā,ūd Khān, Pannī, sent to interview him at San Thome, 251–54; and Dā,ūd Khān, Pannī, a visit at Cudapah, 257; ; and Dā,ūd Khān, Pannī, a visit to Manucci's house at Big Mount, 263; Dā,ūd Khān, Pannī, Manucci visits, with the English envoys, 263, 264; Dā,ūd Khān, Pannī, Manusci goes to take leave of, 265; receives presents, 266; the eunuch Daulat, 159, 160; Deslandes brings MS. of the "Storia" to Europe, viii, suggests to Manucci the writing of his "Storia," 110; at Dhākah, well treated by Thomas Platt, 118; at Dholpur, 36; warned by Agostinho Dias of danger, 91; at Dihlī, v, 38, 39, 74, 97, 110, 271; at Dihlī, acting as a physician, 99, 165; at Dihlī, handsomely treated by Kīrat Singh, 141; at Dihlī, enters service of Jai Singh, v, 125; Dilāwar, warns him of danger, 92; Diler Khān, sends for Manucci to attend him, 212; Dīndār Khān, of Qasūr, Manucci thinks of marrying his daughter, 157; seeks refuge in house of his friend Dulhā, 95, 96; encounter with an angry slave, 211, 212; speaks in defence of the English, 241, 242; at Erivan, 6, 7; at Erzerūm, 5; persecuted by the Europeans, 155, 156; Eusebius, of Bourges, brings home MS. of the "Storia," ix; cures Fatḥ-ullah-Khān, 210; Fidā,e Khān, Manucci is presented to, 149; permits Manucci to have fat removed from two condemned rebels, 153; to Fidā,e Khān, Manucci appeals for protection, 156, 157; and his attorney, J. L. de Figueredo, 217, 218; at Fort St. George (Madras), vii, 196; he marries, 197; appeals for help to Frey Francisco, Father Vicar of Gulkandah, 195; Father Salvador Gallo, of Goa, 217, 218; and Bishop Gaspar Alfonço, 229, 230, 231; visits Ghulam 'Alī Khān at Vellore, 259, 260; allowed to enter the, *Ghusul-Khanah* or private audience chamber, 203; at Goa, v, vi, 135, 137; his illness there, 136; at Goa, he leaves in disguise, 138; decides to return, 166; at Goa, warnings to the viceroy, 167, 168; at Goa, treated as a traitor by Dom Manoel de Souza de Menezes, 169; at Goa, presents Sambhā Jī's envoy to the viceroy, 170; at Goa, sent as envoy to Sambhā Jī, vi, 171, 172; at Goa, helps to frustrate designs of Sambhā Jī and his envoy, 173; at Goa, sent as envoy to the Mogul fleet, off Vingorla, 174, 175; at Goa, sent as envoy to Sambhā Jī for the second time, 175; at Goa, sent to speak with Shāh 'Ālam's envoy, 177; at Goa, meets Mīr 'Aẓam, envoy from Shāh 'Ālam to the viceroy, 177, 178, 179; at Goa, visits Shāh 'Ālam at his encampment near, 179, 180, 181, 182; obtains leave of absence to visit Goa, 188; takes wheat to the Portuguese there, 189; at Goa, jealousy of the physicians there, 220, 221; at Goa, tricked by L. da Cunha, 224, 225; at Goa, stories of life there, 226, 227, 228; his friend Luis Gonzalves, 279, 280; and Thomas Gudlet, 191; his friend Fr. Guety at Gulkandah, 193; Guilherme (William), an Englishman, assists him to demonstrate European mode of fighting, 128, 129; and Mirza Gūl, Governor of Ḥuglī, 119; in Gulkandah, vi, he arrives, 193; flies from and is brought back, 194; in Gulkandah, dealings with the King Abu,l Ḥasan, 193, 194, 195; at Ġwāliyār, 35, 36; employed by Governor Gyfford, vii, 215; visits the Royal Harem as a physician, 203; buries Bellomont at Hoḍal, 37; arrives at Huglī; 118; goes to see Frey Iraõ Bautista, 118, 119; at Huglī, a marriage proposed by the Jesuits, 120, 121; interference of two friars, 121, 122; leaves Huglī, 123; helps Ignatio, a French doctor's son, 269, 270; in India with Bellomont v; at Iṣfahan, 12, 13, 14, 15, 16, 17, 18, 19, 20, 21, 22, 23; and I'tibār Khān, an offer of employment, 110, 111; Jacob, a Dutch surgeon, assists him with a case, 124; enters service of Jai Singh, v, 125; describes European modes of fighting to him, 127, 128; a demonstration, 128, 129; is presented by Jai Singh to Shivā Jī, 132; grief at death of Jai Singh, 141; and the Jesuits, account of their disputes with the Capuchins, vii, meets them at Āgrah, 110; they ask him to take two friars with him to Bengal, 112; ask him to use his influence in their behalf at Huglī, 119; they try to arrange a marriage for him at Huglī, 120, 121; he visits them at Āgrah, 141; at Kaṛapa (Cudapah), visit to Dā,ūd Khān, 257; describes Aurangzeb's march to Kashmīr, 102–10; three days' march with the army towards Kashmīr, 110; spreads false report of death of Khalīlullah Khān, 71; is ordered to proceed to court of Aurangzeb by Kh. Kh., 97; takes service with Kīrat Singh, vi; is generously treated by him at Dihlī, 141; goes to Lāhor, vi; rejoins Dārā at, 77; with Khwājah Basant at, 91, 92; at Lāhor, in great danger, 94; escapes naked, 95; at Lāhor, 141; sets up as a physician, 142; his first patient, 142–4; gains a reputation for skill, 144, 145; at Lāhor, affair of the holy man of Balkh, 150, 151, 152; at Lāhor, story of Thīkā Arāin, a corpulent Mahomedan, 153, 154, 155; at Lāhor, forced to leave in suite of Muḥammad Amīn Khān, 145; returns, 146; falsely accused of theft, 147; at Lāhor, appeals for protection to Fidā,e Khān's troopers, 147, 148; at Lāhor, visits Mirzā Ṣaliḥ, son of Fidā,e Khān, 148; is presented by him to Fidā,e Khān, 149; at Lāhor, story of the eunuch Daulat, 159, 160; at Lāhor, practises as an exorcist, 160, 161, 162; leaves Lāhor, 162, 163; at Lār, 25, 26; and A. Legrenzi, physician, 287, 288; and Ant. Machado, 164; in Madras, vii; his house and garden, vii; he arrives at Madras (Fort St. George), 196; at Madras (Fort St. George), his marriage, 197; returns from deputation to Dā,ūd Khān, 245; warning to the English, 251; at Madras, leaves for S. Thome, 255; returns with a message for Governor Pitt, 257; returns from Tevanapatam, 267; suspected of poisoning Mahābat Khān, 149, 150; receives a visit from Clodio Malier, 39, 40; befriended by Clodio Malier, 46, 47; presented at court of Pr. Dārā, by Clodio Malier, 48; lives in house of Cl. Malier, 50; escapes from Mālkher, vi; and Father Martin, Jesuit, 231–33; Fr. Martin, Director-General, suggests that Manucci should write his autobiography, 110; sends Manucci to Damān in an armed sloop, 166; visits François Martin, at Pondicherry, is advised by him to marry, 196; receives letter from François Martin, 231; replies, 233; communicates with François Martin, 251, 255; treats Fr. Martin when ill, effects a cure, 267; at Masulipatam, vi; Dom M. de Souza de Menezes, treats M. as a traitor, 169; his friend Mirecautaula, 282, 283;

and Mirzā Arjanj, 274, 275; and Mirzā Muḥammad Muqīm, 207, 208, 209; visits Mirzā Ṣāliḥ, 148; is presented by him to Fida,e Khān, 149; called to attend Mirzā Sulaimān Beg, brother-in-law of Shāh 'Ālam, 207, 208; and Khwājah Miskīn, 49; explains why he left the Mogul country, 198, 199; and Muḥammad Amīn Khān, forced to leave Lāhor in his suite, 145; falsely accused by him of theft, 146, 147; assisted by Muḥammad Ibrāhīm to escape from Shāh 'Ālam, 191, 192, 193; askedto treat Muḥammad Ja'far, 257; Mīr Muḥammad sent in pursuit of, 186, 187; and Muḥammad Muqīm, 278, 279; cures Muḥammad Rizā, 210; altercation with Shekh Muḥammad, 183, 184; and Sulṭan Mu'izz-ud-dīn, 186; at Multān, 81, 91; and Mūmin Khān, 195; at Narsapur, vi, he flies there to evade capture by Shāh 'Ālam, 194; at Narwar, 35; interview with Nawāb Bāe Jī, mother of Shāh 'Ālam, 180; writes to the eunuch Nekroz, 215; and Nūr-un-nissā Begam, an accident in blood-letting, 286; his first trial of *pān* (betel), 30; attacked by thieves at Pandharpur, 139, 140; lucky escape near Pānīpat, 75, 76; at Parendā, 140; at Paṭnah, 114; story of the clever Armenian, 115, 116; at Paṭnah, visits Dā,ūd Khān, 116; at Paṭnah, 124; sent as envoy to Rajah of Pent, 129; in Persia, v, 6–27; and Pheliciano de Santa Teresa, Prior of Carmelites, at Goa, 227, 228; appeals for help to Lourenço Pit, 195; employed by Governor Pitt, vii; Governor Pitt arbitrates between Manucci and the Portuguese, 219; Manucci warns him of the approach of Dā,ūd Khān, 251; is asked by Governor Pitt to visit Dā,ūd Khān with the English envoys, 263; and Thomas Platt, of Ḍhākah, 118; in Pondicherry, vii, 251; visits Fr. Martin at, 196; leaves, 197; returns to Pondicherry to treat Fr. Martin, 267; and Joaõ A. Portugal, embassy to Shāh 'Ālam, 222, 223, 224; employed by the Portuguese, vi; and Signor Protazio, 287, 288; at Qāsim Bāzār, 123; befriended by Qāzī Mīr, minister of Shāh 'Ālam, 281, 282, 283; at Qazwīn, 9, 10, 11, 12; arrives with Lord Bellomont at Raguza, 2; receives a warning from Rājāpur, 168; at Rājmahal, 117; story of *satī* at, 123; sent with Rāmāpā on deputation to Dā,ūd Khān, 236; Rāmāpā causes trouble, 238–40, 243, 244; his excuses, 245; generous conduct towards Rāmāpā, 246; sent as envoy to Rajah of Rāmnagar, 129, 130; receives a horse from Manoel Ribeiro, 140; M. and T. Roach, 38, 39, 44; visits G. Roberts, Governor of Tevenapatam, 266, 267; and Heinrich Roth, Jesuit, 112; and the Turk, Rūmī Khān, 78, 79, 80, 81; assisted by Domingo de Saā to demonstrate European mode of fighting, 128, 129; receives letter from Sā'ādatullah Khān, 256; and Sambhā Jī, vi; sent as envoy to, 171, 172, 175; and Diogo de M. de Sampayo, 163, 164; at San Thome, unjust treatment by Portuguese, 217, 218; at San Thome, Governor Pitt as arbitrator, 219; San Thome, sent to receive Dā,ūd Khān, Pannī, at, 248; made a Knight of Sant' Iago, vi, 184; the letters patent, 184, 185, 186; takes part in a rescue from *satī*, 124, 125; warns I. Sermento at Bassain of trouble, 133; I. Sermento testifies as to Manucci's services to the Portuguese, 133, 134; tardy payment of a debt to Manucci, 136; enters service of Shāh 'Ālam, vi, 165, 166; obtains leave, 166; visits him at his camp near Goa, 179–82; and Shāh 'Ālam, 181, 182; attempts to leave Shāh 'Ālam, 186; is recaptured, 187; obtains leave from Shāh 'Ālam to visit Goa, 188; takes a supply of wheat with him, 189; again leaves Shāh 'Ālam, 191, 192, 193; Shāh 'Ālam sends in search of him, 197; Shāh 'Ālam plays a trick on M., 201, 202; Shāh 'Ālam tries to persuade him to change his religion, 204; tested by Shāh 'Ālam, 206, 207; ordered by Shāh 'Ālam to treat different people at his court, 208–10; Shāh Ālam annoyed at his being sent for by Diler Khān, 212, 213; negotiates with Shāh 'Ālam, vi, 222–24; and Shāh 'Ālam, 277–82; presented to Shāhjahān, 42; describes the audience hall, 42, 43; at Shīrāz, 24, 25; meets Shivā Jī, 132; at Sihrind, 97, 163; reference, 285; at Sindī, 28; at Sironj, 33, 34; M. and R. Smith, 38, 39, 44; arrives with Lord Bellomont at Smyrna, 2; Joaō de Souza helps him to prescribe, 100; his "Storia do Mogor," account of the MSS., viii, ix; at Sūrat, 29, 30, 31, 163, 166; as a swashbuckler, 273, 274; youthful escapades, 275, 276; at Tabrīz, 7, 8; Ignacio de Taide embezzles his ship and cargo, 163; and Fr. de Tavora, Viceroy of Goa, 221; sends Manucci to negotiate with Sambhā Jī, 171; Fr. de Tavora, his reports to, 173, 182; sends Manucci as envoy to the Mogul fleet, 174, 175; Fr. de Tavora, sends Manucci to speak with envoy of Shāh 'Ālam, 177; Fr. de Tavora offers Manucci knighthood of Sant' Iago, 184; at Tevenapatam, 266, 267; and Thīka Arāin, a corpulent Mahomedan, 153–55; at Tokat, 3; describes manners and customs of Uzbaks from Balkh, 100–102; at Vellore, 259, 260; runs away from Venice, 1653, v, 1; and Father Damaō Vieira, 228, 229; sent as envoy to Mogul fleet off Vingorla, 174, 175; applies for help to Wazīr Khān, 40, 41; taken to Shāhjahān's palace by Wazīr Khān, 41, 42; and Wazīr Khān, 44, 45, 46; writes to Henry Young at Sūrat, 50; Ẕu,lfiqār Khān sends a present to, 266

Maquari, Monsieur, doctor at Pondicherry, 267

Maronites, musical instruments employed by, 107

Martin, Father, Jesuit, and M. 231, 232, 233; reference, 235

Martin, François, Director-General, suggests to Manucci that he should write his autobiography, 110; sends Manucci to Damān in an armed sloop, 166; Manucci goes to visit, 196; advises Manucci to marry, 196; letter to Manucci from, 231; Manucci replies to, 233; Manucci communicates with, 251, 255; sends an envoy to Dā,ūd Khān, 255; Dā,ūd Khān sends a horse to, 256; letter from Sā'ādatullah Khān to, 257; marriage of his granddaughter, 266; illness of, Manucci hastens to his side, 267; death of, 289

Martin, Senhor Francisco. *See* Martin, François

Masqaṭ, fruitless Portuguese expedition against, 137, 138

Masson, Monsieur, a French pirate, 268

Masulipatam, Manucci at, vi

Maya, Thomas de, of S. Thome, 220

Mecca, Jew's-stones from, 28

Meerman, Baron Gérard, purchases MS. of the "Storia," 1705, viii

Mellos and Mendozas, disputes of, at Bassain, 134, 135

Menezes, Dom Manoel de Souza de, Archbishop, temporary Governor of Goa, 168, 169; treats Manucci as a traitor, 169

Menezes, Manoel da Silva de, of S. Thome, 217, 220

Mīrak Aṭā.ullah, a captain, 150

Mīr Bābā, foster brother of Aurangzeb. *See* Bahādur Khān

Mīr Jumlah, in Assam, 117, 118; Viceroy of Bengal, makes Mirza Janī Governor of Rājmahal, 117; makes Mirza Gūl Governor of Ḥuglī, 119

Mirecautaula, a friend of Manucci, 282, 283
Mirzā 'Abdullah, 146
Mirzā Arjanj and Manucci, 274, 275
Mirzā Janī, Governor of Rāj-mahal, 117
Miskīn, Khwājah, Manucci put in the charge of, 49
Misrī Khān, marries the Paṭhan widow instead of Manucci, 158
Mogul country, the, why Manucci left, 198, 199
Moguls, the, fond of flowers, 22
Monte Grande. *See* Big Mount
Moreira, Souza, custodian, 185
Mota, Ilha de Manoel de, island near Goa, 178
Mozambique, I. Sermento goes to, 13[illegible]
Mu 'Aẓẓam, Sulṭan, on the march to Kashmīr, 106
Mubāriz Khān, Manucci attends the wife of, 209
Muḥammad, 81, 82; the image of, 164
Muḥammad Amīn Khān, 51; on the march to Kashmīr, 104; Governor of Lāhor, 141; forces Manucci to leave Lāhor in his suite, 145; has Manucci falsely accused of theft, 146, 147
Muḥammad Ibrāhīm, assists Manucci to escape from Shāh 'Alam, 191, 192, 193
Muḥammad Ja'far, Manucci asked to treat, 257
Muhammad Mīr, foster brother of Shāh 'Ālam, sent in pursuit of Manucci, 186, 187
Muḥammad Muqīm, chief physician to Shāh 'Ālam, 277, 278, 279, 287, 288
Muḥammad Muqīm Mirzā, and M., 207, 208, 209
Muḥammad Riẓā, Manucci cures, 210
Muḥammad Riẓā, Mirzā, officer of Shāh 'Ālam, 222
Muḥammad Ṣādiq, official at Shāh 'Ālam's court, 222
Muḥammad Sa'īd, *dīwan* of the Karnātik, 237
Muḥammad, Shekh, envoy from Aurangzeb to Viceroy of Goa, altercation with Manucci, 183, 184; reference, 185
Muḥammad, Sulṭan, son of Aurangzeb, 60; routed by Dārā, 66
Muḥsin, Khān, Persian physician in service of Shāh 'Ālam, 207; and Muḥammad Riẓā, 209, 210
Mu'īn Mīr, Uzbak, 246
Mu'izz-ud-dīn, Sulṭān, son of Shāh 'Ālam, Manucci entrusts money to, 186; quarrels with his father, 200; references, 180
Multān, Dārā, starts for, 78; his followers arrive at, 81; and his followers leave, 82; Aurangzeb arrives at, 83; Aurangzeb leaves, 85; Khwājah Basant and Lashkar Khān, Governor of, 91; reference, 116
Mumin, Ḥakīm, physician to Bahādur Khān, 113
Mūmin Khān, envoy of Shāh 'Ālam, tries to carry Manucci off, 195
Mūmiyāī, Shīrāz and its, 25
Munger, rivers at, 114
Murād Bakhsh, prepares to seize the throne, 51; advances with Aurangzeb's army, 60; hard pressed by Rām Singh, Rāṭhor, 66; arrives in Āgrah, 73; starts with Aurangzeb in pursuit of Dārā, 74; made a prisoner by Aurangzeb, 74; Manucci attends the daughter of, 151, 152; references, 54, 59
Murād, Mullā, Mahomedan Governor of S. Thome, 276
Murād, Sultan, 8
Music, instruments of, employed by Armenians, Syrians, Maronites, and Turks, 107

Najābat Khān, one of Aurangzeb's generals, 60; routed by Dārā, 66
Narāpā, sent as envoy to Dā,ūd Khān, 251
Narbadā, the river, 33
Narsāpur, Manucci at, vi; flies to, to evade capture by Shāh 'Ālam, 194
Narwar, Bellomont and Manucci at, 35
Nawāb Bāe Jī, mother of Shāh 'Ālam, interviews Manucci, 180

Negapatam, the Dutch at, asked by Dā,ūd Khān to help him against the English, 254
Nekroz, the eunuch, Manucci writes to, 215
Nelur, the river, 179
Niccolao, Hakīm. *See* Manucci
Noah, the Ark of, 6
Nūr-un-nissā, Begam, accident when Manucci drew blood from, 286
Nutmeg, good effect of, on a horse, 140

Ochu. *See* Uchh
Ormuz, the fortress of, 13, 14, 22; the fortress and island of, 27

Pān (betel leaf), 30, 31; Manucci's first trial of, 30
Pandharpur, Manucci attacked by thieves at, 139, 140
Pānīpat, Manucci's lucky escape near, 75, 76
Parendā, Manucci at, 140
Paris, volume of portraits now at Bibliothèque Nationale, in, ix
Paṭnah, rivers at, 113; Manucci at, 114, 115, 116, 124; factories at, English and Dutch, 115; manufacture and trade of, 115
Pedro, Dom, Prince of Portugal, 184
Pent, the Rajah of, Manucci sent as envoy to, 129
Pereyra, Donna A, wife of Chris. Hartley, 196
Persia, Manucci, accompanies Bellomont through, v; presents for the King of, 6; sheep of the country, 8, 24; water supply in, 8, 26; climate resembling England, 14; Shāh 'Abbās, King of, 9, 10, 11, 12, 14, 16, 20; the King of, references, 7, 8, 138; Akbar's intended flight to, 166, 167; references, 2, 3, 5, 184, 271
Persian cavalry, parade of, 16
Persians, fond of flowers, 22
Peshāwar, Fidā,e Khān at, 150
Pheliciano de Santa Teresa, Prior of Carmelites at Goa, 227, 228
Philipps, Sir Thomas, purchases MS. of Manucci's "Storia" 1824, viii
Pinto, Manoel Texeyra, of San Thome, 217
Pit, Lourenço, Dutch envoy in Gulkandah, Manucci appeals for help to, 195
Pitt, Thomas, Governor of Madrās, employs Manucci, vii; arbitrates between Manucci and the Portuguese, 219; visited by Dā,ūd Khān, 248, 249, 250; warned by Manucci of approach of Dā,ūd Khān, 251; reply to message from Dā,ūd Khān and others, 257, 258; asks Manucci to visit Dā,ūd Khān in company with English envoys, 263
Plato, 160
Platt, Thomas, English boat-builder at Ḍhākah, friendly to Manucci, 118
Pondā, Portuguese, defeat at, 168
Pondicherry, Manucci in, [illegible], 251; Manucci goes to visit François Martin at, 196; he leaves, 197; Father Martin returns to, 233; Manucci determines to visit, 235; Dā,ūd Khān asks French at, for help against English, 254; François Martin ill at, 267; death of François Martin, Governor of, 289
Porto, Domingos do, of S. Thome, 217
Portraits, volume of, sent home with first MS. of "Storia," ix
Portugal, the King of, 132, 181
Portugal, Joaõ Antunes, Portuguese envoy to Shāh 'Ālam, 183; Joaõ Antunio, Portuguese envoy to Shāh 'Ālam and Manucci, 222, 223, 224
Portuguese, in India, 13, 22, 27, 133, 136, 166; employ Manucci, vi.
Primavera. *See* Basant, Khwājah
Protazio, Signor, a German, and Manucci, 287, 288
Pulão, 11, 15, 100, 101
Pūnā-gaṛh, the fortress of, reference, 132

Qandahār, and Shāhjahān, 159
Qāsim Bāzār, English, French and Dutch factories at, 123; Manucci at, 123
Qasūr, Dīndār Khān, of, 157
Qāzī Mīr, minister of Shāh 'Ālam, befriends Manucci, 281, 282, 283

Qazwīn, 8, 14; Manucci, and Bellomont at, 9, 10, 11, 12; the royal palace at, 9, 10; situation of, 12
Qurān, the, references to, 74, 143, 153, 164, 204, 208, 268
Quṭb Shāh, King of Gulkandah, treasures of, 193
Quṭb-ud-dīn, Khwājah, gardens of, near Dihlī, 273

Raguza, Manucci arrives with Lord Bellomont at, 2
Rājāpur, warning sent to Manucci from, 168
Rājmaḥal, rivers at, 114; Manucci at, 117; story of *satī*, 123
Rajputs, the, 67; way of wearing the hair, 126
Rām R[illegible], son of Shivā Jī, 258
Rām Singh, Rāṭhor, advances with Dārā's army, 61; death of, 66, 67
Rāmāpā, sent with Manucci on deputation to Dā,ūd Khān, 236; causes trouble, 238, 239, 240, 243, 244; his excuses, 245; Manucci's generous conduct towards, 246
Rāmghāt, a mountain called, 190
Rāmnagar, the Rajah of, Manucci sent as envoy to, 129, 130
Rāvī, the river, 78
Raworth, Mr., English envoy sent to Dā,ūd Khān, 263, 264
Ribeiro, Manoel, gives Manucci a horse at Parendā, 140
Ribeyro, Augustinho, of Goa, 218
Roach, Thomas, seizes Bellomont's property, 38; his petition to Dārā, 40; pardoned by Manucci, 44
Roberts, Gabriel, Governor of Tevenapatam, Manucci visits, 266, 267
Rodrigues, Bertolameo, of S. Thome, 217
Rorī, town of, 86
Roshan Arā Begam and her retinue on the march to Kashmīr, 107, 108; her travelling companion, 109
Roth, Heinrich, Jesuit, begs Manucci to take two friars with him to Bengal, 112; reference, 117
Roubal, Monsieur de, a French pirate, 268
Rūmī Khān, Turkish officer, and Manucci, 78, 79, 80, 81
Rustam Khān, Dakhinī, advances with Dārā's army, 61; gives prudent advice to Dārā, 62, 63; reinforces Dārā, 64; killed, 66
Rustam Rāo, second in command of Gulkandah forces, 195; imprisoned for allowing Manucci to escape, 196

Saā, Domingo de, assists Manucci to demonstrate European mode of fighting, 128, 129
Sā'ādatullah Khān, writes to Manucci, 256; his letter to Fr. Martin, 257
Ṣafar, Khwājah, Armenian of Āgrah, story of his bankruptcy at Paṭnah, 115, 116
Sakkar, town of, 86
Sālih, Mirzā, son of Fidā,e Khān, Manucci visits, 148; presents Manucci to Fidā,e Khān, 149
Salsette, taken possession of by Sambhā Jī, 170, 174
Salt River (Ryo Salgado), 26
Sambhā Jī, Manucci negotiates with, vi; 166; lays plans to seize Goa, 167, 168; takes possession of Salsette and Bardes, 170; his designs on Goa, 172, 173; Manucci sent as envoy to, 171, 172; he sends an envoy in return, 172, 173; Manucci sent as envoy to, for the second time, 175; reference, 190
Sampayo, Diogo de Mello de, refuses to pay his debt to Manucci, 163, 164
Sanganes. *See* Sanjānīs
Sanjānīs (West Coast pirates), 162
San Marco, Library of, volume of portraits in, ix; Manucci's MS. entered in catalogue, ix
San Thome, Manucci at, 217, 218, 219, 220; Bishop Gaspar Alfonço at, 229, 230, 231; Dā,ūd Khān, Pannī, at, 246; Manucci sent to receive Dā,ūd Khān, Pannī, at, 248; Dā,ūd Khān, Pannī, returns to, 250; Dā,ūd Khān, Pannī, at, 251, 252, 253, 254, 265; Fr. Martin sends Monsieur Desprez as envoy to Dā,ūd Khān, Pannī, at, 255;

Mullā Murād, Mahomedan Governor of, 276
Santiago, fortress of, at Goa, 178
Sant' Iago, Manucci made a Knight of, vi, 184, 185, 186
Santo Estevão, the island of, taken by Sambhā Jī, 175; Sambhā Jī, obliged to leave, 177
Santo Pinto, Manoel de, Portuguese envoy to Shāh 'Ālam, 183, 184
Sarāes, account of, 34
Saraiva, Manoel, sent as envoy to Sambhā Jī, 175
Satī, at Rājmahal, story of, 123; a rescue from, near Āgrah, 124, 125
Sermento, Ignacio, at Bassain, warned by Manucci of trouble, 133; signs certificate testifying to Manucci's service to Portuguese, 133, 134; tardy payment of a debt to Manucci, 136
Shafī' Khān, Governor of S. Thome, 219
Shāh 'Abbās. *See* 'Abbās II., Shāh of Persia
Shāh 'Ālam, Manucci negotiates with, vi; Manucci appointed physician to, vi; Jai Singh joins, at Aurangābād, 129; Manucci enters service of, 165, 166; Manucci obtains leave of absence from, 166; approaches Goa, 175; takes several of Sambhā Jī's forts, 176; arrives at Goa, 177; sends envoy to Viceroy of Goa, 177, 178; visit from Manucci, 179, 180, 181, 182; grants Manucci leave of absence to visit Goa, 188; allows him to take a cargo of wheat with him, 189; Manucci escapes from, 191, 192; requests King of Gulkandah to send Manucci back to him, 194; complains to King of Gulkandah of his failure to arrest Manucci, 196; sends in search of Manucci, 197; Manucci attends the mother of, 199; quarrels with his son Sultan Mu'izz-ud-dīn, 200; plays a trick on Manucci, 201, 202; tries to persuade Manucci to change his religion, 204; and Bhāo Singh, 205; his tests for Manucci, 206, 207; orders Manucci to attend Muhammad Muqīm, 208; orders Manucci to attend the wife of Mubāriz Khān, 209; orders Manucci to attend Fath-ullah-Khān, 210; annoyed to hear that Manucci has been sent for by Diler Khān, 212, 213; Manucci sent as envoy to, 222, 223, 224; and Manucci, 277, 278, 279, 280, 281, 282; references, 141, 185
Shahbāz, the eunuch, advises Murād Bakhsh not to accompany Aurangzeb, 74
Shāhjahān, gives revenues of Sūrat to Begam Sāhib, 31; at Dihlī, 37; Manucci presented to, 42; his audience-hall, 42, 43; illness of, 51; and Dārā 51, 52; writes to Dārā, 58; message from Dārā to, 69, 70; answer to Dārā's message, 70; communications with Aurangzeb, 73; made prisoner by Aurangzeb, 73, 74; in prison, harsh treatment of, 111, 112; in prison at Āgrah, 124; and Qandahār, 159; references, 29, 56
Shāh Shujā', son of Shāhjahān, prepares to seize the throne, 51; 66, 87, 104, 117, 119, 274
Shāistah Khān, appointed Governor of Āgrah, 74; references, 51, 249
Sharīf-ul-mulk, brother-in-law of King of Gulkandah, 193
Sharzah Khān, 134
Shekh Mīr, leads a division of Aurangzeb's army, 64; reference, 104
Shīrāz, the bridge of, at Isfahān, 22; 23; Bellomont ill at, 24; description of, 24; Armenians at, 24; Bellomont leaves, 25; and its *mūmiyāī*, 25
Shivā Jī, has many conversations with Manucci, 132; references, 129, 130, 138, 141
Siam, King of, 267
Sihrind, Manucci at, 97, 163; reference, 285
Silva, Francisco da, chief surgeon at S. Thome, 221
Sind, the river of, 84
Sindī, Manucci and Bellomont at, 28; Dārā at, 85